Heroes Wanted

The Screams of Children Have Not Fallen on Deaf Ears

Jamil Maroun

Publisher: Jamil Maroun

The events in this book have been set down to the best of the author's ability, although some names and details have been changed to protect the privacy of individuals.

First Edition August 2023
Cover design by Jamil Maroun

Teddy Bear Graphic #171057614 licensed under
Adobe Stock Image Extended License

ISBN: 979-8-9888499-0-2

Published by Jamil Maroun
PO Box 801, Pollock Pines, CA 95726
www.jamilmaroun.com

This book is dedicated to God.

I'm always quite amazed at your wisdom and plan; You never disappoint. During the zenith of my spiritual relationship with You, I dared to question Your wisdom, and You responded within three days with an answer so simple it would take me decades to fully understand. Magnificent!

"The only thing necessary for the triumph of evil is for good men to do nothing"

— Edmund Burke

Conventions Used in This Book

1. The phrase "The Body of Christ" and the terms "Christians" and "Catholics" are all used interchangeably throughout this book without distinction and are used broadly to represent all followers of Jesus Christ, no matter their religious affiliation or denomination.

2. Terms used to describe church leaders like Pastor, Priest, Spiritual Leader, and Leadership Team are also used interchangeably throughout this book, without distinction. They are used broadly to signify church leadership or those that lead or influence the Body of Christ.

Contents

Part Two
The Evils of This World

Part Three
Visions of What Could Be

Preface

In 2015, during the lowest point in my life, God compelled me to write this book. During the past eight years of this writing odyssey, no matter how tired I was or when I went to sleep, somewhere between 1:00 and 5:00 a.m., I would find myself wide awake and contending with a barrage of thoughts, ideas, and various messages pertaining to the contents of this book. I quickly learned it was futile to try and dismiss these thoughts because regardless how hard I tried or what methods I employed, sleep always managed to elude me. So I embraced my new schedule, and I started writing. As it turned out, waking up between 1:00 and 5:00 a.m. provided me with a block of distraction-free time to be productive as I began to fulfill my new obligation to God.

In the pages of this book are the story of my life and the details of my incredible relationship with God. I've chosen to be as transparent as possible regarding the intimate details of my life. As with any other human being, I've done things that I'm not particularly proud of. I've made mistakes. I've acted foolishly, and I've definitely embarrassed myself or have been someone else's fodder. I'm not perfect. I have my own peccadillos, and just like you, I'm a human being. If having to share the intimate details of my life with the world is what is needed to fulfill my obligations to God—whether they're good, bad, or embarrassing—then so be it.

In order to honor God, I'm perfectly willing to discuss every aspect of my life in great detail, no matter how embarrassing. The only caveat is that I will do so on God's time or my own time, not at the whim of those who wish to assassinate my character.

Jamil "Jim" Maroun
    July 2023

Introduction

We're told that to have faith, to be a believer, and to gain access to Heaven, we must attend church, embrace church doctrine, participate in church rituals, confess our sins, and unconditionally believe that the contents of the Bible represent the word of God. Interestingly enough, I have failed all of those tests, yet I have developed a personal relationship with God. God has watched over me, and God has intervened on my behalf numerous times throughout my life. At one point in my life, when I went searching to restore my relationship with God, God met me in the southern Utah desert. From that point on, God partnered with me so that I could be an unstoppable force for goodness.

Have you ever imagined what our world would look like if there were no corruption, no murders, no rape, no violence, no thefts, no drug addiction, no injustices, and everyone was working towards making this a better world? I have! Have you ever wondered where God is or why God doesn't intervene when horrible, violent crimes are being committed against innocent victims? Are you curious as to how little girls can be savagely raped and murdered, yet God does nothing?

Introduction

In this book, you'll find the answer to these types of questions, the visions of the world God has bestowed upon me, and much more. Throughout my life, I've sought out God. I've asked God for His protection and guidance, and other times I've begged God to use me as a tool in His work. I've prayed to God, I've cried in front of God, I've asked God for forgiveness, I've asked God for guidance, I've asked God for signs, and I've asked God to allow me to serve Him. I've also asked God to let me be a light in this world, so that I may inspire others, and be a beacon of hope, inspiration, and change. I dared to dream big, and God responded in kind. You're about to read a true story about faith, hope, a relationship with God, and the future of humanity.

Part One
My Life

Chapter 1
My Demise

Does God Exist?

Does God exist? For someone like me, that's a silly question. I've found God out in a field, in a pasture, under a tree, by a creek, on the side of a cliff overlooking the ocean, and high on mountaintops. I know God exists by simply gazing in the Heavens at night, where a vast universe, full of promise, reveals itself. During the day, the warmth of our sun and the beauty of Mother Nature all convince me that the universe and the world we live in is God's creation.

The same question can be asked about Satan. Does Satan exist? For the longest time, I was so focused on God and His magnificent creation that I never paid Satan any mind. After all, I wasn't interested in being evil, and I certainly didn't have any intention of spending an eternity in Hell. Interestingly enough, even though I wasn't paying attention to Satan, Satan was paying attention to me. My indifference nearly cost me my life.

. . .

Just like evidence of God's existence is all around us, so too is evidence of Satan's existence. His handiwork surrounds us. Anywhere there is injustice and people are suffering, you'll find Satan and his minions hard at work. At the same time, God is everywhere. God is not indifferent, God is not dormant, nor is God ignoring our plight. God is listening, watching, and stands ready to engage with those who will seek Him out.

An Epic Battle

Humanity is in the midst of an epic spiritual battle that is taking place between good and evil for the right to claim your soul. Whether or not you're aware of this spiritual battle is inconsequential. It doesn't matter if you believe in God or not; It doesn't matter to what religion you belong, or if you have any religion at all. It doesn't matter if you want to participate in the battle or remain on the sidelines. If you're a human being, you have a soul, and whether you like it or not, you're all in.

Satan and his minions are very cunning, and they're out there, lurking, scheming, and exchanging false promises for the right to claim eternal souls. Indifference, hypocrisy, apathy, a lack of compassion, ignorance, and an unwillingness to do what's right are the tools of Satan, as evidenced by the abundance of tyranny, injustice, corruption, fraud, poverty, and needless suffering throughout the world. For Satan and his minions, times are good, and business is booming.

I've battled Satan at least twice in my life. In both instances, I wasn't aware of it until I began piecing together this story on my life. During the first battle, I was placed in a precarious situation not of my doing.

Given my predicament, I knew only that God could help me, so I reached out to Him daily in prayer to intervene, asking for protection for myself and for the people I loved. Over the course of several years, and on God's time, my circumstances changed for the better. I was victorious, and Satan had been soundly defeated.

My second engagement with Satan was disastrous. Like my first time, I was unaware that I was being engaged by Satan and his cadre. I'd also been tricked into believing that God's assistance was not needed. As a result, Satan was in the process of annihilating me when, in what would have been my final hour, God intervened.

No matter how dire the situation or how many souls Satan gathers, goodness will always overcome evil. In God's arsenal are people like me; those who believe goodness will overcome evil, those who have established a relationship with God and want to do good in this world. Those of us who have a personal relationship with God are not always easy to recognize. We can be rough around the edges and exhibit behaviors that aren't what one might expect from those associated with God; but God knows our hearts, God knows our desire to serve Him, to be used by Him, to abide by His will, and most importantly, God knows He can depend on us.

Satan knows that as long as he can keep humanity divided, distracted, and at loggerheads over both trivial and non-so-trivial matters, those forces for goodness in God's arsenal on whom God depends will be marginalized and rendered ineffective. Satan's biggest fear is that if those with a personal relationship with God figure out a way to unite in their efforts at serving God, then Satan will be banished from his Earthly realm.

. . .

God has compelled me to tell this story. For those of you who want to be a force for goodness in this world, believe that goodness can overcome evil, and want to develop your own personal relationship with God; know that humanity is in peril and that through the telling of my life story, and sharing the details of my incredible relationship with God, God has provided humanity with a roadmap for uniting in our efforts at defeating Satan.

My Awakening

It wasn't until 2015, after I'd depleted the remainder of my 401K, that I began to grasp the reality of my situation. I'd been without a steady paycheck since November of 2014, when I resigned from my position at Apple, Inc. I was on medical leave due to stress, and once I realized my work environment was the culprit, I resigned rather than try to milk the system. I attempted to start my own consulting business but quickly burned through my cash reserves.

I found myself flat broke. I could not make car payments, pay my car insurance or rent, and the cellphone company informed my wife and me that our service had been turned off for non-payment. A month earlier, we had run out of propane. We had no hot water or heat. We had been reduced to showering once a week at my mother-in-law's. Compounding my situation were two excruciating, throbbing toothaches necessitating prompt medical attention. Yet, I had no money and no insurance to seek relief. Within a couple of days, my wife wouldn't have any food to eat.

My current predicament was in stark contrast from where I was in 2000 when I graduated from college—the culmination of a lifetime dedicated to becoming a better human being. I endeavored to be responsible and self-sufficient and live a compelling lifestyle full of abundance. God had blessed me with vision. I developed a superior ability to identify numerous technology-based businesses that were years ahead of their time. I was going to generate abundant wealth and be a force for goodness, and I was going to make this a better world for all.

Yet there I was, 15 years after graduating from college, disheartened and inflicted with raw emotion. The previous 15 years of my life had been for nothing. I was unable to successfully launch a single business, let alone lay the foundation for a technology empire. My life had been enshrouded in a cloud of failure and doom. I'd been isolated from friends and prevented from utilizing my God-given skills, talents, and gifts to achieve the visions God had bestowed upon me. Every one of my dreams, desires, goals, and visions for the future had been destroyed. Instead of making this a better world, I was being forced to watch the world deteriorate all around me, and there was nothing I could do about it.

I was coming to the brutal realization that my lot in life wasn't coincidental or the result of making bad business decisions. Sinister forces had orchestrated and delighted in my downfall. I had been marginalized and forced into a life of poverty and irrelevancy. I'd been manipulated, laughed at, and played for a fool. I was unaware of any sins that I may have committed that I should be deserving of such a fate.

I was overwhelmed by the extent to which evil permeates our world. Given my beliefs, values, the objectives I wanted to achieve, and the significant resources that were expended to stop me, before I even began, I knew my enemies had been practicing their craft since the beginning of time. It was obvious that the forces against me had long ago mastered the art of wanton destruction. I knew their ability to operate stealthily, to remain undetectable, and their timing was impeccable. Satan and his minions had flawlessly squandered my life and covered their tracks. Any claims I made about a conspiracy against me would make me sound like a paranoid fool.

God's Intervention

After much contemplation about my situation and reflection upon the previous 15 years of my life, on March 29th, 2015, I was at peace with myself as I wrapped up my affairs before terminating my existence. I had accepted the fact that nefarious forces had checkmated me, and I was powerless against them. While I once had an incredible relationship with God, the church deceived me into believing God was responsible for my lot in life. In anger, I foolishly trashed my relationship with God. I never completely abandoned my relationship with God. I just stopped reaching out to Him. Whereas I once had a thriving relationship with God and was filled with the Holy Spirit on a regular basis, my relationship with God now lay dormant.

During what was to be my final hour, I glanced out my office door and stared at my wife in the other room. She was on her computer and was completely oblivious to the fact that soon, I would leave to run an errand, and she would never see me alive again. It was during this final hour of despair when God intervened. It was like a lightning bolt from out of nowhere. God had sent me a powerful message that although subtle, was powerful enough to jolt my senses, interrupt my thought process, grab my attention, and make me ponder what had just happened. For several minutes, I sat in disbelief, but facts were facts. God had just intervened in a way that only He could. I had just received an undeniable message from God that I was not to take my life that day. During the next few days, God laid out the path for me to rebuild my relationship with Him, and regain control of my life.

God's Will

I wish I could share with you that the very next morning, when I woke up, I found my bank account flush with cash, I no longer had any debts, and my phone was ringing off the hook with consulting offers. I *wish* I could. Unfortunately, when I woke up the following morning, I was still on a collision course with financial disaster. I did, however, wake up with something I thought I would never see again —hope. God had just intervened on my behalf, which was good enough for me. I immediately went about looking for employment.

I soon found myself waking up in the middle of the night with the same specific and intense thoughts running through my head. Who had I wronged, and how do I resolve my persecution? Was I wrong for not compromising my values, beliefs, and relationship with God by refusing to attend church and abide by church doctrine? Was I wrong not to acknowledge the moral superiority of my family? I would then change gears and reflect upon the visions God had bestowed upon me, my relationship with God, and the magnitude of what had been lost. I'd focus on a specific behavior, action, or offense I may have committed, and then I'd become incredulous about how my life had been purposely squandered. In my head, I'd search for justification, pointing out the blatant hypocrisy in our world, the unchecked spread of evil, and man's severe apathy toward the fate of the world. Sometimes I'd reflect upon my relationship with God and all the beautiful experiences we'd had. I began paying closer attention to all the jumbled thoughts in my head and started putting them to paper. Any attempt to go back to sleep was futile.

Once again, I diligently prayed daily to seek God's guidance. As time passed, I became keenly aware that God's response to my pleas for relief was always the same. There was a correlation between my prayers for relief, my inability to sleep through the night, and God's response. God was going to intervene on my behalf to stop my persecution and restore to me the lifestyle that had been denied to me, but first, I had a new obligation to fulfill. During my midnight brainstorming sessions, a pattern began to emerge. Church doctrine, religious teachings, and the rituals of the church are well-known and documented; however, my incredible relationship, experiences, and commitments to God were not. In fact, until I began writing this story, I wasn't even aware that God had taken me up on the numerous overtures I'd made. I knew God had blessed me with spectacular gifts and talents, and I knew what was in my heart, but I never really gave much thought to the fact that God was working with me for a reason.

I soon realized that God was compelling me to tell the story of my life and share the incredible details of my relationship with Him to the world. Based on my experiences with God, as well as the various visions of the world with which God has provided me, I cannot help but feel that this entire book is nothing short of a message from God to the world. The survival of humanity is at stake, and while I may have been rendered irrelevant in the fight between good and evil, God is undeterred.

Chapter 2
Childhood Experiences

Learning About God

My earliest, albeit faint childhood recollections of any formal introduction to God, was attending catechism and Mass at the Maronite Church in Cleveland, Ohio. I am convinced that at a very young age, the Maronite church was responsible for instilling in me key concepts such as being good, not sinning, and reaching out to God through prayer. In addition, I was taught that God was everywhere and was always watching and always listening. I took these concepts to heart, which laid the foundation for my incredible relationship with God. I also fondly remember eating donuts in the church basement after Mass with my father and visiting the bakery next door.

My earliest memory of demonstrating my faith and trust in God occurred at a church carnival in Ohio. I don't believe I was older than five or six years old at the time. Another kid and I were palling around the carnival when a lady approached us with a stick of cotton candy and asked if we wanted it because she couldn't eat it all. It was a full stick of cotton candy, so we both eagerly agreed to take it off her hands. Before I could take my first bite, my new friend posed the question, "What if she poisoned it?" Without hesitation, I confidently replied, "If she poisoned it, it just means that God wants us in Heaven now!" We devoured the whole thing without further discussion.

The only other church that I feel impacted my spiritual growth was Our Lady of The Pillar in Half Moon Bay, California. Our Lady of The Pillar was located behind my parents' grocery store. On Sunday mornings, I would ride with my dad to our family's grocery store, and then was coerced into attending church and catechism classes by myself. Most Sundays, I was our family's sole representative at church. I believe my attendance in catechism classes reinforced the concepts of being good, praying, and serving God.

Outside of these few impactful childhood experiences, attending church was not a priority for my family and was usually reserved for special occasions or religious holidays. I remember one Christmas holiday, my entire family went to the new Maronite Church in Millbrae, California, and arrived early enough that we could sit in the front row pew. When Father Paul came out to greet the parishioners, he looked at my family and remarked that he could always tell when it was a holiday by the new faces in church.

In addition to early church teachings, there was one other source that influenced my willingness to seek out a relationship with God: my mother. My mother believed in and supported the church, but was noncommittal about attending church regularly. However, praying was a different story. My mother taught me how to pray for God's guidance, wisdom, strength, and protection and encouraged me to do so daily. In addition, every time we went somewhere, my mother would make us recite a prayer in the car that God would bring us safely home.

From the day I first learned about God, I never hesitated to pray and reach out to Him regularly. My faith in God, being good, not sinning, and praying for guidance, wisdom, strength, and protection was all done privately. On my own initiative, I was reaching out to God. There was no fanfare. Unbeknownst to me, God was paying attention.

Memories of Ohio

My family lived on Deerfield Drive in Parma, Ohio, and I attended Renwood elementary school, located just down the street, so I'd walk to school. I had a classmate who would always be the first student in line to enter our class in the morning. One day, I set out to beat him, and beat him, I did. It was wintertime and snowing. I arrived at school so early that the doors to the building were still locked. I stood outside, freezing, without shelter from the elements, but I was the first kid at school. I still remember the look on the janitor's face when he unlocked the school doors and saw me shivering in the cold.

I was a latchkey kid and often came home from school to an empty house. One day walking home from school, my feet were freezing cold. When my mom and sister came home later that day, they found me lying on my back, thawing out, with my feet pressed up against our wall heater.

. . .

Heroes Wanted

Being a latchkey kid, I had a lot of unsupervised time to get into trouble—and I did! One day, I decided I was going to chop down a tree. Barefoot, I walked into our garage and retrieved an axe. I stepped on a rake as I walked out of the garage with the axe in hand. Just like a Three Stooges Movie, the rake handle flew up and smacked me right in the head. I immediately dropped the axe onto my big toe. Thankfully the toe wasn't severed or broken, but I did lose my big toenail.

For fun, my friends and I would climb onto the roof of our garage and then hang jump off the side. The garage had a sloping roof, so we'd start at the lower end and then dare each other to drop further towards the peak, where it was a higher drop. One day, when no one else was home, a friend and I had conquered the garage and decided to move on to greater heights. We decided to see who could jump from the highest step on our stairway. We started from the bottom half of the stairs and worked our way up, one step at a time, towards the top. I managed to jump from the second step from the top. Halfway through the jump, I used my hands to push against both walls to keep my momentum going. I almost cleared the last step, but I spun around in the air, and the right half of my foot hit the top of the last step.

I screamed in excruciating pain. My friend ran home to get help. He lived a few doors down. He returned with a wagon. His mom made him wheel me down to his house. Soon my parents came home, and I ended up in the emergency room with a broken foot. When it came time for the doctor to wrap my foot, he had me put a piece of wood in my mouth to muffle my screams of pain—just like in the movies. Way cool!

. . .

Once I learned how to ride a bicycle, my friends and I would spend the day riding our bikes around Parma. One day, while in the car with my mother, I provided her with shortcuts to get us home. My mother was pleasantly surprised, and was bewildered that I was navigating home down streets she'd never been on before. My mother was delighted when I got us home without getting lost.

I was a Cub Scout, and one day a bunch of us went around the neighborhood collecting old newspapers. I had my older brother's red wagon and somehow went off by myself. I went door to door, explaining I was a Cub Scout, and was collecting old newspapers. After a while, one of the older kids was sent to find me, and when he found me, he couldn't believe his eyes. The wagon had three stacks of old newspapers towering over my head. We hit up a few more houses and then had to return and find the others. If we added more newspapers to the wagon, we took a risk that the whole thing would topple over. In the end, I had collected more newspapers than anyone else.

During Halloween, multiple haunted houses would pop up around the Parma area. I still have a frightful memory of going through one of them with my parents. In one room, an ape was running around, chasing me. I was screaming in terror, clinging to my father's leg for dear life. I remember my poor father trying to pry me off his leg so we wouldn't hold up the line. On another occasion, my mother decided to take me with her to a different haunted house. At one point, the entire line snaking through the haunted house was held up because my mother and I were petrified with fear and refused to enter the next chamber. Finally, staff members, or some fearless men, escorted us through the remainder of the haunted house. I remember both my mom and I had our heads down, so we couldn't see what was coming after us.

· · ·

Heroes Wanted

On weekends, my maternal uncle would pick up my mom and me and take us for a drive in his convertible Cadillac with his wife and son. His son was younger than me by a year. On several occasions, we would go to a place called Marble Rock, and my cousin and I would play next to a stream. My cousin would fall in, and I'd get yelled at. One time, when we were at Marble Rock, I felt the call of nature. Why I didn't say anything to my mom is beyond me. I followed a path that led me into a heavily wooded area. Once I was sure I was alone, I dropped my drawers and did my business. With little concern about not having anything to wipe with, I pulled up my pants and headed back. On my way out of the wooded area, I noticed a man in the shadows, watching me. He was standing there as if in a trance. I said 'hi' to him as I walked by. It wasn't until I was an adult that I realized the potential danger I had been in. The man's eyes were glossed over, and he had the same facial expression as an evil villain in a fairytale right before he was about to pounce on his hapless victim. I don't believe that guy had good intentions, and I'm not sure what prevented him from turning me into his next victim.

Later that evening, when we were driving back home with the top of my uncle's convertible up, there was an awful stench in the car, and nobody knew where it was coming from. It was so bad that, even though it was cold outside, the car windows were all rolled down. Eventually, the stench was traced back to my ass. I had to fess up. My uncle was pissed, and my mother scolded me as she wiped my ass with Kleenex in the back seat of my uncle's Cadillac.

In addition to going to Marble Rock, my uncle took my mom and me to Cedar Point with his family. I ended up ditching everyone and then going on the rides I wanted to go on over and over again. Eventually, they'd find me, and I'd get yelled at. Other times, my mom would take me to Cedar Point, and it would be just the two of us.

During one visit, I found a cool tubular slide and spent hours on it while she watched. On the way home, when Mom got tired, she'd find a car dealership to park in, and we'd sleep in the car until morning and then return home.

I almost forgot to mention that our house on Deerfield Drive had a solid wood swinging door that separated the kitchen from the dining room. A sturdy plastic carpet protector—with plastic spikes on the bottom to hold it in place—ran from the front door through the dining room and terminated at the swinging door to our kitchen. Whenever I observed someone entering the kitchen barefoot, I'd flip the plastic carpet runner over and wait for them to re-enter the dining room.

Not Being Good Enough

In 1972, a week before I turned seven years old, my father moved our family from Ohio to the small coastal town of Montara, California. Montara was situated on the side of a large hill and was surrounded by mountains to the north, the Pacific Ocean to the west, and woods to the east. Montara consisted of a long stretch of beach, cliffs overlooking the ocean, dirt roads, fields, and lots of coastal flora. My youth was spent riding dirt bikes, climbing trees, sitting in fields, exploring coastal trails, and communing with God in His beautiful creation. Some of the best memories of my life were from growing up on the coast. While my childhood was uneventful, like all youth, I had my share of challenges.

My mother could be extremely negative and critical of any situation or person, and she often was. In addition, my mother had a penchant for comparing our family to other families and pointing out how much better they were. As a result, at an early age, I developed a low sense of self-esteem. It didn't take long for me to eventually believe that I wasn't good enough and others were better than me. One of my most demoralizing memories from childhood occurred while watching the Winter Olympics on television with my mom and older sister. In a rare moment of household tranquility, the three of us were watching incredibly talented ice skaters.

For me, part of the joy from watching these professional athletes came from being grateful that I could enjoy the show with my mom and sister without any drama. As the three of us watched in awe, one of the skaters performed a spectacular move that caused the entire stadium to erupt into thunderous applause. We're sitting there, along with the rest of the world, mesmerized by this professional ice skater's feat. As the three of us are savoring the moment, out of nowhere, my mom says, "Jimmy, why can't you do that?"

My tranquility was instantly shattered. I felt like I was just punched in the stomach and could not catch my breath. I went from experiencing feelings of amazement and awe to feelings of inadequacy and failure, and not being good enough. I didn't have an answer for my mother. I just wasn't good enough.

In addition to my family, my classmates in grade school helped reinforce my feelings of inadequacy and low self-esteem. My last name and portly frame provided some of my more quick-witted classmates with ample material for creating rhymes at my expense. I had to endure Maroun the baboon and Maroun the balloon. In addition to the verbal abuse, I had to suffer the humiliation of being the last to be picked for a team sport during recess or my physical ed class. Sometimes, I wouldn't be picked at all. While these experiences did affect my self-esteem and confidence, I never believed for one second that my experiences with my classmates were spiteful or anything out of the ordinary. It was just kids being kids. Nonetheless, I would be self-conscious about my weight from elementary school through junior high up until my sophomore year in high school, the year I first played football.

Rounding out my feelings of inadequacy and not being good enough were my paternal aunts and uncles. At family gatherings, I would be admonished for not being able to speak Lebanese. My aunts and uncles would purposely talk to me in Lebanese and then look at me like I was an idiot because I couldn't understand what they were saying. I'd been in America since I was six months old, and my family lived at least an hour and a half away from our Lebanese-speaking relatives. The only Lebanese community on the coast was my brother, sister, mom, and dad. While my older brothers, sister, and parents spoke the language, they predominately spoke English. Everyone else on the coast spoke English, Spanish, or Portuguese.

My mother was fluent in Lebanese and had a very sharp tongue. At family gatherings with my dad's side of the family, mom would often start arguments with my aunts and uncles in Lebanese. The whole room would erupt in a battle of foreign dialects. I'd find myself embarrassed at family gatherings, and I wasn't even aware of what they were arguing about.

I grew up under the shroud of my paternal aunts and uncles looking down on my family. Apparently, there was some bad blood between my father, older brother Shawn, and uncle. As a result, I was constantly warned not to grow up and be like my father and older brothers. From an early age, it was ingrained in my head that my immediate family wasn't as good as the rest of the family.

· · ·

Heroes Wanted

Reinforcing my feelings of inadequacy around my dad's side of the family was a traumatic event that took place when I was sixteen. I drove to my uncle's house in Menlo Park for a family gathering. My dad's side of the family was quite large, and the living room was packed full of people. There were aunts, uncles, and cousins I had never met, didn't remember, or hadn't seen in quite a long time. Our custom was to greet each other with a kiss on both cheeks. Dreading the ritual, I started with a group of relatives sitting by the front door and began our traditional greeting.

There was an old man I'd never seen before. I don't remember if I kissed him or shook his hand. He was introduced to me as the husband of my aunt, who was sitting next to him. As I went in to kiss my aunt, this old man's leg came up between my aunt and me. I thought the old man was having a seizure or a cramp. His leg came back down immediately, and he gestured like he was sorry, but it was too late. The entire room exploded in angry Lebanese dialect.

All of the adults were yelling. I had no idea what was going on. I stood there embarrassed, watching people argue, then abruptly stop, look at me, smile, and then go back to arguing. The sound of a room filled with angry shouting in Lebanese and not knowing what they were saying was terrifying. I'd never felt so uncomfortable. Eventually, an uneasy calm settled over the room. I later learned that my aunt's husband was a wealthy Muslim. The family was against my aunt marrying him, but love prevailed. Apparently, in Muslim culture, only the man is allowed to kiss his wife. It was news to me and fuel on the fire for my dad's side of the family.

For me, my Lebanese ethnicity was an embarrassment. All my friends were white and were born in the United States of America. Prior to my birth, my folks went back and forth between Lebanon and America. Thus my older brothers Richard and Shawn and my older sister Rachel had formed relationships with my aunts and uncles and could speak the language. Although I was born in Lebanon, when I was six months old, my folks moved back to the United States and never went back. The civil war in Lebanon was fodder for my classmates to humiliate me. The bombing of the American barracks in 1983 didn't make me feel much better about myself or my culture. I wanted nothing to do with Lebanese culture. As far as I was concerned, I was an American. I wouldn't learn to appreciate my Lebanese heritage until much later.

Work Ethic Beginnings

I used to walk to and from my elementary school in Montara. On the way was a new house under construction being built by the homeowner and his wife. Fascinated, I'd stop by and talk to them on my way home from school. The couple had a foreign accent and were nice enough. I must have pestered them to see if I could do anything to help them build their new home because one day, the man had me chisel off excess concrete from a stack of gray masonry building bricks.

When I completed the task after a couple of visits, I eagerly asked the man if there was something else I could do. The man replied that he had nothing else for me to do and stated he was quite surprised that I had finished the job he had given me. He explained that he didn't think I would finish the job. At the time, I didn't understand his response. I had asked to help out, and he gave me a task to perform, and I completed the task. A few days later, he accused me of stealing items from his job site.

. . .

I never stole a thing from this couple. As kids, we'd explore his property when he wasn't there, but I never took anything, and neither did anyone else I was with. I never stopped to visit with him and his wife again. It would be a while before I realized the whole point of him having me clean off excess mortar from his masonry bricks was a ruse to get me to stop bugging him and his wife.

I had another neighbor that lived right next door to us. My mom's bedroom had a private deck overlooking the neighbor's backyard. I would see my neighbor working in his backyard and would wander over to see if he needed help. One day, I was helping him dig holes for plants when my mom saw me from her deck and asked me why I was helping the neighbor with his yard when our yard looked horrible. I didn't have an answer, but my neighbor quickly replied that it was because he was paying me, which he was. At the same time, no one in my family was working on our backyard. It was all dirt with the exception of a concrete patio below my mom's balcony. What the hell was I supposed to do?

An Entrepreneur in the Making

My parents owned a grocery store in Half Moon Bay, and when I was nine years old, I was put to work stocking shelves. I still remember pricing merchandise, rotating merchandise, and working inside our walk-in cooler. I learned that if the shelf was empty, we couldn't sell products. If we didn't sell products, we weren't making money. When I was twelve, I was promoted to a cashier's position. At twelve years old, I interacted with customers and learned about customer service.

I was very sociable with customers and liked to joke with them. To this day, I remember the first customer I ever pissed off. A customer I was ringing up asked me to carefully handle his bag of potato chips.

He didn't want them crushed. The last thing I wanted to do was destroy this man's potato chips. I responded to his request with a smart-ass reply and a smile. I thought I was being clever. To my shock, the customer, in a severe tone, instructed me to remove the potato chips from the sale. He did not want them anymore. I quickly apologized, explained I was joking, and offered to give him the potato chips for free, but he said it was too late. He didn't want them. I finished the sale. He paid with a check and then left. I felt horrible, but I learned an invaluable customer service lesson at a very early age.

Another incident that stood out was with one of my regular customers who would enjoy bantering with me. We both had a lot of fun. One day, he was short on money, and I ended up buying him a 12-pack of beer. He promised to pay me back on his next visit. The next time he came into the store, I excitedly greeted him like I usually did and immediately asked if he had the money for the beer I had given him. I did this in front of a line of customers at my register. He smiled and acknowledged that he did and then went about shopping. When he came through my line, no one else was around, and he explained how I had embarrassed him in front of the other customers. I had a great relationship with this customer, we had a lot of fun giving each other a hard time, and the last thing I ever would have wanted to do was embarrass him. I apologized to him and learned another valuable lesson in customer service.

I remember watching a TV program about how a guy was going around and scamming cashiers out of money by asking for change for a twenty. Once he received the smaller denominations, he'd mix them with a stack of bills he had in his other hand, claim the cashier didn't give him the proper change, confuse the cashier, and then end up walking out with more money than he came in with. A few days later, on a Sunday morning, when no one else was in the store, except for my dad cutting meat in the butcher shop and Shawn in the office, a customer tried the same scam on me.

Initially, I thought the customer was making an honest mistake, I knew I provided him with the correct amount of change for a twenty, but as he persisted and started moving money back and forth between his hands, I informed him that we could settle this by counting out my drawer. At the same time, I hit a button that rang a buzzer in the office. As Shawn approached, the man quickly declined and left. When Shawn asked about what was going on, I related the story to him.

My junior high school was on the street behind my parent's grocery store and across the street from the church. During lunchtime, I had permission to leave campus and walk across the street to my parents' grocery store for lunch. During that time, I'd load up with candy, especially pop rocks, make an inventory of what I was taking, and then go back to school and sell everything for ten cents above what we sold them for in the store. I was making money hand-over-fist until one of my teachers complained to my dad.

When I was around ten years old, I received a Tyco slot car racing set for Christmas. My sister Rachel would take me to the mall with her, and I'd always visit the hobby store looking for slot car and track replacement parts. The hobby store was always out of key parts I needed, and each time I'd ask when they would be restocked, I'd be told the items were on backorder from the factory. After several trips, always with the same answer, in frustration, I took matters into my own hands.

· · ·

I found Tyco's phone number—I believe they were somewhere back East—and I called them to complain. I explained to the customer service representative on the phone how I couldn't get track connecting clips, guide pins, and other parts for my slot car set because the factory was always back-ordered. The customer service representative politely asked if my parents knew I was making a long-distance phone call. I assured her it wouldn't be a problem. The customer service representative then continued and explained that the factory had all of these parts in stock and took my information.

A few weeks later, I received a small box that had all of the parts I requested, with extra quantities thrown in for good measure. In addition, two brand-new slot cars were in the box. I was ecstatic. Up until I received my package of slot car parts, my parents were unaware of my long-distance phone call. I didn't get into trouble, but apparently, it was expensive to make long-distance phone calls back in the day. I believe the customer service representative I spoke with believed it was going to be my ass for making a long-distance phone call and sent me something extra for my troubles. Whatever her motivation was, it was an outstanding example of customer service.

In Junior High, one of my classmates started bringing firecrackers to school. Although they were illegal, he was selling them. He confided in me that he was ordering the firecrackers from somewhere back East, where they were still legal. Armed with this information, I raided my mother's room and found a couple of phone books she had brought with her from Ohio. Sure enough, there were several listings for fireworks companies in Ohio.

I sent away for catalogs and pricing. I will never forget my father shaking his head in displeasure as the UPS driver carried into our grocery store a huge box with "Class B Explosives" plastered all over it. I had scored big time. I had purchased several bricks of firecrackers, several grosses of bottle rockets, and all types of other fireworks not available in California. My older brother Shawn ended up selling some to his friends, and for the next several years, we had an awesome time at the beach on the Fourth of July.

In October, Half Moon Bay would hold its annual Pumpkin festival. All weekend long, the town would be packed with tourists. Behind our grocery store was an empty lot, and every year I'd sell parking spaces to the public at $5.00 a shot. Across the street was an open field, and one of the clubs from Half Moon Bay high school would be out there selling parking spaces for only $2.00 a space. When their lot filled up, mine would fill up. One year I encouraged one of the teachers to raise their price to $5.00, but the teacher declined, stating this was a community fundraiser and the school had to maintain budget pricing. It was a perfect example of supply and demand and what people were willing to pay.

One year, Shawn was running a side business wholesaling produce. During the Pumpkin Festival weekend, he scored a screaming deal on corn on the cob. We were sitting on whole cases of it. At the end of the day, when people were leaving the Pumpkin Festival to go home, the street that ran by our grocery store was in bumper-to-bumper traffic. I was in the middle of the street, peddling corn on the cob. Over the weekend, we sold out of corn on the cob, and I made a small fortune.

The Montara Mountain Pinball Factory

In my fifth-grade class was a clown named Barry Bono. Barry was hilarious and unrelenting. I can thank Barry for 'Maroun the Balloon' and 'Baboon Maroun.' Our entire class can also thank Barry for asking our beautiful fifth-grade teacher, during sex education, what a vagina was twenty times in a row. The entire class would be on the floor in hysterics while our teacher, red-faced, embarrassingly tried to address his persistent question in a professional manner. Barry was quite the character.

Barry knew that I loved to play pinball and used to tell me tall stories about pinball. Barry once claimed to have a pinball machine at his house. I was like, great, when could I come over? But Barry would always have an excuse as to why I couldn't. Barry would like to change it up and once told me that the pinball machine he had at home worked, but the bottom of the machine was missing. The internal components were just dangling by their wires. I indulged Barry and went along with his deception. I knew he was lying.

Interestingly enough, though, I could envision a functioning pinball machine missing its bottom. I'd seen the inside of a pinball machine. There was nothing but actuators, coils, solenoids, and other parts all wired together. I believed that anything was possible, and I could envision a machine with all of these components dangling by the electrical wires to which they were attached. Every time Barry would pass off his lie, I would keep asking him when I could come over. I enjoyed watching his continued deception. Classmates thought I was fooled and warned me that Barry was lying. I assured them that I knew.

One day Barry upped his deception and told me that he knew where there was a secret Pinball Factory in the Montara Mountains. Again, I knew he was full of shit. There was nothing in the Montara Mountains but old dirt roads the military created. I knew this because I used to ride my dirt bike on them. Yet, I still indulged Barry. I had a great imagination, though. I could envision an underground pinball factory in the Montara mountains where pinball machines were assembled. In my head, I saw a production line, the whole nine yards. Anything was possible.

I don't know why I never confronted Barry about his deception. He wasn't bothering me. He was the one that was lying. Tolerating habitual liars would be a trend throughout my life. As long as deceptive people were not bothering me, I'd tolerate them. Their devious ways would eventually catch up to them, and in the end, they'd be the ones answering to God.

Temptation

I loved playing pinball and would play every chance I got. Since I worked for my parents, I collected a paycheck and had my own money; however, most of my pay went into my savings account. To supplement my pinball addiction, I would ask my mom or dad for money. Such requests were rarely denied, and when they were, or if no one was around, I'd scrounge around the house for loose change. There was always plenty of loose change lying around our house. I never thought twice about taking it. The only time I got into trouble was when I raided Rachel's piggy bank. I didn't know the money was for her car payment. The only other time I got yelled at was when Shawn discovered I was raiding his large plastic beer bottle that was filled with loose change.

In junior high, I was forced to attend the Catholic church behind my folks' grocery store. One Sunday, I somehow got roped into collecting donations during Mass. I'd walk up and down the aisle with a wicker basket at the end of a long pole and hold it out so people could donate money to the church. I thought it was a pretty cool gig; it made attending church a little more palatable, but at the same time, I didn't think a kid should be collecting money.

One day, I was the first volunteer to finish collecting donations, and I found myself alone in a room with a basketful of money. I allowed my imagination to run free. There were quarters, dollar bills, and a $5.00 bill sitting on the top of the pile as enticing to me as a cherry on an ice cream sundae. I stared at that pile of money and dreamed of the field day I'd have later at the local pinball arcade. Best of all, nobody would be the wiser. It was pure temptation, but because of my values, I knew this money was intended for God's purpose. No matter how tempting, it wasn't mine for the taking. While I enjoyed the fantasy, I never took a penny.

Hope

Despite having low self-esteem, being overweight, and generally not being chosen for team sports during recess, a couple of significant events in my young life provided me with hope. The first event occurred in the fifth grade, towards the end of the school year. We had a day of games that culminated in a series of foot races. Much to everyone's surprise, including my own, I ended up being the second fastest kid in our school. Even with the extra weight, I could run like the wind. I'd been conditioned to believe I was not as good as everyone else, yet here I was, the second fastest kid in the school. It was a huge boost for my self-esteem.

The second event occurred during junior high. Towards the end of the school year, our teacher announced a day of games where two student teams would compete. When it came time to form teams, my hand went up, but no one else's did. The teacher waited patiently. It was quite an awkward moment, to say the least, until one of the prettiest girls in our class, perhaps in the whole school, raised her hand to be my teammate. It was a pity play on her part, but I was grateful for the gesture.

When it came to game day, the two of us killed it. We were beating everyone and would have come in first place, but during the last race, I fell in my gunny sack and couldn't get back up for the simple reason that I couldn't stop laughing. All I could think about was how no one wanted to be on the "fat boy's team," yet there I was with the prettiest girl in the school, and we were killing it. For the life of me, I couldn't stop laughing. By the time I regained my composure, it had cost us first place, but at least we managed to come in second. My teammate wasn't thrilled about us not taking first, but I was forgiven once I explained why I couldn't get up.

There were other experiences during my childhood that afforded me a glimmer of hope. Our school took a field trip to San Francisco to visit the Coast Guard. During the tour, there was a console with all kinds of buttons, levers, and switches. It looked like something right out of *Star Trek*. When our tour guide finished telling us what the console was used for, I asked what would happen if someone came in and just started pushing all the buttons. The tour guide looked at me with a grin, pushed several buttons on the console, and then replied, "I'm not sure, let's find out." All the kids surged towards the console. Every button, lever, and switch was pushed, touched, and moved with wonderment. It was a good time for all.

The Legend of Peg Leg

I first heard about Peg Leg when I was at Pescadero Memorial Park. My mom would organize a group of kids and drive us to the park.

We'd have a picnic and then spend the day exploring trails and playing in the creek. I don't know who told me the story, but Peg Leg was a doctor who was flying his wife and daughter in a single-engine airplane over the Pescadero forest when he ran out of fuel and crashed. Trapped in the wreckage of his burning plane, the doctor had to sever his leg below the knee to free himself. He survived the crash, but unfortunately, the same could not be said for his wife and daughter.

Apparently, the trauma of crashing, cutting off his leg, and losing his family drove the good doctor crazy, but not before he fashioned a thick tree branch into the shape of a peg. A search party eventually stumbled upon the airplane's wreckage, with the burnt bodies of the doctor's wife and child and the doctor's burnt leg lodged in the crumpled cock pit. There was no sign of the doctor. After a couple of weeks, the search was called off. Not being from the local community, the missing doctor was soon forgotten until the partially eaten bodies of missing hikers started turning up. Forensic evaluations revealed a medical scalpel was used to slash the victims. Despite numerous man hunts, the doctor was never found, but the half-eaten bodies of his victims kept piling up.

In the town of Montara, behind 8th Street, was a large vacant field. To the west of the field, several streets came to a dead end on the edge of the field. To the south of the field was a huge valley that went up to the other side of the town south of Montara, Moss Beach. To the east of this large field was a small forest. I'd ridden my dirt bike in the field before, but I'd never been in the forested area. I soon learned that Peg Leg didn't actually crash his plane in Pescadero Memorial Park. Instead, Peg Leg had crashed in the patch of forest on the eastern side of this big, empty field in Montara.

· · ·

Heroes Wanted

One day, my friend Mike and a bunch of other kids came by my house and informed me that several of us kids were going to track down Peg Leg. I needed a weapon, so I grabbed a huge walking stick my mom liked. Other kids in our posse brought knives, hammers ... even an axe. We walked from my house on 5th Street, up East Ave, to 9th Street. From there, we entered the field and began our trek east toward the forest. Being overweight, I couldn't always keep up with the rest of the posse, so I'd fall behind. As we walked through the field, we discussed the various strategies we'd use to defend ourselves against Peg Leg.

As we got closer to the trees, my heart began to race. I was scared shitless, but peer pressure dictated I back up my friends. The wind was blowing, and the trees were swaying. As we closed in on the trees, a trail could be seen that led into the forest. Within 30 yards of the trail entrance, we saw movement, and someone yelled, "Peg Leg!" I dropped my mom's favorite walking stick, and I ran nonstop all the way home with my dog in tow.

As usual, no one was home. Every time the wind blew, the house squeaked, and I was positive it was Peg Leg coming to get me. I didn't sleep a wink that night. The next day, my friend Mike brought over my mom's favorite walking stick and laughed as he explained the movement we observed was other kids. Mike claimed they all yelled for me to stop, but I kept running. He said they spent the day playing on a tree swing.

The Pumpkin Patch

In junior high, I had to attend summer school at Half Moon Bay High School. I'd ride into town with my parents to our grocery store, and then when it was time to go to summer school, I'd walk. The school was on Lewis Foster Drive, and just to the south was a trail that cut through a large pumpkin patch. The trail was a shortcut from the high school to the street.

One day, a friend I used to pal around with, Kenny Grimes, was walking back to town from high school with me and we used the trail to cut through the pumpkin patch. Being kids, we sat down in the middle of the pumpkin patch and started telling scary stories. From where we sat, we could see a cemetery to the east.

At one point, Kenny and I looked back at the trail toward the high school. Neither of us said a word, but we both jumped to our feet and high-tailed it out of the pumpkin patch, away from the school and toward town. We didn't stop until we were on the corner of Main Street and Highway 92. Out of breath, we kept looking back to where the trail through the pumpkin patch terminated, next to an electrical substation.

When Kenny and I were sitting in the field and looked back at the high school, I felt as if I had been transported back in time. The sky was a vivid blue and skipping toward Kenny and me were two young girls, holding hands and dressed in pioneer clothing similar to what they wore on Little House on the Prairie. I felt like I was in a dream. Everything was slightly blurred, but what was most alarming was that the girls were skipping toward us in slow motion.

Kenny and I carefully exchanged accounts of what just transpired, and our stories matched. We both waited at the corner to see if the girls would come out, but they never did. There was no other place to go in that field. Neither one of us ever cut across that field again. I'm not sure of the significance of this experience. I do know what I saw, and what I saw was enough to freak me out and run out of that field. The fact that both Kenny and I described the same event makes the event even more metaphysical.

Little League

One day, when I was in junior high, I was home watching TV when there was a knock on the door. A man, whom I had never met, informed me that my parents had signed me up for Little League, and he was taking me to baseball practice. I hopped into his van with the other kids, and off to practice we went.

When it came to throwing the ball, I couldn't tell if I was left- or right-handed. I struggled to throw the ball with either hand, but with my left hand, the ball went farther, so I resorted to throwing with my left and catching with my right. Batting was a different story. In practice, every time our pitcher threw the ball, I'd whop that sucker over the fence. In practice, I was a power hitter, and whenever I came to bat, the outfield would move back. I couldn't wait to score home runs for my team.

When it came to playing against other teams, my enthusiasm quickly waned. The first time at bat against another team, and subsequently every other game I played, I got beaned by the ball. At first, I believed the other team's pitcher was making mistakes because the ball was being thrown all over the place. It wasn't like the perfect pitches I'd received during practice. I was clueless.

During one of the few times Shawn, his girlfriend, and some of their friends showed up to one of my games to cheer me on, the pitcher threw the ball so close to my shins that I started balling at the plate. I was so humiliated. I hated the game. All I wanted to do was ride my dirt bike. On the rare occasion that I managed to hit the ball, I got a base hit. I ran as fast as I could to first base and slid before the first baseman could tag me out. I ripped the front of my pants, but I was safe. Everyone was laughing. I later learned that players don't slide into first base. They run past it.

I played center field, and my out-fielding was slightly better than my batting abilities. The first time a low drive ball made it out to me, I scooped up the ball and threw it as hard as I could to home plate. The ball bounced a couple of times before making it to the catcher. I learned later that I should have thrown the ball to an infielder. In another game, two high flies to centerfield both landed in my baseball glove. Both plays were victorious moments for me.

Overall, our team sucked. I got beaned at-bat almost every game. During our last game of the season, I avoided getting beaned and got a double. It was the only game we won that season. Our team finally scored a victory, and our coach took the team out to pizza to celebrate.

I never played baseball again. My experiences at bat traumatized me for years, and it would be decades before I finally made peace with myself over my baseball experiences. I blamed myself for being beaned at the plate, and I was ashamed for crying at the plate. Before our first league game, I'd never been exposed to curve balls or any other type of pitch. After watching me getting beaned and crying during our first league game, our pitcher was probably afraid of traumatizing me further if he threw an aggressive curve ball at me in practice. It was only after I realized I was ignorant of the game that I received any closure.

. . .

I was never asked if I wanted to play baseball. No one in my family played baseball, and no one in my family ever taught me how. I wasn't taught about the various pitches pitchers used. I didn't even know what the protocol was when approaching the plate. Does the pitcher wait for the batter to set up, or does the batter only have a few seconds to get into position before the pitcher throws the ball? I was forced to play a sport I wasn't thrilled about and knew nothing about. My experiences in Little League taught me that dropping a kid off for a sport and not supporting that kid is a losing proposition. Education, the sharing of knowledge, encouragement, practice, and feedback are vital for success.

Juvenile Court

I don't remember how old I was when I received a ticket for riding my dirt bike on a public street in Montara. I may have still been in elementary school, but one thing is for sure—I'll never forget my court experience. I remember sitting before the judge with my father, who had to take time off from work. During the court proceedings, my father started yelling at the judge, questioning why the Sheriff's deputies had time to sit and ticket kids.

I was embarrassed that my dad had to take time off from work on my behalf. After this experience, I either side-saddled my dirt bike and jump off it if I saw a Sheriff's vehicle, or I walked beside the bike until I reached a field. In any case, I made sure I never got caught riding my dirt bike on the street again. I never ran from a Sheriff's patrol car. However, the Sheriff's helicopter was a different story.

. . .

My friends and I loved running from the Sheriff's helicopter. We'd be on Montara Mountain and spot the helicopter coming for us. We'd head for the eastern part of Montara, where the trees provided ample concealment from the sky. Once under the canopy of trees, we'd race across town as fast as we could, using both streets and fields. From afar, we'd watch the Sheriff's helicopter look for us.

Interestingly enough, one of my primary escape routes took me to the backside of the woods that Peg Leg was supposedly haunting. The trail entrance that started at the end of the huge field went through the woods and down a steep hill that terminated on one of the back roads in Montara. I'd race across town to this back road and then get on the trail and ride up the path to the big empty field. There was no cover in the field, but it didn't matter; the Sheriff's helicopter was on the other side of town. I could safely navigate home. I'm not going to lie. The first few times riding on the trail through the woods, Peg Leg haunted, terrified me. You never know!

Montara Nudie Beach

Growing up in Montara, I had two primary friends, Marcus and Mike. Both were a grade ahead of me. During the summer before I became a freshman in high school and Marcus and Mike were sophomores, we decided to go down to the farthest end of Montara Beach, the end closest to Devil's Slide, where all the nudies hung out. Montara Beach was almost a mile long and had the type of sand you sink in when you walk. The three of us walked from my house on 5th Street down to Montara Beach and then began our trek to the far end of the beach.

As we started to get closer to the end of the beach where the nudies were, we encountered a naked man sitting on the beach, minding his own business as he looked out to the Pacific Ocean. We continued walking past him. After several yards, Marcus chickened out and stated he wasn't going any farther. Marcus would wait for Mike and me to return. Mike and I continued. We encountered another naked guy on our trek to the end of the beach. As we got closer to the cliffs at the end of Montara Beach, we hit the jackpot.

A naked couple was on the beach having sex. We climbed on the rocks and pretended we were exploring, but the entire time, we were watching the couple. Every now and then, the couple would look up to see what we were doing, and we'd pretend we weren't watching them. Once we had our fill, we returned to collect Marcus and head home.

We picked up our friend Marcus, and as we were about to walk by the first naked man, Marcus told Mike and me how the guy had walked by him several times, showing off his balls. Marcus was pissed and said when we walked by this guy, he was going to curse him out. As we drew near, the three of us, led by Marcus, took off running and laughing. When we were about 50 yards away, Marcus and Mike turned around and started yelling profanities at this guy. I didn't say a word. I watched. The target of my friend's expletives was looking the other way as if he couldn't hear. My friends gave up, and we all turned around and started walking toward home as if nothing had happened.

I was known for having a loud voice, and I knew this guy would hear me, so I turned around to yell my first string of profanities, and instead of yelling an expletive or two, I screamed, "Now you guys did it!" As the air rushed out of my lungs, the guy was in a dead sprint coming straight for us. Marcus, who was thin, tall, and on the high school track team, shot out of there like a jackrabbit. He was gone. My friend Mike, not quite as tall but very much in shape from playing football, was not far behind. Fortunately for me, Mike stopped, turned around, and screamed at me to get my ass moving. He was like my own personal coach. I needed one, too. I was chubby, and I was out of shape. I'd never exercised. I'd sink in the sand with every step I took, impeding my escape. I couldn't have gone more than five yards before I was out of breath. Mike, God bless him, stayed with me and, from about ten yards ahead, kept imploring me to get my ass in gear.

I was out of breath, and I was running for my life. I never looked back. Mike kept providing me with updates that the guy was gaining on us. We came to a sand dune, and on the other side, my neighbor and his wife were enjoying a picnic on the beach. I wanted to join them, but Mike insisted we keep going. We made it to the cliffs and started climbing. I thought we were safe, but Mike was screaming that the guy was putting on his clothes. We ended up escaping, but I had to run from Montara Beach up a steep hill to the safety of my house on 5th Street. Marcus ran to his house, and Mike ran to his. Later that night, they both came over to my house, carrying baseball bats for protection.

Junior High Bullies

When I was in junior high, this older kid, whom I'll call Paul, lived in Montara and used to pick on me whenever he saw me. He'd punch me, insult me, and even kick me. I never thought to fight back. I never felt threatened by him. I was more intrigued as to why someone would behave as he did. I'd brush him off and do my best to avoid him when possible. After junior high, I never saw him again until my junior year in high school. Not sure what happened to him or where he had disappeared to, but he hadn't grown an inch. He was short. I, on the other hand, had lost my baby fat, was 6'1, and was on the football team. I'd come into my own.

When Paul saw me, he was very apologetic for bullying me when we were younger, and I could tell he feared that I would exact my revenge upon him. I was astonished to see how frightened he seemed. I held no ill will towards him, and it certainly wasn't in me to want to beat him up for events that had happened years ago. The thought of retaliation never entered my mind. I had written off what had happened as us being kids and being some kind of a rite of passage. I assured him I didn't hold any ill will towards him and not to worry about the past.

Unlike Paul, whom I only saw in Montara, there was a kid a year ahead of me in junior high named Sammy. Sammy used to love punching me in my arm every time he saw me at school. He wasn't a big kid, but he did have a wicked punch, and his punches hurt. One day I'd had enough. It was during Physical Ed class. We were standing in a line, and he walloped me in the arm. It hurt. For the first time in my life, I stood up for myself. With tears in my eyes, I started calling him derogatory names, and when he got close to me, I started swinging away.

Apparently, Sammy was trained in martial arts. I never landed a single punch. Sammy dodged every swing, and fortunately for me, Sammy never swung back. He only avoided my swings. Otherwise, I would have gotten my ass kicked. After a few minutes of me yelling profanities, crying, and missing with every swing, the PE teacher, who had been observing the scene, told Sammy to knock it off. Sammy never punched me in the arm again.

. . .

One day, I was at the Quick Stop in Montara playing my favorite pinball game, Wizard. Three or four of us were playing the same game, and it was my turn. I was on a winning streak. I was racking up points, winning games, and playing one ball for what seemed like forever. At one point, one of the other players bumped the machine, causing it to tilt and me to lose my ball. He was like, 'Oops,' but it was a deliberate move. I was devastated that my winning streak had been ruined, but it never occurred to me to knock this kid upside his head or even confront him. I was good at pinball, and he was not. I'd be playing long after he was gone.

My Dirt Bike

One saving grace from my childhood was my Honda XR 75 dirt bike. It was thrilling to ride. Dirt bike riding boosted my self-esteem and confidence, and riding a dirt bike represented total freedom in my life —freedom to ride wherever I wanted; and I went all over. My friends and I would ride our dirt bikes on the various Army roads on Montara Mountain. At the time, I believed Westinghouse or some other corporation owned the property. Public access wasn't allowed, but we knew how to bypass the locked gates and then spend the rest of the day having a field day exploring. I can remember sitting on top of Montara Mountain on a clear, hot day and seeing the El Granda Radar tower.

There were trails on top of Montara Mountain that would lead to the top of Devil's Slide. My friends and I would sit and watch the traffic below. Other trails would take us over the mountain to Pacifica. That trail was way cool but challenging. The Army road to Pacifica had been washed out in three different places. All that was left was a ledge. One of my riding friends showed me you could ride the ledge and bypass the washout, but it was scary. If you leaned slightly to the left, you risked falling off the ledge and dropping about 10 feet into the washout. The alternative was to drop into the washout and climb back up to the other side. The problem was that there wasn't a clear trail through the washout. The first time I brought one of my friends with me on this trail, he chose to drop down into each washout rather than ride the ledge. Each washout proved challenging as he struggled to navigate through them and get back up and onto the road.

My friends and I knew the back roads, trails, and fields so well that we could ride to Moss Beach, the next town over, and then ride all the way to the El Granada Radar station with little fear of encountering a Sheriff's patrol. There was a whole series of trails and fields that no one would ever know existed unless they specifically looked for them. My friends and I would spend entire days riding around and exploring the various fields and trails we discovered.

We'd race our dirt bikes on the gravel road behind the Half Moon Bay airport, and one time, a friend showed me how to access a fire road from the top of Montara Mountain that led to Half Moon Bay. I was impressed and thought it was a cool discovery, but my dad was pissed when I showed up at the store and told him how I got there.

There was a hill on Montara Mountain that was called V-Hill. The Army road curved around the mountain. To the left of the curve was a steep trail going up the left side of the mountain, and on the right side of the curve was another trail going up the right side of the mountain; hence, V-Hill. The difference being that, on the right side, the climb became nearly vertical toward the top. Few ever tried climbing the right side, including me. Those that did were usually much older and rode bigger dirt bikes.

. . .

The left side of V-Hill was challenging enough for me and my Honda XR-75. My friends had two stoke motorcycles that would make it to the top of V-Hill without too much effort. I, on the other hand, with my four-stroke motor, would make it halfway to three-quarters of the way up and then stall out. I'd find myself on the side of a very steep hill. I'd have to turn the bike around carefully and then cautiously go back down the way I came.

The challenge for me was twofold: the dirt was very soft and deep. If I tried to slow down too much and over-braked the rear tire, as I often did, the bike would slide out from under me. If I over-braked the front tire, I'd go over the handlebars with the rest of my motorcycle in tow. My fear of descending too fast was well justified. By the time I reached the bottom of V-Hill, if I couldn't safely veer to the left, I'd end up crossing the road and pretty much fall off a cliff and into a gully. Instinctually, I tried to control my downhill speed and would end up tumbling down the hill. Sometimes I'd flip over the handlebars, slide, or lose my balance fall over, and then slide. It took a while, but I eventually figured out that when I started to climb V-Hill, I needed to downshift to keep the engine's rpm revved to maintain the necessary power and torque to get to the top. Once I reached the top, my confidence grew, and I was able to descend without crashing.

When I went dirt bike riding, wearing a helmet was optional. Most of the time, I wore one, but occasionally I wouldn't. Once, when I was coming down V-Hill, I locked up the front brake of my dirt bike and flipped over the handlebars. At one point, I was lying flat on my back, thinking I had stopped tumbling, when whack, my head flopped back violently against a rock. Had I not been wearing my helmet that day, I would have split my head wide open. I wore my helmet from that time on. Riding without a helmet is a cool proposition and feels fantastic, but it can have severe consequences in case of an accident.

Heroes Wanted

. . .

In addition to V-Hill, My friends and I would drive our dirt bikes as fast as we could over dirt mounds, bumps, and small piles of dirt or hills to see how high and far we could fly through the air. We'd do wheelies, and power slide our dirt bikes through turns to get the bike sideways. Growing up, I crashed every way you can think of on a dirt bike. My experiences helped ingrain into me the dynamics of motor-cycle riding that would last me a lifetime.

Between junior high and my freshman year in high school, all my friends were receiving bigger and better dirt bikes. Even though I had my own money, my parents refused to let me purchase a newer motorcycle. I was told that when I turned 16, I would want a car. They were right.

Chapter 3
High School Memories

Education

In junior high, my friend Danny and I used to race through our math assignments in class. Whoever finished first between us would slam their pencils down on the desk loud enough to announce victory. We had a lot of fun. In high school, I took to business math without issue. I'd already been practicing most of that math from working for my parents in their grocery store.

Pre-algebra was a different story, though. I'm positive my pre-algebra teacher was the same guy I was a smart ass to when I first started working the cash register in my dad's store. He's the one that insisted I take the potato chips off of his order. He never said anything, and I never brought it up.

Pre-algebra was a complete mystery. I can still remember staring at a number line and not grasping the concept of negative numbers. To his credit, my math teacher did spend extra time trying to help me, but to no avail. I felt incredibly stupid, embarrassed, and defeated. I didn't get it, but other students did. The other kids in my class were better than me because they could do the math. My inability to pass pre-algebra would haunt me for years.

I was never a big fan of school growing up. In high school, I was a C and D student. Shawn and my parents discussed me becoming a lawyer, but I never considered it. It wasn't until late in my junior year in high school that something clicked inside me about pursuing higher education. I suddenly saw the value of increasing my knowledge. When I graduated from high school, I did try my hand at college but dropped out during my first semester. I had bills to pay. I couldn't focus on school.

Through the years, I would take a course here or there for self-improvement. Through life experiences, I became aware that knowledge equaled power and that knowledge leveled the playing field. During my mid-twenties, when I'd hear about budget cuts to education, I'd write to my elected officials, pleading with them not to cut education funding.

My Driver's License Test

Obtaining my driver's license was a piece of cake because of my experiences riding a dirt bike. I was comfortable behind the wheel of a vehicle, especially if the vehicle had a clutch. When it came time to take the written part of the DMV test, I studied hard in school and was prepared. On the day I took my written DMV driver's license test, Shawn, also had to take the test. I passed my test and was ecstatic. Shawn, whom I looked up to, did not. I couldn't wait to return to our grocery store and boast to our dad about my success.

. . .

When we returned to our grocery store, my dad was super pissed at me. Shawn had spoken to my dad before I had and told my dad that he had passed the DMV exam, and I had failed it. My excitement, my enthusiasm, and my victory were gone. My dad believed Shawn. Shawn let his little facade go on for a few hours before he finally vindicated me by recanting his lie. My brother betrayed me that day, and I was disappointed in my father for not believing me. On that day, I learned that being deceptive and manipulative was second nature for Shawn.

Hell Hole

When I received my driver's license, Shawn lent me his 1979 Dodge 4x4 Power Wagon. He had a Triumph Spitfire he used to drive around. I did a lot of stupid things in that truck, and it's a miracle I didn't total the truck or get myself and my friends killed. Some of my friends suggested we take the pickup truck down to Montara Beach and go four-wheeling in the sand. There was a dirt road that led from the highway to the beach. As we neared the beach, there was another 4x4 truck parked on the dirt road with a couple of guys sitting in it. I nodded at them and continued on to the sand. As I did so, I wondered why I had never seen anyone else driving a 4x4 vehicle on Montara Beach. About 40 yards away from the dirt road, I figured out why. The truck sank right up to its axles in the sand. The more I tried to get out, the deeper the truck became buried. As far as I was concerned, my life was over. I had no money and no idea how I would get the truck unearthed.

It just happened that farther down Montara Beach, most of the Half Moon Bay High School Track team was having a party. One of my friends walked down to where the party was and came back with several drunk track team members. To my surprise, these drunk kids literally picked up the truck one wheel well at a time so that we could get wooden planks under the tires. With the planks in place, I was able to turn the truck around and make it back to the dirt road.

There were plenty of other stupid moves on my part. Once, I took the truck down to El Granada beach, by the radar tower, and drove it near the surf to do donuts in the sand. I was fortunate I didn't get stuck in the surf. Another time, I went four-wheeling at nighttime in the fog. I attempted to climb a steep hill by the Montara water tower but couldn't make it to the top. I had friends in the cab and friends in the back of the pickup truck. It was too steep to risk trying to turn the vehicle around, so I had to back down the hill in the dark and in the fog with my friends in the back of the truck directing me.

One day, I was giving a classmate a ride home from school when we decided to go drifting in the truck around the dirt roads of Montara. No matter how hard I tried, I couldn't get the pickup truck to go sideways. The one time I finally did, I oversteered and was headed right for a brand-new Volkswagen Jetta parked on the roadside. At the last second, I cut the wheel the other way and barely missed smashing into the parked vehicle. In shock, my friend and I called it a day.

The zenith of my off-roading stupidity came during my sophomore year in high school, when an upperclassman in my typing class named Victor Vincenze said, "Hey Maroun, let's cut typing class and take your brother's 4x4 four-wheeling." Victor, another student and I took my brother's 4x4 down to the cliffs overlooking Half Moon Bay beach. I went up and down a few small hills, we bounced around and were generally having a good time ... and then we came to Hell Hole.

. . .

I'd never heard of Hell Hole. Victor was daring me to see if my brother's 4x4 had what it took to make it through. Hell Hole didn't look ominous. It was about the length of a couple of pickup trucks and one pickup truck in width. I was determined to defend my brother's choice in 4x4s, and not knowing what I was doing, I listened to Victor's instructions and tried to cross Hell Hole by crossing at its narrowest point. When I entered Hell Hole, the truck sank in water right up to the bottom of the doors. Since I was trying to cross the width of Hell Hole, there was no room for maneuvering or gaining speed.

I managed to get the front of the truck out but not the back end. I put the pickup truck in reverse and this time got the back end out, but not the front. No matter what I tried, I couldn't exit Hell Hole. After several attempts, the truck stalled and I would start the motor with the tailpipe submerged underwater. Eventually, the battery died and I couldn't get the truck started. I wasn't working at the time, I didn't have a penny on me, and I can't describe the terror reverberating throughout my body. Victor stayed with me, and our mutual friend hiked back to our high school for help.

One of the benefits of growing up in Half Moon Bay is we had our share of rednecks with 4x4 pickup trucks. After a couple of hours or so, our friend returned with pretty much all of the rednecks from school, along with their 4x4 pickup trucks. Someone hooked up a tow rope to my brother's pickup truck, and several people tried to pull me out, but they were pulling dead weight. No one was successful. My level of panic increased exponentially as talk turned to needing a tow truck to pull me out. I had no money to pay for a tow truck.

. . .

One of the rednecks used his CB radio and contacted a friend. Shortly after, another 4x4 showed up with a couple of guys in their early 20s. Initially, they tried to pull me out but failed like everyone else. Not discouraged, they used their winch and ran the cable through another truck's winch before connecting it to my brother's pickup truck. They created a pulley system and finally succeeded in pulling my brother's Dodge Power Wagon out of Hell Hole. Once out of the water, the pickup truck still wouldn't start. I ended up having to compression start it. It ran like crap. I drove it straight to our family's mechanic.

The next morning I got the call. Half Moon Bay was a small town, and my failed exploit at navigating Hell Hole was the talk of the town. Word got back to Shawn immediately, and he wanted to kill me. In the end, they had to rebuild the bottom half of the engine. A few weeks after this incident, Shawn delivered to me a '68 Camaro that had belonged to his ex-girlfriend. I was in love with that car. Our family mechanic was pissed. He and everyone else thought I would kill myself in that car.

There were several reasons why I didn't kill myself in my '68 Camaro. I was observant and had learned my lessons from four-wheeling in Shawn's pickup truck. TV commercials were full of 4x4 pickup trucks off-roading and conquering the wilderness. I had learned the hard way that those commercials were total bullshit. Pickup trucks, especially 4x4 pickup trucks, were not invincible, and off-roading could be very expensive. I garnered a new-found respect for being responsible with vehicles.

My Camaro came with a 327 small-block engine, a Rochester two-barrel carburetor, and an on-the-floor manual 3-speed transmission. It would be a year before I could swap out the 3-speed transmission for a Muncie 4-speed transmission. The difference was day and night, and I'm grateful I learned to drive the car with the 3-speed transmission.

After high school graduation, I had the engine rebuilt. I couldn't afford an Edelbrock manifold with a Holly Double Pumper carburetor, but I was able to purchase a stock intake manifold from the junkyard with a Rochester four-barrel carburetor attached. By the time the secondaries started opening on the Rochester carburetor, I'd be exceeding 75 m.p.h., and that was plenty fast enough for me. I took the lessons from my exploits with Shawn's Dodge Power Wagon to heart. I never did anything stupid with my brother's pickup truck again, and I never crashed my Camaro.

High School Sports

In high school, because of my size, everyone said I should go out for football. I wanted nothing to do with it. I don't remember how I did it, but I managed to avoid playing football my freshman year. Towards the end of the school year, I did cave to peer pressure and ended up joining the track team. My events were the shot-put and discus throw. I enjoyed being a part of the track team and made friends with upperclassmen. My participation with the high school track team helped me get into shape. It was the first time I had exercised in my life.

My sophomore year in high school saw me joining the football team. Despite my size, I was intimidated by other players. I had never played football before. I watched a few games on TV, but I was never really that into football, and I certainly didn't like the idea of playing a contact sport where bodily injury was a likely possible outcome.

Heroes Wanted

. . .

The first two weeks of the football season start out with what's called double sessions, during which time we would have two practices daily, one in the morning and one in the afternoon. Throughout the day, we would run numerous drills to get into shape. At the end of each practice, our coach would have us run around the perimeter of the football field. Each time the coach blew his whistle, we'd race from the goalpost, around the edge of the football field, to the 50-yard line. Once most of the team was on the 50-yard line, he'd blow his whistle again, and the team would run from the 50-yard line to the other goalpost, following the edge of the field. We continued this drill as long as the coach blew his whistle.

Being overweight and not used to physical exertion, as soon as I started to push myself, I began to wheeze, something I'd never done before. The harder I pushed myself, the louder the wheezing became. It wasn't very pleasant to be running around the field with a high-pitched wheezing sound emanating from my body as I struggled to breathe. It was embarrassing, though, and my teammates certainly found it humorous. The coaches never stopped me, and there was no way in hell I would quit while my teammates continued to run. As my wheezing reached a fevered pitch, I'd be forced to stop and try to catch my breath. It would take several minutes to recover, and if I were able, I'd resume running.

As the season progressed, my wheezing became less severe. I was told asthma was the cause of my wheezing. Until football, I had never experienced any problems breathing, but I had never exercised before. During my junior year, the wheezing wasn't as bad, and by the end of the season, it was minimal and didn't interrupt my workout. During my senior year, the wheezing was non-existent. If I had had asthma, I didn't anymore.

One of my fondest football memories occurred during my senior year. By the end of the first day of double sessions, everyone was in pain and limping around. My friend Danny and I had spent the summer working out at a gym he belonged to. After our first day of double sessions, sore from head to toe, we went to the gym he belonged to and let the onsite physical therapist work on us. He was fantastic. He would isolate a muscle and then apply pressure until the muscle relaxed. Neither my friend Danny nor I were crazy about him working our groin area, but the next day, Danny and I were the only two people on the team that could walk without grimacing in pain.

During the summer before my senior year, when Danny and I were working out together, something inside my brain clicked, and suddenly football made sense to me. I no longer feared being hit by (or hitting) other players. When double sessions began, I would explode from my football stance during hitting drills. Both my team-mates and my coaches took notice. My coaches were so impressed that when it came time to hit the sled, I was moved to the front of the line so that I could set an example. My new-found prowess earned me much more game time during my senior year.

I had a great senior year in football. I received stickers for quarterback sacks and fumble recoveries. It's worth mentioning that even though I did well, I still didn't have a firm grasp of the game. I wasn't always sure what I was supposed to do or who to hit on plays. I remember whining to my coaches several times because the opposing team would double-team me. It wasn't until many years later that I realized that it was a good thing.

. . .

Football was one of the best things that ever happened to me in high school. From the moment I joined the team my sophomore year through graduation, I was now a jock. Throughout the year, we'd all hang out together and show up at all the parties together. My social life and confidence took a giant leap forward. I gained new friendships, had incredible experiences, and created some of the best memories of my life that I never would have experienced had I not gone out for football.

Expanded Entrepreneurial Experiences

In high school, my forays into entrepreneurship continued. My cousin set me up with imported socks and shoes that I would peddle at the Alameda Flea Market on weekends. I'd be at the flea market setting up my wares at 6:00 or 7:00 a.m. When inexpensive LCD watches were being imported, I dropped the socks and shoe line and began selling LCD watches, which I purchased from my cousin for $2.50 each and then turned around and sold them for between $6.00 and $35.00 apiece—whatever the market would bear. I eventually had my own inventory and drove around with a trunk full of display cases filled with LCD watches.

When the San Mateo Fair came around, a high school buddy and I went to the fair and walked around selling LCD watches to the carnies and anyone else interested. I made a small fortune that night. At the end of the night, my buddy and I found ourselves still in the fairgrounds while it was shutting down. One of the carnies who had purchased several watches from me advised us to leave for our own safety. We did so—promptly.

. . .

When my parents lost their grocery store business, I went to work for a family friend who owned a gas station. I was 16 years old and on my way to being a self-sufficient young adult. Thanks to my parents and Shawn, I was business savvy and had a solid work ethic. I saw work through the eyes of a business owner. While coworkers showed up to punch a time clock, I was focused on taking care of the customer and making money for the business.

While I learned much about business from my family, I also learned what not to do. My family made numerous mistakes, and I learned from them. I also had plenty of my own learning experiences. While attending the Alameda Flea Market on weekends, I'd go out with my high school buddies and party on Friday and Saturday nights. The next morning, I'd be at the flea market by 6:00 a.m. with a hangover and then I'd roast under the sun all day because I didn't have a canopy. After about three weekends, I learned to stop drinking at 10:00 p.m.—or not drink at all—whenever I had to get up early the following day. When I turned 21, I made it a point to switch to soda water by 11:00 p.m. at the latest. By 2:00 a.m., when the bars closed, I would be sober, and my hangovers the next day would cause minimum discomfort.

My early entrepreneurial experiences exposed me to business, customer service, sales, and much more. My inclusion in adult conversations with my parents, Shawn, and other adults taught me to be responsible. Engaging with adults on a regular basis helped me weather the ribbings from my classmates. I'm very grateful for the entrepreneurial experiences my parents provided me with at such a young age.

Juvenile Court Revisited

The second time I appeared in juvenile court was when I was sixteen years old. While cruising the El Camino in my 1968 Camaro in San Mateo, I was stopped at the turn-around light in front of Hillsdale Mall. When the light turned green, one of my buddies told me to light them up. Light 'em up, I did, right in front of a motorcycle cop. I received a citation for audible tire friction. Once again, my father had to take time off from work and go to Juvenile Court with me. All I remember from the court proceedings was the judge trying to make me out as a hood and my dad vehemently defending me, telling the judge I was a good person. Once again, I walked away from that court proceeding feeling horrible that my poor dad, who worked very hard, had to take time off from his day to defend me in court. I pledged to myself that I would never compel my father to go to court with me again, and I kept my pledge.

When cruising the El Camino, my friends liked to ride with me because I wasn't afraid to speed-pass between cars, I had a killer car stereo, and after all, it was a 1968 Camaro. In addition, my car-door speakers popped out so we could stash cans of beer in the doors. While my friends enjoyed being able to drink beer while driving around in the car, I noticed an unsettling trend. Whenever we pulled down a side street to park and drink beer, if the police showed up, we'd have to pour out our beer, and one of us would have to perform a sobriety test on the side of the road. After performing about three sobriety tests, this got old. I didn't mind going to parties and drinking, but I didn't want to drive around with open containers of alcohol in my vehicle. I understood who would go to jail. I ended up parking my car in the garage on Friday and Saturday nights.

High School Bullying

During my freshman year in high school, my childhood friend Mike, who egged me on to run from the guy chasing us on Montara Beach, would kick and punch me, call me names, and humiliate me whenever he saw me on campus. I never understood his behavior. We'd known each other since we were kids. We played together all the time and explored Montara and Moss Beach together on our bicycles. By my sophomore year, he wasn't kicking and hitting me, but he could sure embarrass me. He had a superior ability to be wickedly sarcastic. I was actually envious of his ability to be sarcastic off the cuff. It would take me hours or days to come up with comebacks that would instantly roll off his tongue.

One of my favorite memories of Mike was when we were returning home from a football game on the school bus. I started bantering with one of the other football players. When the player gave me crap back, I clammed up from embarrassment because the entire cheerleading squad was sitting behind me. After several brutal insults, my childhood friend Mike let loose on the other football player. Mike's insults were hilarious. The entire bus was roaring with laughter. When we got off the bus that night, the other football player approached me and asked what was up with Mike defending me. We both laughed when I explained I didn't have an answer.

During my junior year, in my home economics class, sitting at one table were five or six of the most beautiful girls in our school. I was in another group but managed to work my way into theirs. I had zero confidence, yet there I was, sitting, laughing, and getting along with these beautiful women. I was utterly amazed. One day, several of the girls and I loaded into my '68 Camaro and went to Round Table Pizza, where we all enjoyed a great lunch.

. . .

When it came time to return to campus, my car ran like crap and kept stalling. We barely made it back. I could have died when one of the girls, embarrassed by the stall outs on the way back to school, remarked that I should learn to drive. What had been a significant win for me was now a major loss. I felt devastated and embarrassed.

I later discovered that while having lunch with these beautiful girls, some classmates switched the spark plug wires around on my engine. I was sure who it was, but I never confronted or retaliated against them. Instead, I rigged up my hood so it couldn't be opened without a key.

Pirate's Cove

When my folks lost their business and their house during my junior year in high school, my dad returned to Lebanon, and my older brother Shawn took in my mom, Rachel, her two kids, and me. At the time, I didn't have a job. Shawn was taking care of all of us. Shawn knew the head chef at a restaurant that was opening soon and arranged for me to get a job there as a dishwasher. It just so happened that the restaurant's owner, an Italian fellow, was our landlord. Shawn was frequently late on the rent, so the owner, Antonio, would often call the house looking for my brother.

One day Antonio called, and I answered the phone. He angrily demanded to speak to Shawn, who happened to be sitting next to me. As I handed Shawn the phone, Shawn asked who it was. I casually replied, "It's hot shot, Antonio." For the next 20 minutes, my brother was on the phone, trying to convince Antonio not to have me killed. It was a very intense conversation. Shawn eventually convinced

Antonio not to kill me, but when he got off the phone, he nearly did. A couple of weeks later, I showed up to work at Pirate's Cove. Harry, the head chef who hired me, knew about my spat with Antonio. It was our secret.

I remember the first day on the job. Antonio had all the staff stand in a circle and then gave a welcoming speech. After his speech, Antonio walked around the circle, made eye contact with each new hire, and welcomed them aboard. Antonio learned my first name that day but nothing more. I was so nervous I thought I would die, but I desperately needed the money.

The restaurant hadn't opened yet. Construction crews were putting on the finishing touches. I was there primarily to assist with the construction cleanup. During my first week on the job, I was loading full five-gallon paint buckets onto the back of a flatbed pickup truck parked on the street in front of the restaurant. Some concrete workers were putting in a new sidewalk and curb next to the truck. I had already loaded several buckets on the truck, and when I went to load one more, the bucket tipped back on me, the lid popped off, and five gallons of white paint spilled all over me, the back of the truck, and onto a popular street in Burlingame, California. The paint spilled on the road and immediately headed toward the new sidewalk that had just been set.

Fortunately, the concrete guys already had a hose out and began diverting the paint from their new curb into a nearby gutter. Several coworkers jumped in to help me with clean up. As we mopped up the paint from the road, a motorcycle cop drove by and started yelling at us. Fortunately, he kept going. I thought for sure I was going to get fired that day, but I didn't. Everyone was pretty understanding and supportive. I was one of the more dependable people on the cleanup crew.

When the restaurant finally opened, I began my position as a dishwasher. We had a tight kitchen crew. We all got along very well, worked hard, and enjoyed the intense banter going back and forth. I soon gained a reputation for being a hard worker. I didn't think I was doing anything special. I just showed up to work each day and did my job. Whenever I ran into Antonio, he would greet me like every other employee. I was terrified he'd discover who I was.

In the back dining room, used for banquets, there was a picture on the wall that intrigued me. It was a picture of a flower surrounded by a wrinkled magenta sheet. The flower was also magenta but was a shade or two darker. Whenever I walked by this picture, I would stop, stare, and admire its beauty. There was something about this picture that mesmerized me.

One day, while I was admiring the picture, one of the waitresses entered the banquet room and saw me. I shared with her my thoughts about the beauty of the flower in the painting, and she just looked at me and laughed. She then proceeded to point out that the sheet was actually draped over a woman's body, and the flower, an African tulip, represented her female parts. I took another look at the picture, and sure enough, it wasn't just a wrinkled sheet. At the top of the picture, under all those wrinkles, were two breasts. Suddenly, I could see the outline of a female's body under the sheets. The African tulip was strategically placed between the woman's closed legs. I'd been looking at this picture for months and was clueless as to what I was looking at. I went to the local gallery and put a copy on layaway. To this day, I have the framed picture hanging on my wall.

. . .

One night, one of the barbacks failed to show up for work, and management needed someone to fill in. I volunteered to stay late and work the shift. Within the week, both barbacks were let go, and I was promoted to the position of barback. I was seventeen years old, had the body of a high school football player, wore tight Pirate's Cove T-shirts, and was working behind the bar at one of the Bay Area's hottest new nightclubs.

The bar had three bartending stations laid out like the three points of a triangle. I was responsible for cleaning drink glasses, emptying trash, and ensuring that none of the stations ran out of ice, glasses, condiments, or alcohol. Every night I worked, I was on an adrenaline high. I was surrounded by gorgeous women who were checking me out. I worked very hard, was great at my job, and the bartenders all loved me and ensured I was tipped very well at the end of the night.

I was well-liked by everyone in the restaurant. I had a great relationship with my coworkers and flirted with all the waitresses. I even went out with a few of them. I remember a few of the older busboys being in awe of my flirtatious ways. When one of them discovered that I had gone out with one of the waitresses, he asked me how I did it.

Antonio sponsored a kickboxing fighter. This guy was a young black man with a very aggressive attitude. He'd threaten to kick your ass if you looked at him wrong. Many employees feared him, and several busboys were on his shit list. As for me, we got along just fine. I remember him remarking to me that he liked how I was respectful to him. I'd greet him when he entered the restaurant, but I stayed out of his way. To this day, I don't know what I did to be on his good side, but I'm certainly glad I was!

One night, Harry, the head chef, and I were in the office, bullshitting. Antonio still didn't know who I was, and Harry and I were discussing that infamous day when I called him "Hotshot Antonio." Just then, Antonio walked into the room. Harry's mouth dropped open, and his eyes almost popped out of his head. I greeted Antonio and then quickly left the room. A few days later, I ran into Antonio in the hallway. Antonio stopped me and said, "So you're Jim Maroun." I thought I was going to die. I said, "Yes," and he reached out, shook my hand, and thanked me for doing such an incredible job. Wow!

At one point, a new general manager was brought in. He was tough, didn't care if he was liked or not, and started cleaning house. A lot of people didn't like him. I got along with him. I knew he had a job to do, and I knew where he was coming from. At the same time, he threw a lot of extra work my way. One day, in frustration, I confronted him. I asked him why he gave me multiple tasks while others stood around doing nothing. His answer floored me. He responded that he was assigning me various tasks because he could depend on me to get the job done. His response wouldn't be the last time I heard how dependable I was.

On My Own

The devastation my parents felt filing for bankruptcy and losing everything they owned took its toll on them and the rest of my family. For them, the world was very dark and depressing. I'd been working part-time jobs after school since I was sixteen. I was young, ambitious, and was just starting out in life. I was going to conquer the world. So on my eighteenth birthday, when Shawn jokingly told me to move out, I surprised him by taking him up on his offer.

It was imperative that I finish high school and receive my diploma. I created a budget and reviewed it with my economics teacher and vice principal. They both signed off on it. I answered an advertisement in the paper for a roommate, and by the end of the month, I had moved into an apartment on Woodside Road in Redwood City. I spent the remainder of my high school senior year working as a dishwasher to support myself. After graduation, I worked various jobs and continued my financial independence from Shawn and my family.

Parking Tickets

One of the many benefits of being raised by entrepreneurial parents is that I was exposed to all aspects of running a business—especially communication and negotiations. I often listened to my father when he was on the phone arguing with a vendor for one reason or another. My father taught me the importance of standing up for oneself when wronged. As a result, I wasn't afraid to engage adults in challenging conversations. If I believed something wasn't right and needed to be corrected, I had the confidence to confront those in authority.

My willingness to seek redress proved to be useful when I was eighteen years old. My work at Pirate's Cove meant I wouldn't get home until after midnight. As a result of my late-night hours, by the time I arrived at my apartment in Redwood City, there would be no parking spaces within a couple of blocks. However, in front of my apartment building was a red zone, the length of at least five cars.

. . .

Heroes Wanted

Out of necessity, I started parking in the red zone, or sometimes, due to how others parked, I'd be parked half in the red zone and half legally. Early the next morning, I'd move my car to an available parking space. I got away with this for quite a while, and then some cop caught on to me. Whenever I parked in the red zone—even if *part* of my car was in the red zone—I'd receive a parking citation. Before I knew it, I had a stack of a mile high. I remembered my dad scolding the judge about Sheriff's deputies having nothing better to do than ticket kids on dirt bikes, so I put on my torn jeans and tennis shoes with holes in them and took the stack of parking tickets down to city hall. I made my case to the clerk behind the counter.

I explained I was a high school student, living independently and working in a restaurant to support myself. I explained I worked late, and by the time I got home, there was no place to park within a few blocks. I claimed it was unfair for this cop to keep ticketing me when there was a huge red zone in front of the apartment complex that could easily accommodate five or more cars. I also explained I didn't have the money to pay the fines.

The clerk behind the counter listened to my story, took one look at me, looked at the stack of parking tickets I was holding, then looked me in the eyes and said, "I never want to see you in here again," as he took the parking tickets from me. I counted my blessings and did a much better job finding a parking space when I arrived late. The clerk never saw me again, and I never received another parking ticket for parking in that red zone.

I love this memory. Being much wiser and fully understanding the importance of red zones, I couldn't even imagine trying to pull this stunt today.

Chapter 4
Select Memories

My Parents

Neither of my parents was educated beyond elementary school, though both were good people and hard-working entrepreneurs. Since I was the baby of the family, both ensured I was spoiled …. until they lost their business. The next sibling in my family was my sister Rachel, who was ten years older than I, Shawn was 12 years older, and my eldest brother Richard, was older by 13 years. The age gap resulted in my older siblings having a much closer relationship with my parents.

I don't have a lot of memories of doing things with my dad. I remember when we lived in Ohio. He'd come home from work, get down on all fours, and let me ride on his back. Sometimes he'd bring me home toys or boxes of football cards. In Montara, I remember him coming home, and we'd watch his favorite television programs like The Dukes of Hazard, Barney Miller, Colombo, Cannon, and other detective shows. We just never really did much together. Dad loved to play poker with his buddies, and he worshipped his brothers and sisters, spending as much time with them as possible.

If I needed help building a Pinewood Derby Car or writing a school paper, I'd turn to Shawn, who was the nucleus of our family. My parents depended on him for everything. Even though I do not recall spending much time with my dad doing things, I have no complaints. He was awesome. We had shelter, food was always on the table, and I grew up in a safe home environment. The one prevalent memory of my father that I cherish is he loved to make people laugh. I definitely inherited my father's penchant for bringing laughter and smiles into this world.

In 1995 I was attending Napa Valley College when I received word that my father had had a stroke and was in the hospital. At the time, I didn't have a car. When I reached the hospital the next day, he had experienced a series of mini-strokes and was in a coma. I never got a chance to speak with him again. I did stand by his bed, though, and tell him how much I loved him and how much I appreciated everything he had done for me. My father worked hard and had a tough life. His heart was always in the right place. He passed away several weeks later.

In regard to my mom, I've got both great and horrible memories. Mom used to take me to amusement parks, state parks, the beach, or to tourist attractions like the Winchester Mystery House. When I was in Cub Scouts and Boy Scouts, my mom volunteered as a den mother and came up with cool projects. In addition, Mom would organize outings and places to visit.

. . .

Mom loved to cook, too. I remember one night, there was nothing to eat in the refrigerator. Mom made a homemade pizza totally from scratch. It was delicious. Mom was also great at making Lebanese food. Whenever we had company over for dinner, she would continuously fill their plate with food, insisting they eat more, no matter how emotional the protest. There was always room for another bite.

At one point, my mom owned a deli in Half Moon Bay. I remember walking in once, and the place was packed. Mom was walking around with a pan of fresh potato salad she had just made and was handing out ladle-sized samples. She was so proud of herself with how delicious it turned out that it didn't matter whether a customer wanted to try it or not. They received a sample. Mom did deserve to feel proud. It was delicious.

On other occasions, when customers tried to order a sandwich, Mom would refuse to make it and instead insisted they order whatever she just made because it was so delicious. She'd even offer them a free sample. Mom was a great cook, had a big heart, and her intentions were in the right place, but she just thought differently. My mother's boldness and sharp tongue would often lead to embarrassing moments.

My mom and dad would fight like cats and dogs. I remember when the three of us were driving to Reno. I was sitting in the back seat, my dad was driving, and my mom was in the passenger seat. They had been arguing the entire trip. At one point, my mom said, "It's okay, Louie, everyone has a little crazy in them." My dad immediately slammed his hand on the car dashboard and exclaimed, "No, Betty, no one is as crazy as you!" I burst out in laughter.

. . .

Heroes Wanted

Once, my mother entered our grocery store and started yelling about what a son of a bitch my dad was in front of a long line of customers waiting to pay for their groceries. Dad was at the back of the store in the butcher shop. One of the customers in line was a friend of Dad's. He stood there staring at me with a huge grin on his face. I could have died from embarrassment.

I remember one year celebrating Christmas at Rachel's house. My parents were separated but not divorced. There was never any reconciliation between them. They lived separate lives, but we were still a family, and at family gatherings, they would both show up. Dad would show up in peace, and Mom would show up prepared for battle. Anyways, it's Christmas Eve, we're at Rachel's, we made it through dinner, and we're all sitting around watching a movie. Dad decided to go to bed. An hour or so later, the rest of us all decide to retire. My mom soon discovered that my dad had gone to sleep in the bed she wanted.

For the next hour, all we heard about was how my dad grew up a peasant in Lebanon and how he used to sleep on dirt floors, and now all of a sudden, that son of a bitch is a king who gets to sleep in the best bed in the house. Mom was merciless as she picked my dad's life apart. Dad never responded, and the rest of us couldn't stop laughing. Mom could be both brutal and entertaining at the same time.

As I got older, I began to pity Rachel. She had a good heart, and she would always host holiday events at her house. We were all welcome in her home, and for her dedication to family, she was often rewarded with my mother's wrath. Mom would shred Rachel just like she would my dad. While it was amusing, I know it had to have taken its toll on Rachel. It was awful.

. . .

During the holidays, Rachel would make dinner plans, shop accordingly, and prepare food. Then Mom would come over with food that she had prepared or partially prepared and hijack the kitchen along with anything my sister had planned. I don't have a single memory of having a family gathering where there weren't any arguments, crying, or drama. My mother always managed to stir the pot.

Even I, her baby, wasn't immune from her wrath. When I was still in high school, I'd go to my mom's deli on my lunch break to get a sandwich. Once, I went to her deli, and the place was packed with customers. As soon as I walked in, she looked at me, and from behind the counter, she yelled, "You son of a bitch, you killed my dog!" I turned around and found another establishment to have lunch at that day.

The dog was a Pomeranian given to my mother by my brother Richard, who lived in an apartment in the Los Angeles area. Richard had trained the dog to "go" on a newspaper in a bathroom. In Montara, we tried to train the dog to go outside and failed miserably. Mom would let the dog out into our front yard. There was no fencing around our yard; just dirt roads. No matter how hard we tried, that dog would always end up making a mess on the downstairs landing in front of my room. The carpet was ruined. It always smelled of urine, and I'd always have to be on guard for little piles of Muffy bombs. Yes, her name was Muffy.

When my mom vacationed in Ohio to visit family, I was responsible for caring for the dog. One night, I let the dog out the front door so she could go to the bathroom. The dog got hit by a car. I found her on the side of the road, curled up and panting. Despite Shawn spending over $500 in veterinary fees, the dog ended up dying a week later. My mom knew I hated the dog, so she blamed me.

I never said anything, but I knew who hit the dog. One of the kids at my high school drove a car with an engine that made a distinctive sound. It was unmistakable. I heard his engine, and I heard his car swerve, as he went out of his way to run over our dog. Such a move wouldn't be out of character for the person driving the vehicle. I never shared my suspicions with my mom and Rachel because, with or without proof, they would have gone "scorched earth" on his ass.

Mom definitely had a sharp tongue and a different perspective. She never shied away from using her sharp tongue, especially if she didn't like you. In my twenties, I remember pleading with her not to be so abrasive. I told her I didn't want to have bad memories of her when I got older. Mom was receptive to my request. She asked me not to yell at her during difficult situations and instead to use logic to explain what was happening. I had varying success. Unfortunately, my mother and Shawn were very close. Shawn loved to provoke my mom and then pour gasoline on the fire to entertain himself. Any progress I would make with getting Mom to behave would be lost once my instigating brother came around.

In 2010, my wife and I flew to Chicago to pick up a 1997 Honda CBR 1100 BlackBirdXX, which I had purchased on eBay and was going to drive back to California. When we reached South Dakota, we got the call. Mom had a brain aneurysm and had passed away. My brothers and sister wanted to have the memorial immediately. My brother Richard demanded we come back home immediately. In a heated discussion, I told Richard to pull his head out of his ass and look at where we were on a map. Even if we drove to the nearest airport, we still wouldn't be there in time for the memorial.

I told my family to have it without us. I personally didn't need to attend a memorial. My wife and I were out in God's country. We were taking backroads on the way home and enjoying nature's magnificent beauty. Out in nature, my wife and I were able to make peace with my mother's passing. We celebrated her life and even prayed for her at Wayside Chapel, a little chapel located next to a rest stop on westbound Interstate 90 in South Dakota. My wife even recorded my mom's name in the guest registry. The family decided to wait another week before having the memorial, so my wife and I could attend.

My brothers, sister, nieces, nephews, and close family friends were in tears during my mother's memorial. Neither Richard, Shawn, nor Rachel were in a state where they could say a few words about my mother. I, on the other hand, had made a conscious choice many years earlier to focus my memories on all the good things Mom did. In addition, my wife and I dealt with my mother's death out in God's country. As a result, I was at peace with my mother's passing and was able to share the following favorite memories:

I once confronted my mom about going out to all-you-can-eat buffets and stuffing her purse with food. I was like, "Mom, why do you insist on packing your purse full of food when we go to all-you-can-eat buffets? You're not discreet about it, and it's embarrassing." Mom looked me in the eye and said, "Jimmy, how come when I get home, everyone asks me what I brought home?" Everyone at the memorial erupted into laughter.

Heroes Wanted

. . .

The second story I shared was when I was in the cub scouts. There was a kite contest. Each Cub Scout was to build a kite from scratch, and it would be judged on various criteria, including how high it would go. Usually, Shawn would help me with my Cub Scout projects, and whatever the project was, it would look cool. This time, mom was in charge, and for my kite, she brought home plastic wrap that dry cleaners used and two skinny tree branches. We put together a kite with two sticks, dry-cleaning plastic, and a cloth tail. She wrote the word Akela with a blue Magic Marker across the kite. Akela meant to follow the leader.

I was in tears, begging her to let Shawn help, but she would have none of it. Sure enough, come kite day, there were kids with all kinds of cool-looking kites. One kite had been made out of newspaper and was as big as an adult. Other kids had fancy box kites, and there I was with my hideous piece of dry-cleaning plastic.

I launched my kite, and it immediately went higher than everyone else's. It was eating through my roll of twine so fast that when I turned my head to ask a friend for another roll of string, my roll ran out, and the kite took off. Several of us chased after it, but we never caught it. Several friends remarked that had I not run out of string, my kite would have been the highest-flying kite of them all.

I summed up my mother's character by saying that, although at times she appeared to be crazy, if you took a step back, thought about what she was saying, or just waited a few days, you'd realize that most of the time, she was right. Mom did a lot of good, cared for us, and made many people happy, but she never received the praise or recognition she deserved.

My Sense of Humor

I love to make people laugh. I see life as a series of scenes, and I'm always looking for what could be funny. I enjoy turning the ordinary in life into the extraordinary. I've developed a penchant for saying what people think but would never say in public. It doesn't matter if I know the person or if the situation is serious or playful; I look for ways to inject humor into the experience.

Like my dad, I love to make people laugh. There have been many comedians that have influenced my life. Some of the more significant ones were Richard Pryor, Don Rickles, Rodney Dangerfield, and Robin Williams. These men were comedic geniuses and were very quick-witted. I started listening to Richard Pryor's cassette tapes in junior high. I loved everything about his sense of humor and his ability to share stories about the black experience humorously.

Nothing was off-limits to comedians during my youth. Except for Richard Pryor and George Carlin, most comedy routines were hilarious without the use of profanity. Racial jokes were the norm, and they were funny as hell. Don Rickles and many other performers would tear stereotypes to shreds, with the audience laughing all the way. Racial jokes taught us to laugh at racial idiosyncrasies as we learned about each other and ourselves. At the end of their performance, no matter how harsh they had been, the comedians would remind the audience that we were all brothers and sisters, and we all needed to respect each other and find ways to get along. I took these end-of-routine remarks to heart.

. . .

Heroes Wanted

I've learned from personal experiences and observation that when you put in the extra effort to mess with someone, especially when they're not expecting it, they're flattered and appreciate the humor even more. Humorous situations provide a quick, harmless break from the harshness and realities of everyday stresses. I've used my twisted sense of humor to build relationships with people for most of my adult life.

One of my greatest joys is seeing people's responses to my humorous overtures. I'll make an outlandish statement, confession, or innuendo and have people respond with an antidote or statement that clearly demonstrates they're just as crazy as I am, if not more so. Other times, they'll respond with an actual life experience based on the topic of my joke. The ending results are hilarious, and more importantly, two strangers have made a personal connection. These are moments in life that are to be cherished.

While I've been told I should do standup, I don't see a comedy club as an appropriate venue for my brand of humor, which is really more story-based. It gives me great joy, comfort, and satisfaction, knowing that I have my daddy's sense of humor, and through humor, I bring happiness into this world.

Girls

Growing up, I had many influences in my life that dictated how I interacted with girls. Unfortunately, none of those influences were beneficial. At a very early age, I read one of Rachel's adult paperback books. One of the passages I read impacted me for most of my life. In the passage, several females complained about guys only wanting to have sex with them. The girls were looking for friendship and were disappointed in having to contend with sexual advances. The remainder of the book described sexual encounters with various lovers these girls encountered. I took the part about girls wanting to be friends to heart without the benefit of any additional context.

Another unhealthy influence in my life regarding relationships was Shawn and his friends. They were all womanizers, and racked up quite an impressive list of conquests. Women were objectified, and having sex was all that mattered. Throughout the years, I picked up additional toxic beliefs about women and adopted self-defeating expectations. I was never taught about courting, relationships, love, or respecting and valuing the opposite sex until much later in life.

My low self-esteem and lack of self-confidence left me susceptible to the whims of my peers. To my detriment, I would seek their validation. In junior high, a girl from my neighborhood would come over to my house after school. No one was home. We'd sit in the family room downstairs and French kiss for hours. Our afternoon romance lasted several weeks until one of my friends discovered that we were seeing each other. He made a couple of disparaging remarks about her, and that's all it took. I stopped seeing her. My unhealthy need for approval from my peers also killed my prospects in high school.

Unbeknownst to me, a cute girl I knew broke up with a mutual acquaintance. During a rally in our high school gym, she found me in the bleachers and made herself comfortable sitting between my legs. I was surprised but delighted. I liked her, and this was a dream come true until one of my football teammates shot me a frown and ended what could have been a great experience. The same thing happened on a school-sponsored ski trip. On the ride up to Lake Tahoe, one of my classmates and I took a serious interest in one another. A disapproving look from one of my friends

... and my chance for romance that weekend ended before it even began.

My fear of rejection prevented me from asking girls out in high school. Other times, my fear of being inappropriate or crossing the friend's line would hold me back. During a keg party at Montara Beach, I was drunk and standing beside the bonfire when one of my classmates, with whom I would flirt in class, stands next to me and positioned her gorgeous ass into my unsuspecting hand. It was an incredibly brave and daring move on her part. For my part, I reward her seductive move with my best impression of a deer caught in head-lights. I stood there, paralyzed with fear and afraid to make a move.

It wasn't until my junior year in high school, when my family moved to a new community away from the coast, that I noticed a change in my interactions with girls. The girls from my high school knew me from grade school. They were all present for the jokes, verbal abuse, and humiliation I endured. I now had a clean slate. I was meeting and interacting with girls who didn't know me, and I was free from the scrutiny of my friends. My baby fat was gone, I was a football player, I drove a '68 Camaro, and I had significantly more confidence than I did when I was on the coast. I suddenly had hope.

During my senior year in high school, when I started working at Pirate's Cove, I met a cute waitress. She would show up to work with her hair in a ponytail, and I'd flirt with her whenever she came into the kitchen. I took her on a date to Santa Cruz, and it turned out to be one of the best experiences of my life. We both clicked. We had similar family issues, shared similar values, and, most importantly, we couldn't stop laughing throughout our entire date. Our date at Santa Cruz Beach Boardwalk was magical.

. . .

Despite her having a boyfriend, she agreed to see me as a friend. I pursued her as a friend because whenever we went out together, all we did was laugh, giggle, and have a great time. She was the best thing that had ever happened to me. When I had my own apartment in Redwood City, she'd come over, and we'd party. We'd end up wrestling around on the living room floor when my roommate wasn't there. I was given numerous opportunities to take our friendship to the next level, but I was petrified. I didn't want to be that guy that broke the "friends" rule. I didn't want to be that guy that was all about sex.

At work, my friend received a promotion and was now a hostess. I knew nothing of her promotion. I only remember coming to work one day and walking by a beautiful girl at the hostess station. As I mentally made a note to come back and introduce myself, she called me out for walking by her. The cute waitress with the ponytail I was pursuing was actually a knockout in disguise. Once she let her hair down and put on a skirt, every guy in the area became interested, and any chance I had was gone. We had some rough times and ended up going our separate ways, but I thank God I made peace with her before she went off to college and out of my life forever.

During my senior year in high school, there was a young lady in one of my classes that I lived to make laugh. She had the cutest, most addictive laugh. We were friends, and it never occurred to me to ask her out. After I graduated from high school, we stayed in touch and went out a couple of times. It wasn't until many years later that I realized this girl had a crush on me. She even said so, quite matter-of-factly, in my yearbook. I had been oblivious. This girl loved me. I missed out on what could have been a fantastic relationship.

Heroes Wanted

. . .

There were numerous occasions in my life when I could have hooked up with a girl, but I was clueless. When I was 19 and living in Burlingame, I hung out a few times with this gorgeous brunette. One night, someone dropped her off at my house at 2:00 a.m. She came over for one thing and didn't get it because I didn't want to cross the "friends" line or more accurately, I was too chicken to cross it. Unfortunately for me, I've had many experiences in my life where a woman was interested, and I was oblivious to her intentions. There were even times in my life when I knew a woman wanted to have sex with me, and I said no because it was the ethical course of action.

I used to frequent a Jewish deli in Burlingame. They had these things called meat Blintz's that were delicious, as well as the best lemon pound cake I had ever tasted. In addition to fantastic food, several beautiful girls worked behind the counter and waitressed. I used to flirt with all of them. There was one girl in particular, a brunette, that I was in love with. I was 18 or 19 and still shy about asking girls out. During this time in my life, I was working two jobs. I'd work construction during the day with my roommate and then work at Pirates Cove in the evening.

My long days got the best of me, and I ended up getting mononucleosis. I was out of commission for a little over two weeks. During the disease's initial stages, I could not get out of bed. It was horrible. When I finally recovered, on my first day back to work at Pirate's Cove, the cute deli girl I was in love with managed to get into the bar with her girlfriends. She planted herself right in front of my workstation. It was obvious she was there for me.

. . .

Having just recovered from mononucleosis and fearful that I could potentially pass it on to her, I went home alone that night. For me, my decision was easy. I knew she worked hard, and there was no way I would have wanted her to go through what I had to endure. Unfortunately, my good intentions that night didn't go over well, and I never had another opportunity to hook up with her again.

I remember the first time I saw Mary. I told myself I would never have a girl as beautiful as Mary, a beautiful brunette who worked in a local restaurant. I never pursued her, but we'd flirt with each other and enjoyed each other's humor whenever I was in the restaurant. One day, an older waiter encouraged me to ask Mary out, so I did, and we went out on a lunch date.

I was twenty at the time, and Mary was about twenty-four. It turned out Mary had been dating the same guy since she was nineteen; they lived together, and Mary was on her way out. We hit it off. One night, we talked on the telephone for over six hours and only stopped because the battery on my wireless phone died. Mary and I went on several magical dates and even spent the day together in Santa Cruz. I'd always have to get Mary back before her boyfriend came home.

One evening when Mary was at my place, we watched a movie and spent most of the evening drinking wine and making out on my couch. We still hadn't had sex. As the night progressed, Mary looked at me and asked if she should go into the bedroom, remove her clothes, and get into bed. My initial response was, "No! I have to get you back before your boyfriend gets home." Way wrong answer. Mary was pissed as she exclaimed, "You mean you don't want to have sex with me?" In a rare moment for me, I experienced clarity of thought and responded back, "I was just kidding," as I led her into the bedroom.

When it came to dating, it was like my instincts were always off. When I went out with a good girl who was seeking a relationship, I wanted sex. When I dated a girl looking for sex, I was the perfect gentleman. When I did get it right, I was amazed that I was having fun and getting laid. Being the thinker I am, I started to analyze what I did to get girls into bed. I pared it down to three primary behaviors: I was nice, I made my dates laugh, and I told them how beautiful they were. It was a simple formula. Being the honest person that I was, I couldn't replicate this model. I had to be authentic with each woman I dated. I had to be spontaneous and genuine. I couldn't lie, fake interest, or be deceptive about my intentions. It wasn't until much later in life that I realized that other guys weren't quite as scrupulous. Whenever I've shared these stories with my wife, she laughs and says that's why she loves me.

My First Computer

In my high school typing class, there was a single Commodore 64 computer in the room. I'm not sure why it was there or what it was used for, but I would sit in front of it and play a Lemonade game. I thought it was the coolest thing. One day, I learned how to make my name appear on the screen and flash on and off. From that day onwards, I was hooked on computers.

Three years later, in 1985, I purchased my first computer—an Apple IIc. I would spend hours upon hours teaching myself how to code. I'd run down to Mountain View to a Tower Records store and purchase books on programming and logic. My brain absorbed the logic behind computer programing. I was enthralled with computer technology and the potential it offered. I got it immediately. I loved that the computer would do whatever I programmed it to do as long as my coding was accurate and logical.

Inspired by the Movie War Games, I created a text version game that simulated various military scenarios. Depending on the chosen answer, different scenarios would be presented. It was a pretty cool game. Another program I wrote was a simulated Roulette game. It didn't have any graphics. A user would pick a number and place an amount to bet, and if the random number matched the number picked by the player, the player won. I was especially proud of this game because I included computer code to check for three consecutive bets with specific number selections. If the three numbers were played, the next spin wouldn't be random but a predefined number of my choosing. It was a great way to win. I never took advantage of anyone, though. I always showed them the trick.

When I sat in front of my Apple IIc, I envisioned the future of the world. Already having a solid foundation in business by the age of 21, I could see how computers would affect every aspect of our lives. As I continued to learn to code, I was told that people had to be good at math to be a programmer. My Pre-Algebra failures returned to haunt me, and I talked myself out of pursuing my passion. In addition, at the time, Shawn wanted me to work for him, and he was throwing money my way.

My immersion in computer programming, and the necessity of writing programs that were logical, actually helped me to become a much better businessman. Until then, I wasn't familiar with the concept of logic. Approaching business problems logically helped me develop efficient procedures at an early age. Programming logic was a skill set I would draw upon throughout my various careers.

I have one memory from this period in my life that haunts me. At one point, I was looking for a place to live. I answered an ad for a room-mate. The apartment was located in Menlo Park, and when I arrived, a young guy answered the door. He had Apple software and computers all around his apartment. He worked for Apple. We got along, and the room was mine if I wanted it. As fate would have it, Shawn convinced me to move in with him instead. I look back at this moment in my life and can't help but feel that if I had moved in with this kid from Menlo Park, my career trajectory and my life would have gone in a different direction.

For me, the 1980s was a magical time to be living in the Bay Area. Apple was a small company taking on industry titans Microsoft and IBM. Everyone was captivated by Apple being founded in a garage by Steve Jobs and Steve Wozniak. The story of Xerox inviting Steve Jobs to check out a new graphical interface that Xerox wasn't inter-ested in is legendary. Bill Gates getting IBM to license its operating system was the stuff of legends. I was living in the midst of the great-est-ever technological revolution.

Communing With God

The Chapters, Childhood Experiences, High School Memories, and Select Memories were not initially part of this book. It wasn't until I began the 4th revision that I felt the need to include greater details about my childhood and young adult experiences. The contents of these chapters describe the experiences in my life that helped define my character. While I did my best to stick to a chronological timeline, some areas more appropriately lent themselves to a thematic approach; hence, the Select Memories chapter.

During the compilation of these new chapters, there were times I'd have to stop and go for a ride to distract myself. There are a lot of painful memories here. As I looked back on my life, I realized that I was a very good-hearted person, but I was also naïve, and people used that against me. I certainly wasn't perfect then, and I'm not now. But back then, like now, I strive to be the best possible version of myself.

I do like to use my imagination, and while assembling these chapters, I did allow myself to ponder the alternative experiences in life I may have had, if rather than turning the other cheek, I thumped a few heads here and there, or if I would have had more adult supervision while growing up. While an interesting train of thought, I realized I'm unwilling to change the essence of who I am. It was because of my good nature, my naiveté, and my prayers that I caught God's attention.

Having my self-esteem and self-image constantly under attack was depressing. Fortunately for me, I found refuge in nature. The sheer beauty of the coastal landscape, Montara Mountain, the various scents from the coastal flora, and the warm sun or chilly coastal fog inspired me and probed my soul at the deepest levels. Out in nature, I had found sanctuary. I'd spend hours basking in the beauty of God's creation by either sitting on a cliff overlooking the Pacific Ocean or on the side of a hill staring at the Montara Mountains. Out in nature, I would find peace. I wasn't being criticized, scrutinized, or ridiculed. Out in nature, I would contemplate life, dream about the future, and ponder the meaning of life.

· · ·

It was during these special moments in my life, out in nature, that I did what the Maronite Church in Ohio taught me to do when I was introduced to God. I reached out to God in conversation and prayer. Out in God's magnificent creation, I learned how to remain optimistic, believe in myself, and imagine a magnificent future. In God's beautiful creation, I discovered that I was good enough.

On clear nights, I'd find myself sitting at a picnic table in my backyard for hours, gazing at the stars, absorbing the magnitude of the universe, and contemplating life. Out of billions of stars, we live on the only hospitable planet in the universe. Between communing with nature and observing the stars, I'd realize how special our world is and what it means to be alive. In addition, I recognized the insignificance of the drama we create in our lives.

Out in nature, I chose to focus on how special life is and the infinite opportunities available to us as human beings. I concluded at an early age that our beautiful planet, with its amazing ecosystems and the infinite possibilities available to us as human beings, are all evidence of God's brilliance.

My childhood and early adult life were split between two distinct worlds. In my first world was my everyday reality of challenges, competition, responsibility, criticism, and degradation. In my second world, out in nature, while I pondered God's magnificent creation, I was filled with a deep sense of optimism about my future and my ability to become incredibly successful. These feelings of hope and success were intense, compelling, and matter-of-fact. I had a bright future ahead of me; of that, I was convinced.

Chapter 5
Battling Satan: Round I

Jack's Auto Parts

When I was nineteen, I went to work for Jack's Auto Parts stores. Jack's was a family-owned chain of automotive parts stores with about 12 or 13 locations from San Francisco to Santa Clara. The first store I was assigned to was in Redwood City. I don't believe I had been working there for more than a month when Halloween rolled around. I enjoyed dressing up for Halloween, so before going to work one morning, I put a lump of scar makeup on my left cheek. The effect was very realistic. It looked like I had an ugly blister on my cheek.

Upon arriving at work, I told my co-workers and manager that my cousin and I had an argument the night before, and my cousin threw down a pan of French fries cooking in oil. Some of the oil splashed onto my face. My manager inspected the scar and couldn't believe what had happened. Other employees were sympathetic. I only told one other associate it was fake. He laughed his ass off. I was working the cash register that morning and informed all my customers it was a fake scar. They all laughed as they left the store.

About mid-morning, one of our area managers came in. This guy was ultra-conservative and strictly business. He pretended to be walking by, but then he was like, "What the hell happened to you?" With a grin on my face, I shared the same story about the fight with my cousin. He, too, inspected my scar and then went to the back of the store.

During lunch, I went into the restroom and moved the scar to my other cheek. When I came out, my manager happened to be walking by and was startled. He exclaimed, "Hey, it's on the other side." Then he realized it was all a hoax. My co-workers were busting up. The following week I was transferred to the corporate headquarters store in San Mateo. One of the other area managers appreciated my sense of humor but warned me never to do something like that again.

My little prank made me an instant legend with employees throughout the company. Word spread like wildfire that I had gotten one over on Carlsfield, the manager of the Redwood City Store. From that day on, I was greeted like a celebrity at any store I was assigned to. Interestingly, I learned that Carlsfield didn't care much for me, and before my prank, he was trying to get me fired. I was under a microscope at the San Mateo store, but I passed with flying colors.

The owners of Jack's liked to visit the various stores. One day, I had already stocked all the shelves and cleaned as much as possible. The rule of thumb was to make sure you were busy when one of the owners came in. I had nothing more to do, so I approached every customer in the store, even the ones I had already helped, and asked if I could help them find something. The owner noticed me engaging customers, and I received recognition for taking care of customers.

I worked in all of the stores in the chain. At each store, I was warned about the Daily City store. There was a guy there named Bernard Stowe, who was ruthless when it came to bantering. Several of my colleagues feared what might happen when the two of us worked together. There was talk of a potential clash of personalities.

Bernard was a black man, and we hit it off immediately. In terms of banter, Bernard was a bully. He was quick-witted and had no problem using banter to destroy associates in front of customers. I never let it show, but I was petrified of Bernard blowing me up in front of customers. However, I understood Bernard. I knew if I could return the banter as quickly as Bernard could dish it up, then he would back off. Those who couldn't keep up with Bernard would be buried. As a result, I'd come to work with my game face on, ready for a skirmish. I had nothing but fun with Bernard. We'd tangle with each other, and then he'd move on to another associate.

My favorite memory of Bernard is when he taped a sign to the back of my 1968 Camaro that read "Official Qaddafi Staff Car." Qaddafi was a despised dictator that ruled Libya in the 1980s. I discovered the sign on my car when I went to check the parking lot for trash before the store closed. I chuckled as I took the sign off my car and placed it on the back of Bernard's brand new, white Cadillac Deville.

The next day at noon, when Bernard entered the front of the store, he yelled, "Maroun! I'm going to kill you!" Up until that moment, I'd forgotten about the sign swap. Bernard approached the parts counter with a huge grin on his face as he shook his head back and forth and announced I had double-whammied him. Bernard shared how he took his son to school that morning and couldn't figure out why people were driving by him, pointing, and laughing. He continued with how he was pulled over by a motorcycle cop who was laughing hysterically. The motorcycle cop made Bernard get out of his car and walk to the back of it. It was priceless. Everyone at the parts counter laughed so hard. I enjoyed working with Bernard. He had a great sense of humor, and we shared many laughs. I had a lot of fun working for Jack's Auto Parts.

One weekend, Shawn took me to Reno with him and his friends. I sat down at a Blackjack table, and within five minutes, I had lost $50. I thought about how many hours I worked at Jack's Auto Parts to earn that $50. Any previous desire I'd had to gamble disappeared in an instant.

Lebanese Culture

After graduating from high school, I attended a family event, and I met this incredibly beautiful girl from Brazil. She barely spoke any English, and I didn't speak any Portuguese. I met her parents and was allowed to date their daughter. We went on several dates. One day, I called her, and she told me she wasn't allowed to see me anymore because my older brother Shawn and I were drug dealers. That was news to me.

It turned out one of my older cousins was friends with the girl's parents. He told her parents that Shawn and I were drug dealers. I was 18 years old and full of ambition and life. I had nothing to do with Shawn's drug sales. My cousin, who everyone on my dad's side of the family adored, trashed my reputation without a shred of evidence.

I later discovered my esteemed cousin had an affair with the girl's married mother. My reputation was tarnished so that my conniving cousin could win favor and have sex with the mother of the girl I dated. My cousin was beyond reproach. My dad's side of the family loved and adored him .... Adored him, that is, right up until the time he decided to get revenge on his ex-wife by killing their two young daughters before blowing his brains out.

From what I was told, the primary reason my parents lost their business and home in bankruptcy was because of Shawn. In the 1970s, my parents had an opportunity to purchase the building our grocery store was in, along with five or six homes on the same block, for $250,000.00. My father told Shawn to make a full-price offer for the property. Instead, Shawn made an offer to purchase the property for $200,000.00. A group of businesspersons came in with a full-price offer. We lost out on the opportunity to purchase the property.

My folks claimed they had a verbal contract for a five-year lease option and sued to have it enforced. It took a few years for the case to make its way through the courts. In the end, my parents went bankrupt—lost the court case and everything they owned. To make good on debts and take care of the family, Shawn turned to drug dealing.

Whatever Shawn was doing at the time was Shawn's business. The accusation that I was involved in drug sales was an outright lie. Shawn was a huge influence in my life while growing up, and I loved him dearly, but we eventually had a falling out. Shawn had convinced me to move out of my Redwood City apartment and into a house with him and a family friend. I was working construction during the day with our roommate, and at night I was working at Pirate's Cove. Meanwhile, Shawn was sitting at home on his ass, getting high all day.

One day, I came home from work, and Shawn asked me for money. I was watching someone I loved dearly, who was smart and business-savvy, deteriorate right before my eyes. He was so much better than the life he was living. Shawn didn't like my response to his request for money. Thank God for my left jab because Shawn was a wrestler, and if he had gotten close to me, I would have gotten my ass kicked. I eventually found another place to live and distanced myself from him. I was self-sufficient and taking care of myself. I lost track of Shawn and his antics.

Around the time I was nineteen, Shawn started a business selling porcelain dolls and brass figurines. He was also driving around in a fairly new Mercedes Benz. My parents demanded that I be loyal to the family by quitting my job at Jack's Auto Parts and go to work for my brother. Lebanese culture places a high value on family and basically obligated me to support my family. When I was growing up, Shawn was the nucleus of our family. He ran my parents' grocery store, and everyone in our family looked to him for guidance and depended on him. Everyone loved Shawn. He could do no wrong, and my family needed me.

I knew Shawn was good-hearted, generous, and business-savvy, but I had learned there were always strings attached to his generosity that wasn't always apparent. I knew Shawn was a master at manipulation, especially when it came to me. So when my parents approached me about going to work for him, I was very reluctant to give up my independence. Since our falling out, we hadn't seen each other in quite a while. Based off of Shawn's new success, I had no reason to believe he was still involved with drugs. He was a successful businessman.

Discontent with being an employee, my entrepreneurial ambitions, along with Shawn throwing cash my way, convinced me to resign from my position at Jack's Auto Parts and go to work for my brother. Despite past differences, I loved Shawn dearly. He was taking care of our family. He was intelligent, entrepreneurial, ambitious, and knowledgeable about sourcing exclusive merchandise. Shawn had a generous heart and was an excellent businessman.

Soon after going to work for Shawn, I learned that, in addition to his porcelain doll and brass figurine gift business, Shawn was also distributing cocaine. While he was willing to sacrifice his freedom for lucrative profits, nothing in this world was worth the price of my freedom. For me, the thought of being locked up in a cage represented ultimate failure and was absolutely inconceivable.

My Faith In God

I believed, with all of my heart, in the potential of my brother's legitimate business and our ability to be highly successful without his lucrative drug distribution business. I was completely devoted to my brother and my family. My belief and faith in God dictated that it would be up to me to get Shawn off drugs, persuade him to give up his illegal activities, and focus on our legitimate business. With unstoppable, youthful zest, I dedicated my life to my brother and worked my ass off for him. I focused all my energy on building his legitimate business while trying to persuade him to give up his drug business.

. . .

For his part, Shawn was adamant that I not be involved in his illicit drug distribution business, which suited me perfectly. And though I had no burning desire to be incarcerated, I wasn't opposed to partaking in a free supply of cocaine for personal use. Although my efforts were focused on running and growing our legitimate business, I found myself in a constant state of conflict and fear. No matter how much I focused on our legitimate business or how successful our legitimate business became, I was still living in my brother's lie. Our financial success was fake, and I hated the fact that we weren't legitimate. I knew with all my heart that we could succeed without Shawn's drug dealing.

On the other hand, Shawn was caught up in a drug dealer's lifestyle and partied with the best of them. Even I wasn't immune from the desire to live large. Nonetheless, I was constantly attempting to persuade him to abandon his illicit activities. As committed and enthusiastic as I was to growing our legitimate business, he was obsessed with drug trafficking and all the perks it brought with it. I was fighting to free both of us from his destructive obsession, yet I could not persuade him to give up drug distribution and focus all of his efforts on our legitimate business. Given my knowledge of Shawn's illicit activities, I found myself constantly having to look over my shoulder.

I knew in my heart that Shawn's path wasn't the path for me. During the six years that I worked with Shawn, I prayed to God day and night. I prayed for God's protection. I prayed to God to keep Shawn safe. I prayed that God would open Shawn's eyes so he could tackle his drug addiction, and I prayed that God would help Shawn reprioritize his life so he would focus all of his energy on our legitimate business. We had a world full of legitimate opportunities. I knew we didn't need Shawn distributing cocaine to be successful. I loathed the fact that our success wasn't 100% legitimate. At no time was I aware that I was engaged in a battle between good and evil, nor was I aware that God was paying attention and listening to my prayers.

A Fool's Errand

My lectures on giving up drugs and going legitimate had varying effects on Shawn. Sometimes, I believed he actually listened to what I was saying and took my advice to heart; other times, I might as well have been talking to the wall. We used to purchase porcelain dolls and brass figurines from a wealthy, successful businessman in the Los Angeles area, who was an importer with a warehouse the size of a football field. He liked Shawn and me very much. We were always treated very well when we visited. Shawn looked up to this businessman and dreamed of one day having a business as large as his.

One day, after concluding our business, as Shawn and I were driving back home in our van packed with porcelain dolls and brass figurines, I asked Shawn if he could ever recall a time when we conducted business with this man, and he broke out marijuana or cocaine? Obviously, the answer was no, but subtle confrontations like this would give Shawn pause, and there would be a change for a few days. Periodically, I would try similar strategies, but always to no avail.

At one point, Shawn broke his shin bone and was bedridden. During this time, he was starting to date a beautiful blonde my age, or 12 years his junior. This incredibly beautiful woman fed my brother's ego. He fell instantly in love with her and wanted to marry her. One day, when I visited him while he was still laid out in bed, he reached into his pocket, pulled out an 8-ball of cocaine, and boasted about how he always had to have cocaine around to keep his new girlfriend interested.

At that exact moment, his new girlfriend became my enemy. Everything I was working for, and any progress I had made in trying to persuade Shawn to sober up, had just gone out the door. If having cocaine around was the key to wooing this woman, then I knew my attempts at getting Shawn to abandon his illicit activities would fall on deaf ears. Although the odds were now overwhelmingly against me, I stuck to my faith in God and my faith in my ability to help Shawn grow our legitimate business to the point he didn't need or want his drug distribution activities. For the next several years, there would be fights and fragile truces between Shawn, his girlfriend, and me. God was observing.

Manipulated

I remarked earlier about what a master manipulator Shawn was. Well, when I was 21 years old, Shawn accepted a plea bargain for the distribution of a controlled substance. He was sentenced to 4 ½ months in prison. Despite not having anything to do with his illicit business, or any desire to get involved with his illicit business, Shawn pleaded with me to keep his illicit business alive by making deliveries for him until he returned. He assured me all of his customers were family friends that I knew. I reluctantly agreed to meet his customers, though as it turned out, I had never met most of the people to whom I was introduced.

Shawn made arrangements, so all I had to do was answer his pager, go to point A to pick up the product, and then deliver the product to point B. I would only have the product on me during a delivery. On the day Shawn left to begin his prison sentence, he handed me two pagers. One pager was for our legitimate business customers, and the other was for his illicit business customers. To this day, I remember vowing to myself never to answer the illicit business pager. I'd focus all of my energy on our legitimate business. In addition to handing me both pagers, Shawn informed me that he never told our mother he was going to prison. He left that very dramatic and emotional conversation for me to handle.

Within days of Shawn's absence, I soon realized I would be solely responsible for having to make multiple vehicle payments, insurance payments, a house payment, pay my father's rent, provide my mother and other family members with money, pay utilities, pay my own rent and living expenses, and cover all of our business expenses. Our legitimate business brought in a substantial cash flow, but it wasn't enough to cover our entire expenses. While our legitimate business pager was silent for long periods, Shawn's illicit business pager wouldn't stop beeping.

At the age of 21, with great hesitancy, reluctance, and enormous pressure created by my manipulative brother, I compromised my values. I did what I needed to do to take care of my family and keep our legitimate business venture going. I was being sucked into a world I wanted nothing to do with. Distributing cocaine certainly wasn't my plan or dream. I doubled my prayers to God daily, asking for His protection and intervention.

During the next 4 ½ months, I ended up partying and living large, but I took care of my family. My brother Richard was struggling financially, and when I stopped by to visit him and his family, I gave him $500 cash and took his kids grocery shopping. We returned with three shopping carts full of groceries. One time, when I visited my mom, I gave her $800 cash and bought her furniture.

The 4 ½ months Shawn was gone turned out to be one of the most intense experiences in my entire life. I was living a double life with the thrills, drama, and personal conflict of an intense thriller. Despite having access to unlimited amounts of cocaine, I never sought to expand Shawn's illicit business. I limited my actions to making deliveries to his existing clientele. I never let on to my friends about my double life.

I remember driving around the bay area one night, high on cocaine, and praying to God. I was making exorbitant amounts of money, I was partying, and I was very popular. However, my life was a sham, and I was conflicted between my beliefs and values and the reality of my life. I certainly wasn't living my life the way I'd envisioned it. I was living in my brother's lie and compromising my values and beliefs. I reiterated to God that I wanted nothing to do with this lifestyle. I wanted out, but I was trapped. I was incredibly naïve, and I was in way over my head. God was listening.

In Over My Head

During this highly intense period in my life, where I was doing my brother's bidding, I started to date a beautiful girl my age that knew I was using cocaine but suspected more. Despite my best efforts at trying to bed this girl, she wasn't one to give in. I have fond memories of her coming over to my apartment, stripping down to her panties, and then spending the next several hours letting me try to get those panties off. She was always wearing Calvin Klein's Obsession perfume. I found her perfume intoxicating, and to this day, if I encounter a woman wearing Obsession perfume, a grin appears on my face as a wave of memories over-comes me.

One night, this young lady told me she wanted to try cocaine. She had never done cocaine before. Here was a perfect opportunity to get her high and increase the likelihood of getting those panties off her. However, no such thought entered my mind. In response to her request to try cocaine, I lectured her about drug addiction and how she was better off not trying it. I refused to introduce her to cocaine; she was okay with that. A month or so later, we parted ways, and I was dating an older woman who wanted nothing to do with drugs and encouraged me to get sober.

One of Shawn's customers was actually a friend of the family I knew from my childhood. When I learned of his financial difficulties, I wiped out his debt to my brother. One of the most heartbreaking but eye-opening moments for me during this period was watching one of Shawn's customers exploit another human being. I watched in disgust as he taunted this individual, whom I knew, with a small bindle of cocaine while teasing him about getting high. Shawn's customer had no remorse or sense of wrongdoing. Watching one human being exploit another so cavalierly made me sick to my stomach.

I never confronted my brother's customer. I figured God would deal with him on His time. I later reached out to the exploited person, encouraging this poor soul never to let anyone demean them, espe-cially over drugs. I felt sorry for this person who was hard-working—a good person, but addicted to drugs. One night, while at home getting high, I watched a Frontline episode about the war on drugs. I attempted to call into the show and voice my opposition to the war on drugs in support of drug prevention education and treatment programs.

Despite my brother's assurances and planning, I'm fortunate I didn't get killed or end up in prison. I had several close calls that could have ended up either way. I didn't know most of Shawn's illicit business customers, but I loved and trusted my brother. Still, I had no business making deliveries on his behalf, and his taking advantage of my love and loyalty to him revealed much about his character.

I look back on those 4 ½ months and believe, with all of my heart, that the only reason I survived this period in my life unscathed was due to the grace of God. When Shawn returned from his vacation at "camp," we had a huge argument over his girlfriend and parted ways. I sought refuge in Napa.

Chapter 6
A Reprieve: Napa 1986

Begging For God's Intervention

I once went dancing all summer long.
I'd dance all night and dance all day.
She was a beauty, with long snow-white hair.
She made me feel good, she made me feel bad.
She gave me energy, she wore me out.
When fall fell upon me I realized what she had done.
She robbed me of my dignity.
She had emptied my pocket.
Anything I valued was gone.
All for pleasure.
She lied to me, but I caught her.
For the devil shall not dance with me again.

— Jim Maroun, June 1987

Heroes Wanted

Shawn and I owned a house in Napa that had a granny unit above the garage. We rented the main house while our mom lived in the granny unit. I moved in with her, and for several months all I did was eat, sleep, cry, pray, and beg God and Jesus to intervene in my life. God had used the previous 4 ½ months of my life to open my eyes to the extent of wickedness in this world. I was appalled and frightened by what I saw. Human beings could be so selfish, superficial, and ruthless.

The extent of the extremely superficial world in which we live overwhelmed me. People were so incredibly fake. I was a fake. The lifestyle I had just lived was fake. My experiences during the previous 4 ½ months allowed me to witness firsthand people's raw desire for success and what they're willing to do to be successful and part of the "in crowd." Madison Avenue was doing a spectacular job of defining what success looked liked. I observed a world where people were willing to take advantage of others, exploit others, manipulate others, and do whatever it took to achieve success, no matter the cost.

The lifestyle I had just experienced was absent of God. I felt so empty. I was provided a glimpse into a world I wanted nothing to do with. Unfortunately, that world was all around me. It wasn't just limited to drug dealers and drug users. I begged God to protect me, to shield me from evil, to shield me from evil people, and to prevent me from ever compromising my values again. I desired meaning in my life. I wanted nothing to do with being superficial, petty, or having to be immoral to make money. I prayed to God to protect me and allow me to live a life where I could serve Him. God was listening.

Healing

After several months of detoxing, I decided to register for a few college courses at Napa Valley College. I had become a big believer in self-improvement and the acquisition of knowledge. The first time I stepped onto the Napa Valley College Campus, my life was changed forever. I met an assistant in the English department who encouraged me to enroll in a couple of classes. She helped me decide which ones to take and how to register. This person's single act of kindness helped change my life forever.

At Napa Valley College, I met professors that cared about other human beings and were committed to making this a better world. I took an English class, where I discovered my penchant for writing, and I did a research paper on the history of drug addiction, which helped me conquer my own struggles with cocaine. I took a study skills class that taught me how to read a book and extract meaningful information (I would find good use for these study skills later on in life). The support staff and instructors I met at Napa Valley College were incredible human beings. Their unselfish kindness and dedication to their profession was inspirational. I'll always be grateful to these folks for their huge impact on my life.

While living in Napa, I purchased my first street motorcycle; a red Yamaha Radian 600. I discovered the beauty of the Napa Valley on my new motorcycle. When my classes were done for the day, I would jump on it, ride up Silverado Trail to Calistoga, and sometimes go over the mountain to Middletown. Other times, I would explore the Lake Berryessa area.

· · ·

Heroes Wanted

With its picturesque hills, vineyards, climate, flora, and rural atmosphere, the beauty of the Napa Valley was a testament to God's magnificent creation. While exploring the Valley, I would find myself in heightened states of spirituality and could sense traces of God all around. Basically, I was communing with God on the backroads of the Napa Valley.

For a brief period, I was living the life of a typical 22-year-old. Life was simple, I was learning, and I didn't have to look over my shoulders. I'd contrast my current life to the time when Shawn was in jail. I'd think about my professors and their dedication to improving humanity. I'd think about their daily struggles to make a living, provide for their families, and do what they love to do. These were honest, hard-working individuals. Then I would reflect upon the realities of the world I had escaped from. I believed most people were clueless about what was really happening in our world.

Those 4 ½ months of my life, when Shawn was in jail, provided me with the most intense experiences of my young life. The emotions, the enormous power trip from living a secret life, the partying, and the intensity of living on the edge all proved to be mind-boggling and made me feel like I had lived a lifetime in very short order. I was extremely grateful and content to leave that world behind me, unscathed more-or-less.

Before I could attend a second semester at Napa Valley College, I was called back to the Bay Area. Shawn needed my help. I returned invigorated and more determined than ever to help grow Shawn's legitimate business. Once again, I prayed daily that God would keep Shawn safe, open his eyes, and rid us of all of his illegal activities. God was paying attention.

My Yamaha Radian 600

My decision to purchase a street motorcycle wasn't taken lightly. The dynamics of riding on the street were considerably different from riding off-road. There was traffic, concrete, and steel—lots of it. Crashing in a field or on a dirt trail would be nothing like crashing on a paved road with curbs, metal posts, and oncoming cars.

My experiences riding a dirt bike during my childhood, however, did provide me with invaluable lessons for riding a motorcycle on the street. I learned, for instance, that riding a street motorcycle would demand the utmost respect for the street motorcycle's capabilities as well as a heightened sense of my surroundings at all times. I knew the moment I disrespected the capabilities of my street motorcycle or did something stupid, it could kill me, and not think twice about it.

One day I was stopped at a red light. There were four lanes of traffic: two going in my direction and two going in the opposite direction. I was in the second lane from the right. When the light turned green, I accelerated. As soon as I crossed the intersection, out of nowhere, a green station wagon pulled out from the K-Mart parking lot right in front of me. Once the lady behind the wheel realized she cut me off, she panicked and stopped. Both traffic lanes in my direction were effectively blocked, and I was accelerating right toward her front fender.

My first reaction was to hit the brakes. I applied too much pressure to the rear brake, so the bike started to slide out from under me. I was still heading toward the front fender of her car. In my mind, I envisioned how I would hit the front of her car and then try to use my hands to propel myself over the hood. The next thing I knew, my instincts kicked in. I unconsciously down-shifted the bike into a lower gear and opened up the throttle. The motorcycle immediately came out of its slide, and I threw my weight to the left and swerved sharply around the stationary vehicle. It was an incredible move that was purely instinctual. It happened fast, without me thinking about it. My years of dirt bike riding as a kid had paid off big time.

Chapter 7
Battling Satan: Round I, Part II

Expanded Business Opportunities

While I was gone, Shawn expanded his legitimate business offerings to include cutlery products. We now carried porcelain dolls, brass figurines, cutlery products, and assorted gift items. Shawn recruited our eldest brother, Richard, to run the new cutlery line and moved him and his family from Southern California to the Central Valley.

The new cutlery line proved very profitable and opened up new avenues of revenue. We began exhibiting our product lines at four major trade shows a year and added a few gun shows in addition to the various flea markets we attended. In between the trade shows, we depended on Richard to reach out to our growing list of customers to generate sales.

· · ·

In addition to expanding product lines, Shawn opened up a beautiful showroom in San Francisco that also served as our warehouse. The entire building was a restored warehouse converted into offices, restaurants, and retail shops. While our showroom was close to the San Francisco Gift & Jewelry Center, we were still off the beaten path. Rent was cheap enough for San Francisco, but only a few businesses were open. Walk-in foot traffic was non-existent. We were driving our existing customers to our showroom.

Despite the numerous legitimate opportunities before us, Shawn just couldn't resist being involved in the drug trade. I know Richard didn't partake in getting high and would have preferred it if Shawn wasn't involved with drugs. We never talked about it. He did his job, and I did mine. No matter how hard I tried or how persuasive my arguments were, I could not persuade Shawn to give up his illegal activities. He was caught up in a drug dealing lifestyle, and there wasn't anything I could do to change his mind. I continued to live in fear, knowing that our lives could come crashing down at any moment. Every day, I continued to pray to God for protection for my family and to get Shawn off drugs and out of the drug distribution business.

An Early Innovator

While it was Richard's responsibility to handle the cutlery products, it was my responsibility to manage the porcelain dolls, brass figurines, and assorted gift items. In addition to my duties, I took on numerous projects designed to help enhance our efficiency and productivity. Being the youngest brother by 12 years, my ideas weren't received very well by my older brothers. Egos were involved, and I often had to fight with them even as I was trying to make their jobs easier. Fortunately for me, a much older and wiser business consultant would usually side with me. Below are a few of the contributions I made over the years to our business:

. . .

Monthly Flyers

I created our monthly, multi-paged flyer, promoting our latest products and sale items. A computer store in our building would allow me to use one of their Macs. I'd use a desktop publishing program to create each page's text and product placement. I'd then print out a master copy of the layout. Next, I'd cut product images from a vendor's catalog and paste the pictures onto my flyer. Once the printing was done, I'd fold them in thirds and take them to the post office to be processed as bulk mail. At one point, we had a mailing list of nearly 2,000 customers.

Shipping Department

Our shipping department needed to be more organized and efficient. There wasn't any logical organization to how Shawn and Richard set it up. When an order was pulled, boxed, weighed, and labeled for shipment, it was farthest from the main door. As a result, the UPS driver was forced to navigate through our warehouse, load up packages on his dolly, and navigate back out without running anyone over.

My solution was simple. I reversed the direction of the flow of our shipping department. In addition, I put the materials necessary for each stage of the packaging and shipping process in a logical order. When orders were packaged and ready for shipment, they were stacked right next to the door, ready for the UPS driver to pick them up. As simple as this process sounds, I had to fight like hell with my brothers to get it implemented.

Trade Show Preparation

When I did my first trade show, during setup, I spent the entire day unpacking products, labeling them, and creating show signs. By the time my second trade show rolled around, I knew to prep my merchandise before it left our warehouse. As a result, when I arrived at the trade show, all of my products were labeled and ready to go.

All I had to do was unbox them, set up displays, and hang the pre-made signs. Setup took a few hours, and I now had the rest of the day to spend at my leisure. As much as I tried, I could never convince Richard to do the same for the cutlery line. Nor would he accept my assistance with setting up at the trade shows. Only he knew what needed to be done. As a result, I'd be free to roam about, and he'd be stuck labeling and pricing merchandise right up until the start of the show.

Display Cases

Our portable display case system for cutlery products was horrible. We were using cheap wooden stands that were falling apart. Once the wooden stand was set up, it would hold six 8"x 14" jewelry glass display cases. Cutlery products that didn't fit in these glass cases would be laid out on a couple of tables inside their opened boxes.

I partnered with a guy who used to sell cassette tapes displayed in 2' x 3' glass display cases with adjustable shelves. We devised an A-frame that would hold two glass displays on each side. Each display case would lock onto the A-frame. We could now transport our cutlery products in eight display cases. Once we were on site, all we had to do was set up the A-frames and snap the display cases into place. We no longer had to open a few dozen boxes and lay out cutlery products.

For our smaller pocket knives that fit in the smaller 8" x 14" jewelry display boxes, I reached out to a friend who worked with aluminum and had him build me a couple of aluminum A-frames. They were beautiful. They folded up, and they could each hold twelve 8" x 14" jewelry display boxes. Transporting display products was now easier, less of a hassle, and saved considerable time.

Customer Contact System

I came up with a coded system for tracking customer interactions. I created sales scripts and developed a filing system to note customer conversation highlights efficiently. It might be a month before I contacted a customer again, but when I did, I'd have information from our last conversation right at my fingertips. It was an excellent system for building rapport, establishing relationships, and keeping current on my customers' business needs.

My Compensation

Richard was drawing a healthy salary each month so that he could pay his mortgages and feed his family. I had no problem with that. For the entire time I worked for Shawn, my pay fluctuated between $300 and $400 weekly. I drew enough money to pay my rent, car payment, and utilities. I never demanded more money because I knew how much money the legitimate business was generating. I knew what our monthly expenses were, and I knew where the cash came from to cover any shortfalls. As far as I was concerned, I was putting in sweat equity. I believed in our legitimate business and worked my ass off trying to make it successful. Once the company was legitimate and we were free from Shawn's illegal activities, I would look at filling my pockets with gold.

Friction

There is absolutely no doubt that Richard was a great salesman. He was very personable and was a phenomenal bullshitter. He was family, and both Shawn and I trusted him explicitly. However, it wasn't always smooth sailing. Richard, being the eldest in the family, believed he should be calling the shots because he was the eldest. Richard lacked the business experience Shawn, the business consultant, and I had. In addition, some of the business decisions he did make demonstrated his ignorance of business strategies. None of this mattered to Richard. He was the oldest. Therefore he should be in charge.

Another point of contention for Richard was our business checking account. Richard felt he should be a signatory on the account. He felt slighted that I was, and he wasn't. Even after Shawn and I explained that I was only on the account in cases of an emergency. It didn't matter. He still felt he should also be on the account. One of the most telltale signs that Richard didn't understand our business was his insistence that when we did trade shows in Las Vegas or Reno, he'd be given extra cash so he could gamble. We're not talking about some paltry sum. He wanted $2,000 per show on top of his already generous salary.

There was no logical explanation or justification for giving him extra cash so he could gamble other than he felt entitled to it. Shawn and I were in complete disbelief. Eventually, there was a falling out between my two older brothers, and Richard was fired for cause. I took over the cutlery product lines and was now responsible for every aspect of the business.

God Answers My Prayers

Soon after Richard was no longer associated with our business, God provided me with a vision of incarceration that was so powerful, I knew it was a warning. The clarity, intensity, and belief that this vision was a real possibility caused me to double my prayers to ask God for His intervention. Nothing in this world was worth my freedom, especially Shawn's illicit activities. I begged God to rid our lives of drugs once and for all. Most importantly, I asked God to protect me.

Within a couple of weeks of my vision of incarceration, Shawn boasted to me about an upcoming drug deal he would soon transact. Shawn seldom, if at all, discussed the specifics of his illicit activities with me. However, this time he was very excited. This upcoming drug deal involved significantly more quantities of drugs than what he normally distributed. In addition, the profits from this transaction would be substantially less than what he would typically gain from his smaller, regular distributions. If this was a setup, the quantity of drugs involved would guarantee a lengthy prison sentence. Increasing my suspicion of a setup was that the person Shawn would transact this deal with wasn't a long-time family friend. Instead, he was someone Shawn had met at the Pescadero prison camp several years earlier.

A few days before my brother's big announcement, I watched a *Frontline* news program documenting how the FBI & DEA were using informants in the war on drugs. I matter-of-factly pointed out to Shawn that this upcoming drug transaction included significantly more amounts of cocaine than he usually distributed, his exposure to increased jail time was significantly increased, and his profit from this one transaction was substantially less than what he usually made. I reminded him that he didn't have a relationship or know the guy he would transact this deal with. I shared with him everything I had just learned from watching the *Frontline* television documentary. I specifically told him how the FBI & DEA planted informants in prisons. I did my best to talk Shawn out of transacting this upcoming drug deal. Shawn failed to heed my warning, and the following week my brother's illicit drug activities were shut down permanently.

God had answered my prayers; not how I would have liked or envisioned, but nonetheless, they were answered. My days of having to look over my shoulder, and living in my brother's world of lies were soon ending. Shawn's final illicit drug-selling deal went down exactly as I had predicted.

Chapter 8
Penance: The Cost of My Freedom

Grand Preparations

As I predicted, Shawn was going to jail for a long time. It took several months to arrange his bail. During this time, I shut down the San Francisco showroom and set up operations in a small warehouse we maintained down the street from Shawn's house. I kept our legitimate business operational by keeping up our attendance at trade shows and gun shows, sending out flyers to our customers, and making sales calls.

When Shawn finally did make bail, we moved into our house in Napa and opened a retail cutlery store to continue operating our wholesale business. Shawn's wife was pregnant, and the game plan Shawn pushed was that she and I would share the house, and she would help me run the business. Until this point, she had never been involved in the company's operation.

. . .

Heroes Wanted

Neither my sister-in-law nor I believed in this proposition. We both had our doubts. Despite our protests, Shawn was persistent. There were no other options available, so we'd have to learn to depend on each other to make it work. I was hesitant but willing to try. The first sign that Shawn's wife wasn't on the same page was when he and his wife returned from a weekend getaway. I had moved in over that same weekend and had just finished setting up my new waterbed. When his wife saw my room and giant waterbed, she immediately burst into tears. He was feeding her lies too.

Several days later, I was incredulous when Shawn begged me to move back to the Bay Area and restart his drug distribution business. He knew I wanted nothing to do with his illicit drug dealing, but he was willing to risk my life and freedom to achieve his objectives. I flat-out refused his numerous requests.

God had answered my prayers, and I was extremely grateful to have the scourge of drugs removed from my life. After I made it clear to Shawn that I would not be reviving his drug distribution business, I did my best to convince him that his fantasy arrangement between his wife and me wouldn't work out. My protest fell upon deaf ears. He wouldn't hear it.

Unfortunately, our options were limited. Financially, we had no choice. We all had to compromise and do our best to make it work out. I loved my brother and believed in my ability to make everything work. Through extensive negotiations, I had Shawn and his wife Quit Claim their half-interest in the home to me. In exchange, I had to sign a lease agreement with his wife to prevent me from evicting her. To help with the expenses, my sister-in-law's brother moved into an extra room attached to the home. I would be able to count on rental income from both my sister-in-law and her brother.

Ambition & God

When Richard was fired several months earlier, we began transitioning out of the porcelain doll and brass figurine lines and focused exclusively on the cutlery product line. We went from three brothers working full-time to two brothers, and now it would be me and my sister-in-law. It was sheer ambition, over-confidence, and my unwavering belief that with God's blessings, I'd successfully legitimize our cutlery business. The company generated substantial revenues, and we had a healthy profit margin. The biggest challenge I would face was keeping expenses down while maintaining enough cash flow and reserves to get through the dreaded months of January, February, and March, where cash flow would be almost non-existent, but bills still had to be paid. Without Shawn, there would be no extra cash to get through these traditionally slow months.

Each month, I would be responsible for the house mortgage, household expenses, such as water, garbage, cable, electricity, homeowners' insurance, rent and utilities for the retail location, business insurance, car payment & insurance, truck payment & insurance, business expenses, telephone expenses, and taxes. I'm sure other expenses have slipped my mind after 30 years. In hindsight, as I write this, I must have been bat shit crazy to take on this nearly impossible task, especially with what transpired on the day Shawn reported to prison.

Sabotage

I believe that the day after my niece was born, Shawn had to report to prison to begin his ten-year sentence. He turned himself in on a

Heroes Wanted

Monday because on Tuesdays, I would get up at around 4:00 a.m. and drive out to a wholesale flea market in the central valley to sell our cutlery products. I could depend on the Tuesday wholesale flea market to generate revenues of between $1,500 and $2,500 weekly. On the first night Shawn turned himself in, his wife went on a rampage, attacked me, and purposely punctured my waterbed with a sharp item. Water was everywhere. I had no idea of what provoked her. My nerves were shot, I didn't get any sleep, and I failed to make it to the wholesale flea market the following day. From day one, I lost needed revenue.

The next day I went about draining my water bed, patching the hole, and then filling it up again. Not a simple process for a king-size waterbed. When I spoke with Shawn by phone, he stated my sister-in-law denied putting a hole in the waterbed. Shawn pushed the narrative that I had somehow accidentally punctured it myself. Furthermore, Shawn informed me that my sister-in-law had attacked me for telling her mother that I was happy the baby was healthy, considering that in all the time she was pregnant, she hadn't missed a single day of smoking marijuana. The truth of the matter is, I was relieved. The newspapers were full of stories of babies with health issues when the mothers used drugs or alcohol during pregnancy, and since she smoked pot all the time, I assumed her mother was aware of her drug use. Yes, I'm that naïve.

The delicate truce between my sister-in-law and me had been shattered, and my brother wasn't there to keep the peace between us. I don't remember if I had the sheriff out on that first night, but our fighting continued, and there were plenty of other times when members of the sheriff's office responded to my calls for assistance.

.   .   .

After the second hole in my waterbed, I put a lock on my bedroom door. Shawn still didn't believe she was responsible. Any possibility of my sister-in-law helping out with the business was now nonexistent. The responsibility to keep everything running fell upon me. I was up for the challenge. I had no problem getting up at 4:00 a.m. and working until 8:00 p.m. I would take a nap for an hour or two during the day. I also didn't mind working seven days a week. I was doing what I had to do to legitimize the business.

One night, shortly after the second puncture in my waterbed, I went to the bathroom but forgot to lock my bedroom door. When I returned to my room and lay back in bed, I splashed right into a puddle of water. Despite having the sheriff out several times, nothing could be done. She had a signed lease and had a right to be there. At least on the third attack, Shawn came to his senses and yelled at his wife. During the next several months, Shawn's wife and I tried to kill each other. It was a crazy time. I was constantly stressed out, my stomach was in knots, and my reward for working my ass off all day was to come home to a house in disarray and a battle brewing.

For the lease between my sister-in-law and me to be valid, she was required to make a token rent payment each month. Her brother, though, despite having a rental agreement, felt no obligation to pay rent ... and didn't. I don't believe I received a single rent payment from him. Once again, I was missing out on needed revenue, but bills still had to be paid, and someone had to keep the business going.

During these dreadful first few months, I engaged the services of a local attorney to look at my options for breaking the lease I had with my sister-in-law. The lease was solid. My only option was to file a restraining order against my sister-in-law in hopes of having her arrested when she attacked me. I also had the attorney handle the eviction of my sister-in-law's brother. All told, I spent several thousand dollars on attorney's fees for evicting my sister-in-law's brother and filing a restraining order against her.

There were many times when I had the sheriff out to enforce the restraining order, but they never arrested my sister-in-law. The sheriff's deputies were in disbelief that I could even have a restraining order placed against someone I was living with. I even made an appointment and met with sheriff's representatives. While they were sympathetic, they were unable to assist me. I had no legal recourse or relief.

There were many nights when I'd come home not knowing what to expect. One night I came home, and she had three men over. The four of them were sitting in the living room with a fire going in the fireplace, only the fireplace damper was closed, and the entire house was filled with smoke. I called the sheriff. The sheriff came, kicked out the guys, and did nothing else. I couldn't get her arrested for violating the restraining order, even while my home was being destroyed.

On several occasions, my sister-in-law would arrive home with my niece and my niece's older step-sister, and then the three of them would proceed to scream and cry as loud as they could. With my sister-in-law's bedroom right next to mine, the noise was deafening ... and more than a little concerning. For whatever reason, probably just to annoy me, my sister-in-law was pinning both girls down on the floor and pulling on their hair until the three of them were all screaming and crying. I called 911 several times, only to have the CHP show up within minutes, do a safety check, and then leave.

Nothing else would happen. Adding to the turmoil was my mother, who lived in a granny unit at the back of the property.

My mom didn't like my girlfriend and was very clear about her disapproval. During my entire life, my mother never liked anyone that dated or married one of her children until after they split up. Only then would they gain favor with my mother and be welcomed. So I had to contend with my mother always complaining about my girlfriend and anything else she could think of.

One night during one of my big fights with my sister-in-law, her mom and stepdad drove up from the Bay Area. I believed they were coming to calm down their daughter. Instead, I found myself under attack from my sister-in-law, her mother, and her stepfather. What a night that turned out to be. Then there was my sister-in-law's ex-husband. My home had two driveways, one on each side of the front yard, but not connected. When my sister-in-law's ex-husband came to pick up his daughter, he'd park in one driveway, and instead of backing out, he'd drive across my lawn and leech lines to the other driveway to make his grand exit. I'd come home from work and see the tire tracks from his car across my lawn. He was never there when I was.

At one point, my sister-in-law found a new boyfriend, and she wasn't shy about bringing him around the house. My brother went to great lengths to provide for his wife. I'm working my ass off every day, and she starts bringing home a boyfriend. On the nights she didn't come home, the following day, I'd observe her lone car parked in the local bar's empty parking lot while on my way to work. At least my niece was safe with either my girlfriend or mother. I was powerless to do anything.

. . .

During this horrible period of my life, when everything was in turmoil, I started to receive phone calls from Richard. Each time he was in tears and begging me to loan him money for his mortgage because he had gambled his paycheck away and his wife was going to leave him. He promised me he would pay me back within a week.

I believe I was deceived twice before I finally told him no more. Richard had a gambling problem and was out of control. Me sending him money that I couldn't afford to part with, or would never see again, wouldn't solve anything. I never saw a dime of the money I had sent.

My Niece

After several months of pure hell, numerous calls to 911, and frequent visits from the Sheriff's Department and CHP, my sister-in-law was arrested for driving while under the influence of alcohol. At the time of arrest, my niece was with her in the car, prompting Child Protective Services (CPS) to become involved. At her mother's request, my niece was placed in my care. Per Child Protective Services, my sister-in-law wasn't allowed near my niece while she was being investigated and was therefore prohibited from returning to my home. My sister-in-law's alcohol addiction finally caught up to her.

I knew my sister-in-law needed help getting her life back on track. In earnest, I met with her case manager at CPS and shared everything that had transpired. I pleaded with CPS to ensure my sister-in-law received the needed treatment. After a few weeks, Child Protective

Services contacted me and informed me that they were going to unite mother and child.

I protested and told them it was much too soon and that they would get my niece killed. My objections fell on deaf ears; the law was the law, and CPS was obligated to unite mother and child as soon as possible. Child Protective Services reunited my niece with her mother on a Friday. Two days later, on a Sunday, CPS contacted me and requested I pick up my niece again. Her mother had been arrested for driving under the influence a second time!

I was livid, and I'll never forget the sight of my niece when I went to pick her up. She was still in her car seat, fast asleep. She was so tiny, innocent, and helpless. I didn't think for a minute that she was tired and needed sleep. She was traumatized by the experience, and sleep was a natural defense.

The very next morning, I went down to the courthouse and tried to get in to see the Judge handling my sister-in-law's case. When his receptionist asked why I wanted to see him, I informed her that I wanted him to meet the baby he was going to get killed, and then I burst into tears. I couldn't see the Judge, so I sat out on the stairs of the Napa County Courthouse, balling like a baby. The system kept failing me, and now it was failing my niece. My sister-in-law had a severe drinking problem, and if she didn't receive the help she needed, she would get herself killed, and possibly her children and others as well, if she was involved in an accident while driving under the influence.

· · ·

After I composed myself on the courthouse stairs, my next stop was the District Attorney's office. I remember standing at the lobby window, pleading to see anyone so I could introduce them to my niece, whose death they would be responsible for if she were killed. As I spoke to the receptionist, a man came walking in from the street, took one look at me, took one look at my niece, and became incensed. He demanded to know if the baby in my arms was Carla Maroun. I confirmed it was her, and that I'd just been given temporary custody again because her mom had received another DUI.

I'd never seen a more livid government employee in my life. He turned out to be the district attorney. Within the next few weeks, my sister-in-law had all her things moved out of the house. I would no longer be terrorized at home, and my sister-in-law would get the treatment she so badly needed. It would be many years before I would ever see my ex-sister-in-law again. Thankfully, she was eventually able to turn her life around.

Business Challenges

It wasn't enough that I was fighting with Shawn, who was behind bars. I also had to contend with his wife, her family, and my mother while working 12-to-16-hour days to pay the bills, amid juggling a plethora of business challenges.

California Employment Development Department

Before Shawn began his prison sentence, we started receiving notices from California's Employment Development Department regarding an employee. As we had never had employees, we discarded the notices. After Shawn began serving his prison sentence, the notices kept coming, and the amount of the fines kept increasing. It didn't matter to me. We never had any employees, so I kept throwing away these documents. Finally, when the penalties reached $75K, I contacted the Employment Development Department to inform them they were nuts.

As it turns out, the California Employment Development Department wasn't 'nuts.' When Richard was fired for cause, he filed for unemployment. To the best of my knowledge (and that of Shawn), our business was structured so that we were all independent contractors. However, the Employment Development Department auditor reviewed our business structure and tax filings and informed me otherwise. After correspondence and meetings, the auditor explained that Richard's job description, duties, and responsibilities classified him as an employee. It only cost me $3,600.00 to learn this valuable lesson.

At the time, I had to hire part-time employees to help keep the store open when I was at a trade show, gun show, or flea market. I had no idea about payroll taxes and believed all employee taxes would be figured out when I did my taxes at the end of the year. Wrong! I now had payroll penalties to pay, I had to ensure all payroll tax paperwork was completed, and I was required to make quarterly payroll tax payments.

Wholesale Flea Market

The weekly wholesale flea market I would attend every Tuesday was losing its financial luster. Sales were barely breaking $1,000.00—sometimes a lot less. I believe the seeds had already been planted for the decline in sales revenue before Shawn turned himself in to begin his prison sentence. Shawn had been attending this wholesale flea market for years, was well known, and was known to have money and spend it! Before turning himself in, he was still helping me with the business, and he would help out at this flea market. On one occasion, as we're walking around the flea market, he's acting like a celebrity as he informs vendors and our customers that he will be imprisoned for the next ten years for distributing cocaine. I had to pull him aside and tell him to shut up. I reminded him I still depended on this flea market for revenue, and not everyone believed drug dealers were cool.

Soon after Shawn was gone, a couple of good old boys started showing up at the flea market, as well as some of the gun shows I exhibited at, and bragged to all of the vendors, some of who I used to supply with cutlery products, about how they could purchase the same products I was selling from importers located back east, at significantly lower prices. I also discovered that more and more of the vendors I had previously sold to at the guns shows were now purchasing directly from the same importers I bought from, at my cost. Flaws in our business model were starting to materialize.

A Flawed Business Model

When we were selling porcelain dolls and brass figurines, Shawn managed to score exceptional deals. We'd start with very healthy profit margins, but competitors would kill our margins as time progressed. All of our porcelain dolls and brass figurines were imported from either Korea, Taiwan, or China. Our sources for these products were based out of Los Angeles.

We had no control over pricing or distribution because we weren't importers. When Shawn acquired the cutlery line, it was a little different. The country of origin for most of the cutlery products we initially sold was Japan or Pakistan, and most importers were on the East Coast. As a result, for several years, we could maintain healthy profit margins. As time progressed, cheaper imports started coming from Taiwan and China and flooded the market. In addition, the East Coast importers we purchased from began to expand West. Our exclusivity bubble had burst.

Our vendors provided us with very competitive discounts on the products we were purchasing. Still, we missed significant discounts because we never purchased single items in bulk quantities. A typical order would be for multiple products and styles with minimum amounts. I didn't discover until late in the game that if we purchased 200 units of a single product, our discount was significantly more, allowing us to be more competitive. A few vendors I dealt with encouraged me to make bulk purchases. While I did manage to purchase in bulk a few times and receive generous discounts, it was late in the game, and I didn't have the financial bandwidth to focus only on a few select products. My customers expected variety.

Before Shawn got busted a second time, we had talked about importing directly. It made the most sense and would have been a logical step, given the volume we were selling. The challenge for us was back in the 1980s there was no Internet. We had no idea where to begin or what the process might look like. Shawn would have been perfect at figuring this out, but he was too caught up being Joe drug dealer. He had no incentive. As a result, we were beholden to importers.

At one point, one of my primary vendors started including contact information in the boxes of every cutlery product they sold. Before I knew it, I had lost my best customers and a significant source of my cash flow. The vendor agreed to refer the customer to me, but the damage was done, and the writing was on the wall. My customer preferred purchasing directly from the importer.

The Truth

At one point, Richard started reaching out to me with offers to come back and help me run the business. After telling him 'no' several times, I politely explained that the company couldn't support his salary requirements. I offered to put him on commission if he brought in new sales, but I knew that bringing in another salesperson wouldn't solve our problems. We weren't importers, and our suppliers were making inroads by selling directly to our customers. I tried to explain this to Richard, but it fell on deaf ears. Richard was persistent and aggressive; he would be the hero and save the business, and I was standing in his way.

Richard recruited my parents to advocate for him. Suddenly I wasn't doing a good job, and everything was my fault. I remember the last conversation with Richard on the subject of him coming back to work. I informed him that while he worked for our brother Shawn, his paycheck was funded by drug sales. I reiterated the challenges I was facing and repeated to him that there was no money to pay him a salary. I'll never forget how dramatic and "shocked" Richard became when he heard drug sales funded his salary. Richard was great at theatrics. As for his paycheck, all one had to do was look at the numbers to realize I was telling the truth. Our legitimate wholesale business always generated significant revenues with a healthy profit margin. The problem was that our expenses were always out-of-hand because Shawn wanted to care for everyone. The chances of my success were astronomical and were a testament to my faith in God.

The Final Blows

I had racked up an enormous amount of personal credit card debt. I was pushing vendor invoices out to 90 days with vendors that allowed me to do so, and I was losing sales to those very same vendors as they expanded west. Early on, I had implemented cost-cutting measures. I exchanged our Grumman work truck and my beautiful Firebird Formula for a Ford Van, saving approximately $600.00 monthly.

Despite my best efforts and long days, I was being undermined by my family. The very people I supported with my hard work and long hours were sabotaging me; making my life unbearable. The odds of my success were already stacked against me, and while I devoted every ounce of my energy to making a go of it, I was forced to contend with a bunch of ingrates. Shawn had successfully manipulated me and forced me into a no-win scenario.

After months of abuse, I began to question why I was killing myself, trying to take care of ungrateful, apathetic people dedicated to undermining me at every turn. I began to ponder what would happen if one day, when I woke up, I just let it all go and didn't turn up for work. While mulling these types of questions over and over again in my head, the final blow to the business came when I exhibited at a Las Vegas trade show.

For the first time since attending these trade shows, one of my vendors from the East Coast was exhibiting and selling most of my popular cutlery products at my cost. At this point, the game was over. I was devastated, demoralized, and tired. I didn't have the knowledge, financial resources, support, or energy to figure this one out. My brother's dream, which I tried to legitimize, was in its death throes.

. . .

My girlfriend, mom, and I took turns caring for my niece. My mom wouldn't let up on her criticism of my girlfriend, and my girlfriend started talking about marriage. She was remarkable, and I did love her, but when I began to think about marriage, I knew she wasn't the one. Rather than prolonging the relationship, I chose not to waste her time and broke up with her. My mom was now the primary caretaker of my niece until I came home.

I'll never forget the day my mom came to me complaining about how she was tired and couldn't be responsible for taking care of my niece all the time. I screamed at her about when I had a girlfriend, all she did was bitch about my girlfriend, and now that my girlfriend was gone, she was still bitching. I was done. Listening to my mom complaining about having to watch my niece was the final straw. I contacted Child Protective Services and informed them that I could no longer take care of my niece. I explained to them the situation and told them I was out of options. My mom flipped out, and the Child Protective Services person I spoke to read me the riot act, but I had no choice. Apparently, that day was the day I woke up and stopped caring and just let it all go.

For the remainder of my life, I have to live with the memory of turning my niece over to Child Protective Services. Within the week, my sister Rachel and her husband stepped up and took custody. Within a few months, I closed the business, sold all assets, and distanced myself from my toxic family.

No amount of compensation was worth what I had been put through. I vowed to God that I would never compromise myself or fight over money or property again. I walked away from my family and my past. A new life awaited me, and I was finally free from my brother's influence, control, and manipulation.

Debriefing

Lebanese culture, family pressure, and my brother's lies and manipulation all exposed me to drug dealing. My faith in God, and my belief in goodness overcoming evil, dictated that I try to get Shawn off drugs and focus on his legitimate business. For several years, I busted my ass off running our legitimate business. I warned him not to do that final drug deal, and I resisted and declined his insistence that I continue his drug dealing when he went to prison. I tried to take care of his wife, daughter, and our mother. I worked tirelessly to keep the family together and legitimize our business, but I was sabotaged from day one.

After liquidating all assets, paying off vendors, paying off all my personal and business credit cards, and purchasing a used vehicle, I had enough cash to start a new life, and I did. Unlike Richard, who used to draw a hefty salary every month, my compensation was minimal. I was investing sweat equity into the business with my 12-to-16-hour days, seven days a week.

After more than six years of my life dedicated to "family" and the hell I'd been put through, I wasn't about to walk away empty-handed. As far as I was concerned, the remaining funds from the liquidation of assets were compensation for the sweat equity I had invested into the business over the years. I was embarking upon a new career, and if I were successful in my new endeavors, then my brother Shawn, my business partner, would be successful, too.

. . .

Heroes Wanted

If you listen to my brothers, you'll hear a tale about a fortune, a vast inventory, and how I lost everything. The narrative I've provided is the truth. There was no massive inventory of products. The business was sustained on credit card debt and generous vendor terms. There certainly wasn't any fortune under my control. I took over a company propped up by drug money and tried to make it legitimate. When I was being put through hell by Shawn's wife, neither of my brothers was there.

From the first day Shawn reported to prison until I walked away from everything, my life was hell. Every day I paid a high price for Shawn's manipulation and lies. When I walked away from everything to begin my new life, I had no qualms about using any leftover monies to fund my fresh start in life. After everything I went through, if you offered me all the money in the world to go through it again, I'd decline and explain my decision with a few choice words for you.

When Shawn was released from prison, I offered to debrief him. I had all the records, receipts, expenses, copies of the restraining order, attorney fees, Sheriff's reports, EDD statements, and everything needed for a complete accounting. Shawn declined and stated everything was good between us. I immediately discarded the box of receipts and records. The box was toxic, and I couldn't wait to get rid of it.

I never looked back, and at no time did I ever consider asking Shawn for forgiveness for the way things transpired between us because I didn't owe him shit. He manipulated me, lied to me, and set me up for failure, and I still did my best to make everything work. For those who may be sympathetic to Shawn's plight, keep this in mind. If Shawn cared about taking care of his wife, daughter, and business, then he should have quit dealing drugs way before he got busted. He could have focused on making a legitimate living to support his family, but he didn't. Instead, he lied and manipulated me into trying to do it for him.

Lessons Learned

Looking back, I now know that God had used Shawn's illicit activities to test my mettle and open my eyes to the realities of our world. I was nineteen years old when I went to work for Shawn, and like all nineteen-year-olds, I was very impressionable. I was looking for leadership and direction and wanted to be a part of something great.

I could have readily accepted my brother's illicit activities, but I didn't. I sought out God daily and never lost focus of how things could be. I did what I had to do for my family. I focused my efforts on expanding Shawn's legitimate business. I tried to open Shawn's eyes to his drug addiction, and I tried to persuade Shawn to stop dealing drugs. While there were times when my behavior was less than exemplary, my faith and commitment to God never waned, nor did it go unnoticed.

In fact, I believe my agreeing to take over the business when Shawn began his prison sentence was an epic display of my faith in God, and God was paying attention. The odds against me were enormous; unbeknownst to me, Shawn was setting up my sister-in-law and me for failure. I was put through hell for over a year, but God was listening and watching.

The years spent working with Shawn in our legitimate wholesale business taught me much. I learned about business, business administration, sales script development, customer tracking, processes and procedures, and more. Most significantly, I learned about the importance of controlling distribution. We had our lunches handed to us because we weren't manufacturers or direct importers. We existed and prospered on the whim of other organizations and had no control over market conditions. All of these experiences proved to be invaluable as I moved on.

In regard to Shawn's illicit drug dealing, God used my brother's drug dealing to open my eyes to the unjust and immoral war on drugs. Unfortunately, when Shawn was busted the second time, I arrived at his house to drop off our work truck and pick up my car. As soon as I stepped out of our work truck, I had a gun pointed at my head. For the next few hours, I endured power-crazed DEA & FBI agents who didn't seem all that concerned about the Constitution of The United States. I was forced to sit and watch these federal drug agents search my brother's home without a search warrant, claiming they were "securing the premises." These government agents' behaviors, actions, and disregard for The Constitution traumatized me, as they proclaimed there wasn't a Constitution and they could do whatever they wanted.

In the coming months, as more and more information about the drug bust became available, I learned how these arrogant government drug agents, who claim to be protectors of the public, especially children, from the scourge of drugs, regularly cut deals with violent criminals with lengthy arrest records, as long as those violent criminals become informants. Basically, our government was letting violent criminals in and out of jail, no matter what their crimes, as long as they became an informant. Those who we trust to protect us, instead exploit us, and use their positions of power to create more work for themselves off the pain, suffering, and victimization of others. The agents' abhorrent, un-Godly behavior, arrogance, lawlessness, and disdain for our Constitution haunt me to this very day.

Finally and most importantly, I learned through my own experiences with drug abuse that drug addicts eventually end up fighting for their souls and don't even realize it. I learned through my own experiences that drug addiction affects people differently. For those who have no control over their addiction, their only remedy is to seek out a higher power. God used my experiences to open my eyes to the hypocrisy of the world. People are suffering and dying from drug addiction while entire industries prosper from the misery of drug addicts. I took these lessons to heart and pledged to God that I would address the injustices taking place because of the war on drugs and that I would be a force for goodness and help people understand and overcome drug addiction. God was listening and knew in me He had found a champion.

Chapter 9
A New Life

A New Beginning

W hile I was growing up, my mother would often boast about how her nephew, my older cousin, was a very successful real estate broker. Subsequently, my mother always encouraged me to get into the real estate profession. While in the process of liquidating assets from the cutlery business, I enrolled in a real estate training course from Century 21. For several months, I studied very hard and then passed the real estate licensing exam.

As soon as I received my license, I walked into the number one real estate company in the Napa Valley at the time, Castle Realty, and introduced myself to the sales manager. I looked the sales manager right in the eyes and told him I wanted to work at Castle Realty because their parking lot had the most BMWs and Mercedes Benzes. I got the job. Castle Realty was full of very successful realtors, each in their own right. I was incredibly lucky to be exposed to so many wonderful people, and even luckier that some of them encouraged me and took me under their wings.

I embraced my new real estate career wholeheartedly and learned as much as I could about real estate. I'd sit in the office conference room and watch real estate sales training videos. I'd take notes and then make copies of them available to anyone who wanted them. I also attended several real estate training seminars. I purchased Mike Ferry sales tapes and discovered Tony Robbins' self-improvement tapes. My passion for computer technology soon made me the go-to guy for computer assistance.

There was a two-person real estate team in our office that was incredibly successful. These ladies, Beth and Samantha, were money-making machines. I used to caravan with both of them and have them rolling on the floor with laughter. These ladies took me under their wing and did what they could to assist me with my new career in real estate. Since I didn't have any listings, I'd hold open houses on weekends with theirs in hopes of picking up buyers.

In order to help me get my own listings, Beth took me out canvassing one day. We picked a neighborhood, and Beth knocked on the doors of the first two houses. After a short, pleasant conversation with each homeowner, we determined neither homeowner was interested in selling their home. I eagerly took the 3rd house. As soon as I introduced myself, the homeowner promptly slammed the door in my face. Beth couldn't stop laughing, and I was done for the day.

At one point, Beth and Samantha brought me in on a new condo subdivision. They were extremely busy and needed someone onsite. I needed the experience ... and the sales. I remember when Samantha brought a client of hers to the property. The three of us were walking around, looking at the different units. As we walked back to the main office, Samantha pointed out the trim on one of the condos and remarked to her client, "Isn't that a beautiful shade of Fuchsia?" I was dumbfounded and had no idea what she was talking about. All I saw was trim that was painted dark pink.

In order to promote myself and gain greater exposure in the community, I spent a small fortune each month on advertising. I ran advertisements in the local real estate magazine and a small advertisement in the Napa Valley Register. Most of the time, I didn't have my own listings, so I'd advertise on one of my colleague's listings that I was going to hold an open that weekend. I loved to get creative with my marketing efforts and started to invite people to come by my open houses to see a great house and enjoy some Rice Krispy treats.

The young woman who worked in the classified advertisements department at the Napa Valley Register liked me and would help me with my advertisements. One day, I brought her an advertisement that she liked so much that she hooked me up. I came up with an advertisement of a picture of me in a suit, leaning back, with a pair of Maracas. The caption read something to the effect of, "This Realtor Knows How To Command Attention." It was a clever advertisement, and my friend placed it in the center of all real estate advertisements in the Sunday Newspaper. You certainly couldn't miss it. I only ran it once. I didn't get any business from it, but everyone in the real estate industry got a kick out of it. Even my boss told me he liked it when he informed me that moving forward, I'd have to have my advertisements approved by management before running them.

. . .

There was one other person in my real estate office that took me under her wing. Her name was Candice, and she was another top-performing realtor in the Napa Valley. Candice was very attractive and very much a professional businesswoman. Candice commanded attention when she entered a room. She wasn't a flirt. She dressed in business attire and was a bulldog. Candice could hold her own with the best of them and possessed confidence I could only dream of. My attraction to Candice was her business acumen. Like Samantha and Beth, Candice would land exclusive clients. Candice mentored me, believed in me, and turned out to be a great friend.

On a personal level, Candice and her boyfriend, Terry, were very good to me. They'd have me over, take me out to dinner, and would take me to concerts held at some of the wineries. I'd caravan with Candice and hold open houses on her listings, too. Candice was a former educator, and she liked the fact that I was trying to learn as much as I could about real estate, as well as share my knowledge with others. Both Candice and her boyfriend Terry were well versed in the way the government functioned and shared their insight with me, as well as encouraged me to get involved with our realtors' Local Government Relations Committee.

In order to create some excitement and generate sales in our office, our boss would periodically have sales contests. We'd be split into two teams. Basically, half the office would be treated to a nice meal. I definitely had my fair share of victory dinners and margaritas at Compadres in Yountville. One of the best contest prizes I was fortunate enough to participate in was dinner on the Napa Valley Wine Train. Our dinner turned out to be a murder mystery dinner. Several colleagues brought their own wine, and before the train left the station, we were all feeling pretty good.

· · ·

Heroes Wanted

Part of the festivities that night included the tasting of a secret wine. The person who correctly guessed the wine's name would win a prize. One of the Murder Mystery staff members walked around the train car and poured samples of the wine from a brown paper bag. We were given a small piece of paper to write down our names and our guess as to what the wine was we had just sampled. As one of my colleagues and I waited for our turn, some of our other colleagues were given a sample of the wine.

As soon as they sampled the mystery wine, they started yelling out names such as Robert Mondavi Reserve, Opus One, and several other premium brands. It became a giant snooty convention as my colleague connoisseurs tried a bit of one-upmanship on their knowledge of Napa Valley's exquisite wines. When the young lady finally made it to my colleague and me, as she poured some of the wine into my glass, I observed the wine was a light shade of pink. I took one sip, looked at my colleague, and proclaimed it was a 1989 Beringer White Zinfandel. The young lady gave me a startled look and encouraged me to write my name on the piece of paper with my answer. I was pretty much drunk and indifferent. I declined her offer.

When it came time to announce the contest winner, the Murder Mystery staff member unwrapped the wine bottle—a 1989 Beringer White Zinfandel. She then pointed at me and let everyone know that I was the only one that correctly guessed the answer. I didn't win anything because I neglected to submit my answer on a piece of paper, but it didn't matter to me. My colleague and I were on the floor laughing. Everyone was spouting off these premium Napa Valley wines, and in the end, it turned out to be a bottle that retailed for ten bucks. My mom loved Beringer White Zinfandel and often had a bottle in her refrigerator. Every now and then, I'd have a taste with dinner.

A New Reality

The contrast between my past life and the new life I was embarking upon was astounding. I was no longer living under my brother's lie, I no longer had to look over my shoulder, and I had rid myself of all the people sabotaging my life. I was beginning to create a life of my own choosing. I was associating with incredibly successful people—people who liked me, people who mentored me, and people who welcomed me into the community. I was making new friends and discovered my desire to get involved in the community.

During this time of rejuvenation, there were never any specific questions asked about my past, which seemed only fair, as the past I had left behind was of my brother's making. It was a lifestyle I didn't want anything to do with, and had I been left to my own devices, it was a lifestyle I would never have embarked upon. While I never went into any great details about my past, I certainly wouldn't have dodged any hard questions had they come up. Just like my relationship between myself and God was private, my experiences with drugs and my brother's illicit activities were between God and me. I was moving forward with my life and wasn't looking back. I knew when the time was right, on God's time, I would readily disclose my experiences from that intense period of my life.

As I settled into my new life in the Napa Valley, I learned that I possessed a unique point of view regarding the war on drugs compared to my new friends and colleagues. While I grew up around drugs, the people I was associating with were stringent in their points of view regarding drug use. I would often hear how people didn't want their tax dollars being spent on drug treatment programs for people who made poor lifestyle decisions.

. . .

Heroes Wanted

During the 1990s, there wasn't much information out there about the abuses taking place under the guise of the war on drugs. At this juncture in my life, it certainly wasn't my place to try and inform people how our Constitution was being systematically undermined, how our government was partnering with criminals at our expense, and how tax dollars spent on drug treatment would have been a great deal, compared to the amounts of money being depleted from government coffers by the penal system and by law enforcement agencies. My arguments would have fallen on deaf ears simply for the fact that people weren't ready to believe the level of scandal involved in the war on drugs.

I was curious about the differences between my point of view regarding drugs and those of my new friends and society in general. I was interested to know why the government would enact such ineffective, draconian laws. My curiosity would lead me to take law enforcement classes in order to learn why my values and beliefs were so different from others.

Power

As a member of the Realtor's Local Government Relations Committee (LGR), I often sat in on meetings where local policy recommendations were debated in our committee and then presented to local government officials. I was enthralled with the process. At the time, preserving open space was a hot topic. During one of our LGR committee meetings, the conference room at our local Board of Realtors office was packed with several high-profile Realtors. I remember sitting at the conference table mesmerized as I watched the issue of open space vs. property owner rights being hashed out right in front of me.

. . .

There were Realtors on both sides of the argument, and there was a lot at stake. Whatever point of view our committee took on the issue would represent the view of the Napa County Realtors Association. It became apparent to me that this small group of people, regardless of what was agreed upon, would influence local government policy that would impact the entire community. It was a total rush, and I'll never forget the enormity of power a few people held in their hands, as well as the moral and ethical responsibility to do what was best for the entire community. I'm extremely grateful for the experience, as well as working with people that were both moral and ethical.

When the city of Napa was about to experience a budget shortfall and reached out to various community organizations for ways to increase revenues, I was fortunate to be on a subcommittee responsible for drafting recommendations. Our subcommittee consisted of fiscally conservative, former government employees. I participated in several committee meetings and was always impressed with my fellow committee member's dedication to doing what was right.

The members of our subcommittee were very intelligent and had crafted an esoteric report that would be understood by government officials but not members of the general public. I explained to the authors that, as a layman, I could not understand the report. The report's authors revised their work and crafted a final report that was much more accessible to the layperson. Rather than come up with ways to increase revenues, our subcommittee pointed out excessive government waste and provided several recommendations for lowering government expenses. Once again, I appreciated being involved with such an incredible group of individuals.

. . .

Heroes Wanted

My boss was extremely busy and very much involved with local community events. When he couldn't participate on a committee, he would send me. As a result, I got to participate on committees that involved business leaders and government officials from throughout the Napa Valley. It was a very special time for me. I was living the life I knew Shawn and I could have experienced without his illicit activities. My dreams were coming true.

Holiday Celebrations

I was incensed at my family for all of the tribulations I had been subjected to. For the most part, I kept my distance. When I had the cutlery store in Napa, I met Brad, a businessman my age. We were both single, I was new in town, and we hit it off. We had a lot in common, yet we came from two different worlds. When I met his parents, I hit it off with them, too, and before I knew it, I was invited to a family holiday celebration.

When I arrived at his parent's house, I found a table set for 20 in a holiday theme that looked right out of a movie. Brad's father made homemade wine. Just one glass would give us a buzz, and we were drinking bottles of it because his father didn't add sulfites. Meaning no matter how much we drank, there was no hangover the following day. Brad's grandmother made a concoction that she called rocket fuel, which was served in a Grappa glass with a chunk of pineapple in it. I don't believe any of us had more than three of those, especially those who ate the pineapple.

I'd never eaten at a five-star restaurant before, but I would wager that the meal served at Brad's family holiday meals was worthy of a five-star rating. We'd drink, eat, ... and we'd be very merry. I was astonished that a family could gather and sit through dinner, engaged in conversation and humor. It was the first time in my life at a family gathering without any chaos, arguments, drama, or crying. Throughout the years, I'd be invited to many of Brad's family events, and some of the best times of my life were spent with his family. I'll never forget their hospitality, generosity, love, and awesome sense of humor.

Life was good. My past was behind me. I was embracing my future, I was experiencing personal growth, and for the first time in a very long time, I was living my life, and it was real. I had nothing to hide, and I wasn't living in fear of the police crashing down my door. I was on my way.

Yamaha FJ1200

Back in the late 1980s, I ran into a friend I hadn't seen in years. At the time, he had a white and red Yamaha FJ-1100, and he let me take it out for a ride. I had never experienced anything like it in my life. I felt like I was sitting on top of a rocket ship. The entire bike was vibrating beneath me, and all this motorcycle wanted to do was go fast. It was one of the most intense rides I had ever had, and I was never able to get that experience out of my mind. I had to have one.

In 1992, I purchased a used 1990 Yamaha FJ 1200. The bike was black with blue trim and looked like a piece of fine art. Like its predecessor, this bike vibrated under me, and all it wanted to do was go fast. What I especially enjoyed about this particular motorcycle was that it was classified as a sport-touring bike. The position of the foot pegs allowed for a more upright seating position, meaning I could ride it all day long without killing my back.

. . .

I'd connect with local riders, and we'd go riding all around the Napa Valley. Other times we'd ride out to the coast by cutting through Sonoma and Santa Rosa. I even connected with my friend who turned me on to Yamaha FJ's, and I'd go riding with him and his friends. We'd ride from San Mateo, down Skyline to Santa Cruz, and then come back up through Pescadero and Half Moon Bay.

My favorite activity, though, was riding the FJ1200 throughout the Napa Valley, especially when I finished my last open house on Sundays. I'd run home, throw on a pair of blue jeans and a t-shirt, and then head up Silverado Trail on the FJ1200. I'd have a nice dinner in Calistoga and then come back home on Silverado Trail just as the sun was setting. It was magnificent and very spiritual. The warm air, the various smells, the vineyards, and the picturesque scenery ... all contributed to an incredible experience. I'd be on sensory overload. It was truly a magical time in my life.

My Forte

The real estate training seminars I attended encouraged agents to pick a neighborhood and then go door to door asking if the home-owner wanted to sell their property. If the homeowner said no, move on to the next house. It was generally agreed upon by my colleagues and me that while this formula worked in large metropolitan areas, it was a recipe for disaster in a small community like Napa. I certainly wasn't that bold. Given my previous sales experience from calling on customers when I owned the cutlery business, I began devising indirect sales scripts for contacting homeowners.

I eventually started assembling sellers' packs. I'd purchased inexpensive colored paper folders with two pockets and would include my custom-made brochure, a printout of recent neighborhood homes pending and sold, along with home-selling tips. When someone answered their door, I'd introduce myself and then ask if they were interested in current real estate market conditions in their area. If they were, I'd hand them my packet and start a conversation. I managed to give numerous listing presentations to homeowners but only managed to get one or two listings.

The challenge I had with listing a home for sale was that I was inflexible when it came to the listing price the seller would want for their home. I would exercise due diligence and provide the home-owner with a reasonable price range their home would sell for. I'd have comparable sales to back up the price I was recommending. Sellers often believed their home was worth much more because of the upgrades they had made. I'd try to explain to the homeowner that their home looked great, but it wouldn't sell at the higher price. I was inflexible.

Unfortunately, other real estate agents would come along, indulge the seller, and list the home for an amount much greater than the home was worth. Six months to a year later, the owner would eventually drop the price of the house down to what I had recommended, and it would sell. I wasn't good at that game, and I refused to purposely deceive people to make money.

Buyers were a different story. Most of my real estate transactions were with buyers. I'd meet buyers in the various open houses I did on weekends. Like my home seller packets, I created a buyer packet that included my brochure, a map of Napa County, and a printout of five to ten houses in the same price range, along with home-buying tips. I don't think these packets cost me more than $1.25, and they were a hit. Early on, I discovered that most home buyers were stressed out, didn't feel appreciated, and were looking for someone to reassure them and guide them through the home-buying process. I was their guy.

I'd set appointments with homebuyers and take them out to look at five or six different listings. Based on what they liked or didn't like, I'd spend the week searching for a home that would meet their expectations. I'd then take them out again and only show them houses that met their criteria. It was a pretty successful model, and it worked. I managed to close several transactions as a buyer's representative. As good as I was with buyers, though, the only people making money in real estate were the agents that had the listings.

One day, I received a letter from a Sacramento title company. There were five new homes under construction, in various stages of being built, that were in foreclosure. The title company wanted me to provide them with a proposal for selling the properties. I remember when I shared the letter with my boss, he couldn't believe it and was curious how they had picked me. Someone was looking out for me.

Unfortunately, I was still pretty green, and this project was way over my head. My boss helped me as much as he could, and in the end, the listing went to my good friend Candice. Candice belonged to a realtor service that did referrals, and the property listing came to her through the referral process. I didn't have a problem with the way this went down. I didn't have the experience, but Candice did. I remember thinking, in hindsight at the time, that if I had shown the listing request to Candice and partnered with her, I might have gotten involved with the project. I was counting on those listings to jump-start my foundering real estate career.

My Essence

In hopes of boosting my real estate career, I purchased a set of Tony Robbins self-improvement tapes. I was both impressed with and in awe of Tony's program. I was learning how my brain processed information and how to evaluate my beliefs and values. I learned how to eliminate disempowering beliefs and values and replace them with new, empowering ones. I was learning how to create a compelling future for myself.

One of the exercises in the program required us to brainstorm who we were. We were instructed to take a blank sheet of paper and brainstorm answers to the question, "Who am I?" In 1992, per my instructions, I sat in front of my word processor and brainstormed about who I was, what I believed in, and what I stood for. I ended up with a little over a page of one-line sentences describing the contents of my heart, soul, and essence. I printed a couple of copies, filed them away in my filing cabinet and forgot about them.

Over twenty years later, I rediscovered my brainstorm printouts and instantly recognized the significance of my writing. I was so impressed that I created a poster with all of the sentences and titled it "I Am the Miracle. It's hanging on my wall. Below is a copy for your review. As far as I'm concerned, the words in the "I Am The Miracle" poster are profound and revealing. I wasn't attending church. I wasn't trying to compete with who could be the most pious, who was the best Christian, or who among us was closer to God. I attribute much of this to the success of the Maronite Church in Ohio for introducing me to God and instilling in me a desire to want to be good, to avoid sinning, and that God was everywhere, watching and listening. I further believe all of the statements I brainstormed are derived from all those years I spent on the coast communing with God.

. . .

I had no agenda when writing down these sentences other than to discover my essence, my core being. These thoughts were between God and me. Given my life experiences up until these thoughts were put to paper, I believed the poster title "I Am The Miracle" was appropriate. One thing I wasn't aware of when I brainstormed these thoughts was that God was paying attention.

I Am The Miracle

My life is about drug addiction and the injustices burdened by addicts. My life is about love of all living creatures. My life is about human nature and acceptance of all human beings. My life is about being open and honest. **My life is about goodness overcoming evil.** My life is about helping out fellow human beings. My life is about stopping the hate and manipulation of people. My life is about everyone working together and having acceptance of one another no matter what the distinction. My life is about doing what is best for human beings, not corporations or governments. **My life is about helping other human beings.** My life is about preventing pain and suffering. My life is about making other people feel good. My life is about stopping all of life's injustices. **My life is about helping the child prostitute.** My life is about feeding the hungry. My life is about government which actually helps its citizens. My life is about helping drug addicts. My life is about sheltering the homeless. My life is about inspiring people who need and want to change their lives. My life is about overcoming the perceived impossible. My life is about contributing. **My life is about breaking down barriers that separates us all as human beings.** My life is about ending racism. My life is about teaching the acceptance of others. My life is about judging people on their actions not their race race or skin color. **My life is about being human and that we are all similar in our desires, needs, and ambitions.** My life life is about nothing is so serious that it reduces existence into a dreadful experience. My life is about looking for a better solution. My life is about moving on and progressing. **My life is about the betterment of mankind.** My life is about the human spirit. My life is about all the goodness in the world. My life is about self sacrifice. My life is about going the distance. My life is about making the difference in someone's life. My life is about inspiring people. **My life is about putting a smile on someone's face every day.** My life is about progress. My life is about becoming powerful individual who has the clout to tackle social issues and make a difference. My life is about learning to practice what I preach. My life is about lessons in life to master, conquer and share. **My life is about preventing murder.** My life is about stopping violent crime. My life is about helping the battered wife. My life as about helping the abused person. **My life is about helping the distressed.** My life is about Goodness triumphing over evil. My life is about putting back the dreams for someone who has lost them. **My life is about becoming successful without screwing somebody over.** My life is about not having any enemies. My life is about we are all the same. My life about the ocean. My life is about the mountains. My life is about mother nature. My life is about earthquakes. My life is about rain. My life about hurricanes. My life is about embarrassing moments. **My life is about happiness.** My life is about sadness. My life is about this planet not being ours and we are guests. My life is about believing in a higher power which has a plan for all of us. My life is about people helping people. My life is about not harming others. **My life is about angels entering our lives and helping us through tough times.** My life is about seeing what is great about every situation. My life is about world leaders coming to terms with each other. My life about eliminating race separation. **My life is about human beings.** My life is about being an individual who is in a position to make changes. My life is about being one of the worlds most richest persons. My life is about success. My life is about overcoming. My life is about commitment. **My life is about making a difference.** My life is about spirits using me, higher powers are calling me. My life is about enjoying life. My life is about enjoying the process. **My life is about pulling the rabbit out of the hat.** My life is about ultimate destiny. My life is about destiny waiting for me to make it there. My life is about opportunities around every corner, beckoning to me. **My life is about kicking ass and making it happen.** My life is about life and the process of living. My life is about learning from my mistakes. My life is about learning from my family's mistakes. **My life is about triumph.** My life is about pleasure. My life is about Montara beach and the view of the mountains. My life is about Silverado Trail on a hot sunny day riding the FJ. My life is about my inner strength. **My life is about my commitment to God and abiding by His will.** My life is about listening to my inner self and always acting from my heart. My life is about moving on. My life is about beautiful women. **My life is about experiencing life and all of it's pains and pleasures.** My life is about avoiding traps and living a full life filled with an abundance of love, wealth and contribution. My life is about immediate gratification. My life is about learning. My life about mastering self control. My life is about overcoming addiction. **My life is about learning to love myself.** My life is about overcoming compulsive behavior. My life is about experimentation.

Jamil Maroun

Circa 1992

A Door Closes

The early 1990s were a tough time to be in the real estate business. There were 400 real estate agents in the Napa Valley and only 25 sales pending a month. Most of the homes being sold were listings by top producers. Most of the top producers in real estate had been in the game for quite a while and had an extensive client base.

While I had a fairly decent first year in real estate, my expenses exceeded my income, and I was quickly burning through my cash reserves. By the end of 1992, I had developed some solid marketing strategies, such as my buyer and seller packs, along with some effective sales scripts. I was laying the foundation for a successful real estate career, but I had my challenges. I was running out of money and would soon be broke, and I wasn't willing to acquiesce to the unreasonable expectations of home sellers. So I was grateful when my boss hired a sales consultant to help out struggling agents in our office.

My first and last meeting with this sales consultant was very revealing and brutally opened my eyes. When I met with the sales consultant, I immediately explained why I wasn't making any money. After about five minutes of rambling, the sales consultant politely interrupted me and said, "Jim, stop. Tell me something good about Jim Maroun." I couldn't think of a thing. I was stunned. I had no self-confidence, my self-esteem was gone, and just like my mother unintentionally instilled in me, I believed others were better than me.

My roommate at the time suggested on more than one occasion that we move to Las Vegas and start life anew. Las Vegas was booming, and he believed a new beginning awaited us both. Up until my meeting with the sales consultant, I'd resisted moving to Las Vegas, but now it sounded good. Several factors were driving my decision. My parents lost their business, I wasn't able to keep the cutlery business going, I wasn't making it as a real estate agent, and I was about to run out of money. In addition, I still had not forgiven my family for the hell they'd put me through. Maybe a fresh start in Las Vegas was just what the doctor ordered.

I informed my roommate that I was ready to embrace a new life in Las Vegas, and he confirmed he was ready for a change, too. At my next weekly office meeting, I announced that I was resigning and moving to Las Vegas. I was astounded by the collective " Oh no" response in the room. Many of my colleagues were disappointed that I wasn't sticking it out. Apparently, I was liked by more people than I had imagined.

As soon as I decided to quit my job and move to Las Vegas, several incredible things started happening to me. A quiet calm came over me, and I suddenly had the compulsion to visit the Grand Canyon. I'd never been there—never even gone camping in my life, but I couldn't escape the feeling that something spectacular would happen to me once I was there. I discussed this urge to visit the Grand Canyon with my roommate, and he agreed to go camping there before heading to Las Vegas.

Within a week of resigning from my position at the real estate company, I sold everything I owned except for a few personal items, some clothing, and my motorcycle. As we started to make our initial preparations, our detour to the Grand Canyon expanded to include a tour through Utah, Colorado, New Mexico, and Arizona. When I shared these plans with Brad's mother, she told me to check out Zion National Park in Utah, so I incorporated that into my itinerary as well.

Two weeks before we were set to depart, my roommate informed me that he'd landed a job in Napa and wouldn't be joining me. I was undeterred. I was excited that something incredible was about to happen in my life. I scrapped Las Vegas as my goal and decided to take off and see where my travels would take me. While I shared with everyone that I would look for opportunities to settle down and start a new life, I confided in my two closest friends that I had lost my spiritual connection with God and was going to look for it.

As my departure date neared, several real estate colleagues asked me about the sanity of the adventure I was about to embark upon. One even went so far as to ask several questions like, "What if you run out of gas? What if the bike breaks down? What if you run out of money? What if it rains?..." Before committing to this journey, I would have agreed with this person and not moved forward on such a ludicrous idea. However, I was at peace with myself. I looked my friend in the eye and stated I would deal with any issues as they came up. Even I was amazed at the confidence in my reply.

My family's luck in California wasn't that good. I felt my fortune might be found out of state. I wasn't sure where I was going. I was going to see what Providence brought my way, and I didn't even know if I'd ever return to California. All that changed when Brad announced he would be getting married in six months. There was no way I would miss his wedding. I now had a return date and a reason to return.

Chapter 10
God's Calling

The Beginning of a Journey

May 5th, 1993, leaving Napa California.

On May 4th, 1993, I left Napa on my 1990 Yamaha FJ 1200 motor-cycle, loaded down with enough camping gear and personal posses-sions to allow me to settle down anywhere to start a new life. I had no agenda or expectations. I had several AAA maps with points of interest I'd highlighted as possible routes. The weeks leading up to my departure were filled with calm, anticipation, and excitement. I was about to embark on a journey. I had no idea what was going to happen, how it was going to happen, or when it was going to happen, but I knew something incredible was going to happen.

The morning I left Napa, my sense of excitement had intensified. By the time I crossed the California and Nevada border, I was hiding a huge grin under my full-faced helmet.

> *While riding the Yamaha FJ 1200, I couldn't help but grin, thinking of what I've embarked upon, what I'm already experiencing, and what awaits me, and then contrasting what I'd be doing if I hadn't resigned from my position, and what my friends and colleagues were doing this same minute, as I zip through Nevada. I could hear the mountains calling out to me as I drove by, Your problems and head trips don't matter out here. We don't give a damn about anything, you can destroy yourselves, but we will still be here. We and what we have to offer is all that matters. God is all around me.*

— 5/6/93 Journal entry, Eagles Nest Park, Nevada

In my journal, I originally wrote "the mountains are calling out to me." Many years later, as I document my life experiences for this story, I now know the mountains were not calling out to me. The Holy Spirit was engaging me.

An Encounter with God

On the fourth day of my journey, I entered Southern Utah from the Nevada side. I'd never seen red rocks before, it was like entering a beautiful, mystical kingdom. By the time I entered Zion National Park, I was overwhelmed by the beautiful landscape surrounding me.

I was mesmerized by the monolithic canyon walls, the crisp, clear, dreamy blue sky, and the exhilarating beauty of mother nature that surrounded me. I had never experienced such majestic beauty before.

My campsite in Zion National Park had a picnic table that provided an unobstructed view of one of the magnificent canyon walls. It was so close and vivid that I felt like I could reach up and touch it. I could see every crack and crevice on the canyon wall and discern the various colors of red. Throughout the day, and depending on the sun's location, the canyon walls would change colors. I would sit for hours, mesmerized by the magical beauty surrounding me.

Each day in Zion National Park brought a greater sense of wonderment and an increased expectation that something spectacular would occur. I went on various hiking trails throughout the park. Each trail provided its own breathtaking, awe-inspiring view. I would sit for hours at a time in solitude, exploring my thoughts and communing with God.

During my initial days camping at Zion National Park, I still felt a lot of pain and anger. I was mad at my past, upset that I wasn't financially stable, and extremely angry at Shawn and the rest of my family. One day, while sitting on a large rock in front of a beautiful waterfall that was surrounded by towering red canyon walls, the Holy Spirit reached out to me:

"What can't you handle? You're going to be here for fewer than 100 years. Creation has been here since the beginning of time."

Heroes Wanted

The complexity of this message perplexed me. On the one hand, you can accomplish quite a lot if you have all of eternity. However, our life spans are typically less than a century, so I took the message to mean I'd better get busy and live a purposeful life. Once I depart this life, the world will continue on without me, as it has since the beginning of time. In the grand scheme of things, I took this message to mean that I have a small window of opportunity to make an impact in this world if I'm going to make one at all.

I climbed over a bees' nest and sat on a boulder resting in front of a waterfall, red rock canyon walls towering above me. It was incredibly beautiful and serene. A friend had provided me with a 12-step book. I was trying to quit chewing tobacco. I began reading about step two, seeking out a higher power, and began to giggle. At that moment in time, I realized I was completely surrounded by Him. God was all around me. Little by little, I'm finding myself opening myself up, my entire being to God. I'm experiencing love, joy, serenity, and a wholeness I've never experienced before. I now know this trip has purpose. I was there for a couple of hours, contemplating life while absorbing the sheer beauty of the scenery surrounding me. What an incredible spiritual experience.

— 5/13/93 Journal entry, Zion National Park,
Springdale, UT

Inside the magnificent canyon walls of Zion National Park, I began to realize I was being engulfed by a supernatural force. I felt safe, protected, and loved, as my mind, body, and soul were being rejuvenated. In Zion National Park, I found myself in the presence of God. I evaluated every belief, value, and thought that went through my mind. If they were good and empowering, I'd keep them. If they were bad, I'd pawn them off to God, who was more than willing to take them off my hands. By the grace of God, I was able to forgive myself, my brother, my family, and all of those childhood slights I'd experienced growing up.

I managed to stay in Zion National Park for about 60 days, with the last two weeks spent in a state of bliss. For two weeks, I managed to get through each day without a single negative thought. It was astonishing. I entered Zion National Park with an angry, closed heart. I left Zion National Park with an open heart and a new direction for my life. I'd just experienced an encounter with God, and I was full of the Holy Spirit.

> It's hard to explain, but it's like we're all brainwashed into thinking what life should be about - work, accumulating wealth, success, complex organized lives, but here in nature, these values don't amount to anything. The beauty of nature, trees, birds, mountains, mother nature, life, the seasons, those are the things that really matter. Life is to be enjoyed and experienced. There is a higher power, God does exist, and you must be in touch with yourself, and love yourself. What good is wealth if you're not appreciative of what you have or are happy.
>
> — 5/13/93 Journal entry, Zion National Park,
> Springdale, UT

My incredible journey around the country on my motorcycle lasted approximately five-and-a-half months. I experienced America by traveling on backroads and avoiding freeways, highways, and interstates. I met wonderful people, found love, had incredible experiences, and was given a roadmap for my future. During my journey, I was never alone for long. People would enter my life when needed, and everything fell into place. I returned to Napa in time for Brad's wedding and was ready to begin a new chapter in my life, starting with obtaining a college education.

. . .

For the longest time, when telling the story about my journey around the country on a motorcycle, I was hesitant to state that I had an actual encounter with God. After all, who was I? What did I do to merit or be blessed with an encounter with God? It was only during the writing of this book that I realized that, yes, God did meet me in the Utah desert, and yes, I did merit such an encounter. God had been observing me and listening to my prayers since childhood.

When I prayed to God and communed with God out in nature, it wasn't because of church doctrine. It wasn't out of a desire to be voted "Best Christian." I was reaching out to God because of my faith and my belief in Him. I was reaching out to God because I wanted to do good in this world. He knew my spirit was true and my heart was pure. It turns out my relationship with God is special.

When I prayed as a young child, God was listening. When I communed with God out in nature, God was paying attention. When I prayed every day while resisting temptation and evil, God was watching. When I brainstormed what was in my heart and how I wanted to live my life, God took note. When I shared with a couple of close friends that I was going on a journey to renew my relationship with God, He made it so, and used my circumstances to lay the foundation for a life-long partnership.

An Educational Journey Begins

I returned to Napa, California, with a renewed spirit. I had confidence, focus, and a new direction for my life. I was full of the Holy Spirit and was ready to dedicate myself to earning a college education in Computer Engineering so that I could create the lifestyle I deserved.

It took a few months of looking for work before I was ready to focus on my quest for a college education. On the day I visited Napa Valley College to inquire about when the next semester began, I was surprised to learn that it had started that very same day. Most of the Monday, Wednesday, and Friday classes I wanted to enroll in were already closed to new students.

I hadn't planned on attending classes on Tuesdays and Thursdays, so I started to leave campus, thinking there was always next semester. I was thinking I'd work and save up some money. Before I reached the parking lot, however, I spun around and headed back into the admissions building. I signed up for whatever courses were available on Tuesday and Thursday. I had just boldly interrupted my pattern of procrastination and excuses and took the first steps toward my quest for a college education.

My stated major was Computer Engineering with a minor in business. I had so many incredible visions of how computer technology could impact our lives from when I played on my Apple IIc, that I was now determined to bring these visions to life. My memory and fear of not getting past pre-algebra in high school was now perceived as an obstacle I would overcome, along with any other academic challenges thrown my way. I was now a mature student with several years of life experience under my belt. I was dedicated to achieving my educational goals, I was filled with the Holy Spirit, and I knew with conviction that anything I couldn't do, God could.

. . .

Heroes Wanted

In order to ensure that I'd be successful academically, I dedicated myself to attending school full-time and working part-time. I would keep my life simple and focused on achieving my educational goals. Wealth and material possessions would come later. During the first few weeks of classes, my new girlfriend totaled my car—one that I had purchased with the proceeds from the sale of my Yamaha FJ1200. My only transportation was gone, and soon after, my new girlfriend followed.

Before my encounter with God, I would have been devastated about losing my only mode of transportation, and my girlfriend would have been made aware of my displeasure. However, I was full of the Holy Spirit. I was grateful that she wasn't injured in the accident, and I embraced the reality of my situation. Until I could afford to purchase a bicycle, I walked or caught public transportation to get around. I was unstoppable.

Eventually, I saved up enough money to purchase a nice mountain bike. My mornings would begin with a brisk bicycle ride to the Napa Valley College Campus. Napa was still a rural community then, and the Napa Valley College Campus was surrounded by large fields bristling with wildlife and vegetation. I would arrive on campus early in the morning, find a spot to sit in solitude, and then commune with God. The brisk morning air, the scents and sights of mother nature waking up all around me and communing with God was an inspirational way to start my day.

At this point in my life, when it came to acquiring knowledge, my brain was like a sponge. I soaked up as much information as possible. Each class I took increased my knowledge. I no longer had a cloud of failure hanging over my head. I was coming out of my shell, shedding my past academic failures, my phobias, and my low self-esteem. I was learning about the world, I was learning about myself, and I was building a better me. As I had predicted, math and science were not easy subjects for me to master, but I was prepared to do whatever it took.

My counselors at Napa Valley College were spectacular and encouraged me to engage my professors. I spoke with all of my math and science professors about my challenges. In turn, they provided me with additional learning materials and math books that publishers had provided them with for review. I now had several different math books to draw upon to help me understand and learn how to solve mathematical equations. I utilized the math lab on campus and any other available resource to help me overcome my academic challenges and succeed.

In order to get through my math classes, I would spend inordinate amounts of time studying. Sometimes I'd spend the summer reviewing math. Other times I'd have to repeat a course. Math wasn't my only challenge. Science turned out to be a complete mystery to me. I worked my ass off trying to pass my required science class. I utilized all the resources available to me. The assistant professor even met with me. I remember her asking me a basic science question, and I was clueless. When I received a D in the class, I was in tears. I worked very hard, invested a lot of time, and came up empty.

The following semester, I had a different science teacher and a different science class. Once again, I was provided with extra materials to help nurture the learning processes. The new books I received actually helped me understand formulas much better. I don't remember my final grade for the class, but I did pass. My academic struggles with math and science proved to be a huge learning experience. Math and science forced me to examine how I learned, my strengths, weaknesses, self-perception, and how I dealt with adversity. I performed a self-analysis of my math and science struggles in order to identify limiting, self-defeating beliefs. Below are excerpts from the journal I kept:

Struggle, push, cry, fight, but do not give up on science and mathematics!

Remember, you're developing new learning strategies and new ways of thinking! You are smart, and you do deserve to succeed! Be good to yourself! If life is not up to your expectations, drop your expectations - it's only mathematics.

Mathematics is Power. Manipulation of data is Power. Looking at a formula and knowing how to manipulate it is Power. It is okay for you to demonstrate your success in mastering mathematics.

I'm an intelligent human being. I'm good enough, I can approach problems from a mathematical standpoint. Others are struggling with mathematics just as you are. Like them, you will be victorious!

Mastering Mathematics requires self-confidence. Mathematics is all about concepts. Mastering Mathematics is now a goal you desire to achieve because your dreams are on the other side of mastering Mathematics!

Life is wonderful. Enjoy the process and have some faith in yourself. I will build my self-esteem and self-confidence by mastering mathematics. I will talk to others who have mastered mathematics and think in mathematical terms. I will learn the thought process required to be successful in mathematics.

. . .

My quest for a college education was invigorating. I was dedicating myself to learn, improve, and make myself a better human being. My overall success at Napa Valley College could be attributed to two things. First, God was there for me. Every obstacle and challenge I faced, I put into God's hands, and every single time, God delivered. I was triumphant. The second factor that ensured my success at Napa Valley College was my professors, counselors, and support staff. The professors and staff I interacted with cared, were nurturing and strived to make a difference in the lives of students. Once again, my time spent in Napa and my experiences with Napa Valley College proved to be life-changing.

My dreams were coming true. I had great friends, was on the path to obtaining a college education, and was successfully mastering subjects I never imagined I could conquer. I was alive, learning, working, and communing with God in the beautiful Napa Valley. Everything was going my way, my life was on track, I was happy, full of the Holy Spirit, and life was great.

Not Everyone is Happy

One morning, while in between classes, I found myself in the Napa Valley College cafeteria reading a USA Today newspaper story about a little girl the newspapers dubbed Girl X[1]. Girl X was a little nine-year-old girl who had been raped, strangled, poisoned, and left for dead in a stairwell of the Cabrini-Green Projects in Chicago. When found, Girl X was naked, had gang signs written on her body, and had her panties wrapped around her neck. She was foaming at the mouth from the poison that had been forced down her throat.

. . .

After reading about Girl X, I skipped the remainder of my classes that day and went back home and cried. I was devastated. All I could think about was how this little girl must have been crying, pleading, begging for help, begging for someone to come to her rescue, and no one did. Girl X was on her own, to suffer at the hands of monsters. I contrasted what had happened to Girl X with what was going on in my life.

Everything was going my way. I was overcoming my academic challenges and accomplishing my educational goals. I was living in the beautiful Napa Valley, and I was communing with God on a daily basis. Everything was perfect. Yet, where was God for this little Girl? Where was Superman, Spiderman, Batman, or any other hero, to stop this little girl from being viciously attacked and violated? Why wasn't someone there to prevent this horrible crime from taking place? Why didn't someone step up to intervene and save this little girl? Where was God? Why did God abandon this little girl? For three nights, I prayed, "Why God, why are you here for me, yet you weren't there to protect this little girl?"

God's Provocative Response

On my third night of prayer, God responded with a simple, matter-of-fact answer, "Why should I intervene in what humanity allows to happen?" The implications of God's succinct response changed my life forever. I pondered God's answer. The society that we live in is of our own creation. Society tolerates these types of horrendous crimes and does nothing to prevent them. An image of a kid being busted by five cops for smoking a marijuana joint came to mind. Meanwhile, predator monsters are allowed to roam freely among the population. I saw God's point.

. . .

It wasn't God who had abandoned this little girl. Society had abandoned her. Society had failed to protect the weakest among us by allowing a predator to ravish her. My eyes were opened to God's perspective. Why should God intervene in what society tolerates? For the next few days, I couldn't stop pondering the ramifications of God's response. The rape, abuse, and murder of little girls are preventable, but society chooses to look the other way. Society is responsible for not intervening in these heinous crimes, not God.

I reflected upon my five-and-a-half-month journey around the country on my motorcycle and how God had met me out in the southern Utah desert. I thought about how I was filled with the Holy Spirit daily and how I was overcoming all of the obstacles placed before me. At this point in my educational journey, it was becoming clear that I was being blessed with some amazing gifts and talents. I then thought about how God had responded to my prayers regarding Girl X by opening my eyes to the realities of our world.

In order to honor God for all the blessings He had bestowed upon me, I pledged to God that I would use the gifts and talents He blessed me with to protect little girls from being abused, raped, and murdered. I pledged to God that I would be a force for goodness, and with His blessings, I would make this a better world for all. God took note. My adoration for God, along with my commitments to God, were made in private, between God and me. I didn't run down to the local church. I didn't seek the counsel of a priest or pastor. I didn't run around town shooting my mouth off to everyone about how holy I was. I made a commitment to God, and it was kept between the two of us.

Chapter 11
College

Acknowledging My Limits

W hen I began my academic journey at Napa Valley College, people would ask me what I wanted to do with my life. My answer was an emphatic, "Anything I want." I was filled with the Holy Spirit, I was communing with God on a daily basis, I was pursuing a technology degree, and I was overcoming all obstacles in my path. In addition, it was becoming evident to me that I had a knack for identifying technology-based business opportunities. With all my heart and my entire being, I believed that anything was possible with God, and I was now unstoppable. For me, life was great, and it would only get better. When I wasn't studying, I occupied my time with visions of what could be.

When I transferred to CSU Sacramento, I discovered my limitations in math and science when I enrolled in differential equations and physics. Differential equations was a complete mystery. Even with a tutor, I was lost. Physics was very interesting and stimulated my imagination when presented to me in English, but as soon as the topic turned to the math behind it, I was lost.

For each math class I took at Napa Valley College, on the first day of class, I would announce I was forming a study group and was looking for other students to join. Often, several students would raise their hands, and there were always at least one or two students that understood the material and would assist the rest of us. At CSU Sacramento, I had no such luck with my differential equations class. Only one other student raised his hand to form a study group with me, and he was just as lost as I was.

My favorite memory of this person was when we were in the student union building, trying to do a differential equations homework problem. Every few minutes, my study partner would crumple up his piece of paper and throw it away. After his fifth or sixth attempt, he triumphantly slid his paper across the table to me, looked me in the eyes, and announced that he had just proved negative one equals zero. I had never laughed so hard in my life. The entire field of mathematics would now have to be rewritten. I love sharing this story with those who have a science or math background and watching their faces light up with laughter.

I hired a tutor for differential equations, but it didn't help. My Physics teacher was the head of the physics department. When I reached out to him, he quickly had some of his top students tutor me. When I was being tutored, physics made sense to me. Unfortunately, the very next day, it would once again be a mystery. I was starting to hate life. The kicker for me was when one day, I observed how happy my physics tutors were. They were all cheery and loving life. They couldn't understand why I was struggling.

. . .

At that point, I realized I needed to switch majors. I didn't have it in me to try and repeat both classes. I had reached my limits and knew it was time to move on. I should have switched my degree to Information Technology, but I was so burnt out on the sciences that I chose business administration with a focus on strategic management.

Human Trafficking

In my continued quest to better understand the criminal justice system, I enrolled in a couple of classes at CSU Sacramento. During one of these courses, I authored a research paper on the inciting factors that led young girls into prostitution. It was quite disturbing. In most cases, a young girl is molested by a family member and, out of desperation, runs away from home. In some instances, the young girl is apprehended by law enforcement and is either placed in foster care, where she encounters further molestation, or returned to her family, where she's subjected to additional molestation. This vicious cycle repeats until the child eventually encounters a pimp or human trafficker, who psychologically and physically abuses her, purposely addicts her to drugs, and then forces her into prostitution.

During my research, I came across a story describing how a pimp controlled his victim. The narrative I read was about a young girl recounting to a crisis counselor how one night, she hadn't met her quota, and when the pimp found out, he beat her, forced a bottle into her vagina, and then broke it, causing excruciating pain and bleeding. The young girl shared how the pimp demanded she go back out onto the street and not come back until she had more money. In a burst of tears, the young girl shared that when she protested to the pimp that she was bleeding from her vagina, the pimp responded that she should use her mouth.

. . .

As I delved into the causes of prostitution, I was disheartened to say the least. As a society, I questioned how we could design institutions that failed us so miserably. More importantly, as a society, why do we tolerate these types of horrible behaviors? Society is failing to keep our most vulnerable safe and failing to prevent crimes that are utterly preventable. Once again, I pledged to God that I would use the skills, talents, and gifts He bestowed upon me to honor Him by addressing these injustices and by being a force for goodness. God was listening.

A Prayer is Answered

When I worked with Shawn, we depended on importers and distributors. These same importers and distributors would sell to our competitors and eventually to our customers. We were not in control of manufacturing or distribution, and that is something I didn't take lightly. While attending school, I prayed that God might enable me to be a manufacturer or originator of businesses. I didn't want to contend with middlemen or have my business dependent on the whims of others. God began responding to my prayer. As I neared graduation, I began recognizing innovative, technology-based business opportunities all around me. Best of all, I didn't need to create new technology. I was identifying ways to take existing technology and apply it in different ways to satisfy the needs of both consumers and businesses. God was blessing me with the gift of vision.

CSU Sacramento

When I was attending Napa Valley College, I was fortunate to have had counselors that ensured I selected great instructors. As a result, I never had a bad experience there. I wasn't so lucky at CSU Sacramento. While I did have my fair share of excellent instructors, there were enough bad apples, that my once unblemished advocacy of seeking out higher education became blemished. Some of my professors had no business being in front of a classroom.

I had a professor shirk his responsibility for teaching my major's core concepts and instead spend the entire class time reminiscing about his life experiences under the guise that his life experiences were somehow relevant to the subject matter of the class. The class had to endure the professor's ramblings while learning nothing about the course topic. I had another instructor who didn't trust or like students. I had an accounting teacher that provided a handout, which looked like scratch notes. It was pretty much unreadable. Several students dropped that class immediately. I wasn't one of them. One of my most traumatizing experiences was with my advanced statistical class. Advanced Statistics was one of the first upper math classes I had taken that actually made sense to me. The professor was strict, and I liked him. He was good at teaching. He did have shortcomings, but if you understood where he was coming from, you could easily overlook them.

My problems started when I was assigned to a group with three young ladies. We had to come up with a statistical project; one that met his approval; and then later on in the semester, one of us would have to present the findings to the class. The instructor would randomly select the presenter. I did not mesh with these young ladies. We met a few times, and then I could never get in touch with them. When it came down to crunch time, they ditched me, and completed the project on their own. I had no input, and had no clue as to what they had come up with. When it came time to turn in the project, I refused to put my name on it. The professor sided with the young women, and I was given an incomplete. The professor informed me that if I came up with my own project over the summer, I'd be able to present it the following semester, and receive a grade. I had made a significant sacrifice to obtain a college degree. I had dedicated myself to overcoming numerous obstacles to pursue my dream of a college degree, and here was this tyrant unjustly penalizing me, and letting these three other students off the hook.

I spent my entire summer working on that project. I was able to select my topic, and I chose real estate since I had experience in the industry. There were numerous times over the summer when I was working on this project when I would literally see red because I was so incensed at the injustice being perpetrated against me. This professor had hijacked my summer. I had been singled out and unfairly punished for someone else's transgression.

The following semester, I turned in my paper and gave a presentation to one of his classes. I believe I received an A- on the report. I remember him remarking that he was surprised that I had completed the project. He didn't think I would. I remember thinking that was because he was arrogant and on a power trip. The really crazy part of this story is when I was asked about identifying one of my best teachers; I selected him because he did help me understand statistics, which was a pretty incredible feat.

During my last semester, I had an upper-level Strategic Management class that was a complete mystery. The teacher's lectures were focused on one subject. Our reading assignments focused on another subject, and the questions in our reading assignments appeared to be based on a different subject. A classmate summed it up beautifully when he said, "We read about all of the elements that make up the earth, and then we're asked to describe the elements that make up the moon."

. . .

Heroes Wanted

Increasing the stress levels for my classmates and I was there would only be a mid-term and a final. There were no quizzes or tests in between, so as students, we had no idea about the style of tests, or what the teacher was looking for. Fortunately, about five or six of us met weekly to decipher the homework questions. We'd spend a couple of hours together in the library, trying to figure out answers to one or two questions. We were all seniors, we were all intelligent, and we were all stressed out.

Later in the semester, we learned that our instructor was working to make his class an extension of a lower-level strategic management class, which many of us had taken a couple of years earlier. If memory serves me correctly, the class he wanted to link to was the class I took, where the professor reminisced about his life. As students, we now understood the disconnect. Our professor expected us to draw upon concepts we hadn't used in a couple of years and we were never informed a future class would draw upon our previous knowledge. Not telling students two courses are dependent on each other and should be taken back-to-back is very irresponsible. I passed the class and graduated from CSU Sacramento, but for many years, I had nightmares of failing to graduate.

During my senior year in college, I utilized the CSU Sacramento Career Center to assist me in finding a job after college. When I had job interviews, I'd walk from my apartment across the river to the Career Center on the opposite side of campus. I'd wear a suit, and it was summer. By the time I'd get to the Career Center, I'd be sweating. I'd have to spend fifteen to thirty minutes cooling off. I planned accordingly.

. . .

One day I had an interview scheduled for 2:00 p.m. When I arrived, I was informed that my interview had been canceled. I was in disbelief, and the person delivering the bad news had a big smarmy grin on her face. I was incredulous that no one could pick up the phone or send an email letting me know the interview had been canceled, especially since the staff was aware of cancelations at 8:00 a.m. I felt disrespected.

At one point during my stint at CSU Sacramento, the school rolled out a new marketing mantra titled "Opportunity To Learn." Apparently, students were attending school for an opportunity to learn. Given my experiences with so many inept instructors, I called bullshit. I drafted a report based on my classroom experiences and countered that "Opportunity to Learn" was a fraud. Students weren't attending CSU Sacramento for an opportunity to learn. They were attending CSU Sacramento to be taught by qualified instructors, who were good at their jobs and wanted to impart knowledge to others.

My motivation for writing this report was because, as an older student, I knew from experience what good instructors were like and the impact they could have on young minds. Good instructors changed lives, inspired, created engaging learning experiences, and motivated students to learn. Most college kids wouldn't know the difference between a good instructor and a lousy instructor or would be indifferent. To illustrate my point, one of the best instructors I had at CSU Sacramento was my business writing instructor. Students would often complain about his class. He handed out homework assignments like they were candy. His course was very challenging. He set high expectations, and students had to work hard to keep up. He was providing students with real business world experiences. For young adults, the workload for this one class may not appear to be worth it or may, in fact, be overwhelming. In contrast, a non-challenging course given by an unqualified professor, not interested in educating young minds, may be experienced by young adults without scrutiny.

I felt terrible for the parents of the students. Parents sacrificed and saved money to send their children to CSU Sacramento, thinking their kids would receive a first-rate education from instructors who were inspiring their children to learn and expand their minds. Parents and students were paying money and making sacrifices for a quality education being imparted by qualified, world-class instructors. No one was spending money and making personal sacrifices for an "Opportunity To Learn." To be fair, there were some pretty incredible instructors at CSU Sacramento, and I'm grateful for all of them. They're the ones that make a difference in the lives of students. The acquisition of knowledge, the sharing of knowledge, and the development of young minds are of the utmost importance for developing a healthy, thriving civilization.

Chapter 12
Visions of Grandeur

A Promise is Made

As my educational journey progressed from Napa Valley College to CSU Sacramento, my visions of different technology-based business models kept increasing. I started to realize that my financial strategy to get through college would leave me with no seed money to fund one of my new ventures. Instead, I'd be burdened with debt upon graduation.

As with every other challenge that presented itself to me, I placed my concerns into God's capable hands and prayed about it. God assured me that the money I would need to start a business would be available to me once I graduated. The matter was settled. I had complete confidence in God's word. The funding I needed would be available.

During my senior year of college, I was accepted into the Sacramento Entrepreneurship Academy (SEA). The SEA was a mentoring program for college seniors interested in starting their own businesses. Students would meet once a week, form teams, and develop a business plan under the mentorship of several business leaders from the community. The SEA was an incredible organization, and I'm very grateful for all the local business leaders I was able to meet through this organization. During my participation in the SEA program, my brain went into creative overdrive. I started to experience numerous visions for what could be. Everywhere I turned, I saw innovative business opportunities. Every day I was amazed by the visions God was blessing me with and the impact these blessings would have on humanity.

My exposure to community leaders from both Sacramento and Napa, along with my relationship with God, instilled in me enormous confidence. All of my business ideas were industry-disrupting, and in most instances, I would be first to market. Not having money to invest in my own startup, I realized that initially, I might have to trade equity for investment dollars. I wasn't too concerned with this, though. I was generating so many different business ideas that it would only be a matter of time before I had the cash to negotiate better terms with investors. In addition, I had God's promise that upon graduation, money would be there for me. I also knew that God delivers, even if not necessarily in the way we expect it. I had to keep my options open. Knowing that my business ideas were blessings from God, I attempted to get my business concepts in front of as many people as possible. I knew there was going to be an investor, a strategic partner, or someone that was going to invest, and together, we would accomplish great things.

Social Businesses

During this incredible time in my life, as I'm experiencing personal growth, discovery, and the acquisition of knowledge, I'm unable to contain my commitments to God. The Internet was in its infancy, and I was receiving visions for ways to leverage the Internet to advance humanity. Listed below are the synopsis of various social business concepts I was blessed with:

Human Spirit 1997 – 2000

Human Spirit would have been an online magazine celebrating everything great about the United States of America, from our Constitution to the Bill of Rights to the Declaration of Independence. It was designed to celebrate America's success and give all citizens a sense of pride for being a part of the greatest nation in the world. Each issue would profile great American leaders, great Americans, and great American companies. In addition, the secondary thrust of the magazine would be to recognize America's everyday heroes—those who make a difference each and every day. Candidates would be submitted from participating colleges, high schools, and non-profits from all across America.

Human Development 1997 – Current

The concept for Human Development was to create a website resource portal where parents and soon-to-be parents could find the resources and support necessary to provide their children with love, confidence, and respect for other human beings. In addition, the offerings would include courses on nourishment, exercise, self-esteem development, and ways to instill a desire to learn and be better.

The Advocate 1997 – 2002 (Precursor to DebateMe.com)

The Advocate would profile victims of rape, violent crimes, bullying, drug addiction, and prostitution. It would tell the story of the victim's life before and after the crime, with details as to how the crime impacted the victims and their families. Members/subscribers would be encouraged to attend court dates and support victims in their local communities. In addition, The Advocate would publish dedicated exposés that would identify deficiencies in the criminal justice system that perpetuate crime and would encourage members/subscribers to lobby Congress for change. Other aspirations of The Advocate would be to explore gun control , the war on drugs, the death penalty, prostitution, and other controversial issues.

Sanctuary City 1997 – Current

Victims of domestic violence and prostitution, drug addicts, and the homeless would be provided with shelter and an opportunity to reclaim an independent, normal life. Sanctuary City is the conversion or renovation of a warehouse or abandoned building. The ground floor would consist of a mini police station, a medical clinic, a counseling center, an employment development center, a college extension, a coffee shop, a café, a community daycare center, and public recreation center. The second floor would be a dedicated call center training facility that would be supported by various corporations. The third floor would provide housing units for those needing assistance. The fourth and higher floors would be a combination of office space and apartments with premium rents – to help cover operations costs.

Bicycle Sanctuary 1997 – Current

Initially, based on my three years' experience as a pedestrian/bicyclist, the original concept was to have street signs that would alert motorists to the presence of bicyclists on the roadway, the precursor to today's Share the Road signage. Today, the concept has been expanded to include intelligent highways, proximity sensors, real-time traffic control, improved driver training, and several innovations to make commuting greener and safer.

· · ·

End-of-Life Quality Care 2013 – 2014

Assisted living and hospitals can be very lonely and depressing for senior citizens nearing the end of their lives. With a little creative effort, end-of-life care can be significantly improved and less stressful for the patients, their families, and caregivers.

Visionary Business Concepts

On God's time, I was bombarded with innovative business models that were revolutionary, visionary, and years ahead of their time. The beauty of my visions is that they didn't require technological breakthroughs. I was simply looking at existing technology and developing new business models. Most, if not all, of my business concepts were going to disrupt existing industries, create new industries, enable my business to be first to market, and provide consumers with the products and services they desired and businesses with the products and services they needed for healthy profit margins.

I generated over 25 different business opportunities between 1997 and 2014. Below are three different business summaries I developed. At the time of their conception, nothing comparable was on the market. Had I been able to launch any one of these businesses, I would have established myself in the technology sector.

Platinum Websites 1999 - 2000

I originated this concept as a final project for my team for the Sacramento Entrepreneurship Academy. At the time, a basic website cost around $3,000.00. My idea was to offer website templates starting at $600.00. Each template was basically a cookie cutter of common elements and graphics used to create a website. Each template would be customizable to the purchaser's needs. One of my teammates talked me out of pursuing this business model after graduation. I believe it was less than a year later when website templates exploded across the Internet.

Digital Signage - Grocery Store Television Network 1998 – 2000

While attending Napa Valley College, I worked as a part-time meat clerk in a butcher shop. I observed that customers, especially housewives coming in around dinner time, were looking for meal suggestions. Based on my favorite meals, I'd hand out meal suggestions and recipes while selling groceries from behind the meat counter. I was creating a great customer experience. Building off my observations and experiences with grocery shoppers being highly receptive to dinner ideas, I envisioned video displays strategically placed throughout a grocery store.

A short, engaging video providing meal suggestions would loop all day long. Corresponding meal recipes would be available for printout from a nearby kiosk, along with manufacturer coupons. Today, the natural extension of this concept is easily identifiable everywhere, from digital menus and digital signage to video product presentations.

DebateMe.com - 2002

I envisioned a website enabling everyday citizens to interact with mainstream media news. Any story that was published on the web, in print, on the radio, or on television would promote a DebateMe.com code. Users would log in, enter the code, and then could debate the topic of the hour. Debateme.com would have been the first social media website to market. Unlike other social media platforms, it would have promoted rational discussion, taught people how to debate, and taught people to find common ground and build a consensus. DebateMe.com was all about people coming together and finding solutions to the challenges facing our world. I envisioned politicians, community leaders, and business leaders sponsoring weekly debates where anyone could join in and debate topics they were passionate about. It was easily a billion-dollar idea. Debate-Me.com would have focused on upholding our Constitution and backing up arguments with facts.

A Mission in Futility

During the early 2000s, everyone was looking for ways to make money off of the Internet, and there I was, walking around with a treasure map from God. One of the biggest challenges I experienced with my business concepts was putting together financial models. My business concepts were all going to be first to market. As a result, there were no established revenue models to reference. For example, when I came up with DebateMe.com, there were no social media companies.

Posting a comment on a news story was years away. With no comparable revenue models, I had nothing concrete to show investors. While I identified potentially numerous revenue streams for DebateMe.com, trying to convince a potential investor my revenue streams were valid would require a leap of faith by the investor. At the same time, all around me, big money investors were pouring money into Internet startups with zero revenue models.

I had the revenue models. I had visionary business concepts, and I was counting on God's promise that money would be available after I graduated from college. My business concepts were always well received. People's mouths would fall open as they recognized an ingenious business solution right before their eyes. Yet, no matter how impressed people were or how excited they became, there was always an excuse for not partnering or investing.

Eventually, I'd become frustrated and tired of people turning me down or questioning my business concepts. I dismissed people's willingness to invest or partner with me as their inability to grasp the vision, the opportunity, or the market potential of my business concepts. As a result, I continued to look for investors or strategic partners, or I would focus my energy on trying to code the project myself.

For well over a decade, I diligently tried to master the programming languages necessary to build a web platform. I tried to master PHP, MySQL, HTML, and CSS. My passion became an obsession. I'd work a regular full-time job, come home and rest for an hour or two, and then be up until 1:00 a.m. or 2:00 a.m. coding. I'd code for several months at a time and either get overwhelmed, lost in my code, or encounter a challenge I couldn't overcome before eventually shelving the project. A few months later, I'd be re-energized, and the vicious cycle would repeat itself.

I had the program logic down. It was the coding that killed me. Rather than keep my coding simple, I'd get extravagant and generate so much additional code I'd get lost. After years of trying to complete a program, I finally convinced myself that no matter how much I enjoyed coding, a coder I was not!

For the longest time, I was running around with a million different ideas jumping around in my head as I attempted to process these incredible visions from God into some type of business plan. I was always on the hunt for that special person or group of people that would rally behind me. Unfortunately for me, I was oblivious to other people's motives.

It never occurred to me that I was possibly being refused because I didn't belong to the right political party or the right church, was a sinner, or people had ulterior motives. It wasn't until much later in life that I gave any thought to the fact that nobody was partnering with me or investing. I had always assumed it was because they didn't understand the potential of the business concept I was promoting—that they just didn't 'get' it. I was perplexed because at no point during my interactions with God did He ever inform me that there would be conditions attached to the funding I sought. It never crossed my mind that I was being manipulated, played, or laughed at.

Chapter 13
Battling Satan: Round II (2000-2014)

Safe Environment

I grew up in a safe, protected environment, and my faith, belief, and experiences with God led me to adopt a perspective of the world where everyone wanted to do good, everyone wanted to defeat evil, and everyone wanted to make this a better world. With all of my heart, I believed that goodness would overcome evil. From an early age, God showed me that we are all human beings and that we are all very similar in what we want for life. It's our experiences, values, beliefs, and our approach to life that differ. I took it to heart that as human beings, we have far more in common with one another than we have differences.

During my youth, society was focused on bridging the gaps that divided us and building relationships based on what we had in common as human beings. I wholeheartedly believed that if society was united, we could achieve anything, overcome impossible barriers, and triumph over evil. Armed with visions from God, I was positive I would attract the right people into my life—people who held similar beliefs and desires for doing good in the world.

Further blinding me to the intent of those around me is that I was being utterly overwhelmed by visions from God. I was receiving vision after vision of ideas that would have been first to market, industry-disrupting, revenue-generating business concepts that would change the world. I was receiving visions for ways to make this a better world, improve humanity, end injustice, and empower people. How great is that?

For years my brain was going a million miles a second, trying to determine how to realize any one of these magnificent visions. As a result, I never looked deep into the motives of those around me, especially those I loved and trusted. I was blinded by my beliefs and my experiences with God. I thought that the people in my life shared my vision of wanting to do good and do what's right. I believed the people in my life wanted to work with me, and together we would work toward the betterment of humanity. My focus was trying to accomplish the visions God had provided. I figured everyone else would be on board, too. I was wrong, and if it weren't for God's intervention on my behalf, it would have cost me my life.

A Rough Start

Throughout my college years, many supported and encouraged me. During my senior year, numerous opportunities were presented to me that I either declined or I botched. I was driven by the visions God had blessed me with. The technology industry was my future and where my fortune was to be found. To my dismay, without a technology degree, most of the jobs that I qualified for were in sales.

Heroes Wanted

Having been in sales for most of my life, I wasn't really eager to go back. However, the rent needed to be paid.

As part of my graduation celebration from CSU Sacramento, I vacationed in Zion National Park. I stayed at a motel in St George, and one night I found myself standing on the sidewalk on the main boulevard. I must have been out there for a couple of hours, just standing there, mesmerized by the sounds of silence. It was so incredibly peaceful. There was no noise from traffic or any other distractions—just silence and peace. I was once again out in a rural area—the desert—and I felt great.

When I returned home from my vacation, I sent several resumes out to businesses in the St. George area and landed a job with a dietary health supplement company. While I had every intention of pursuing the visions God had planted in my heart, I desperately wanted to live in a rural environment. I loved the St. George area, and out in nature is where I've always found God.

My job in St. George, Utah, lasted approximately 90 days. During that awesome time, when I'd get off of work, I'd ride my bicycle out to an overlook above Snow Canyon Park. The view of the canyon below me was spectacular. I'd sit there for hours in sensory overload, enjoying the warm wind rushing up against my body while I took in the beauty of God's creation. I'd sit on the side of a cliff and watch as the sky faded from deep blue to gray to black while simultaneously watching the walls of the red canyons change colors. On my days off, I'd head out to Zion National Park and hang out at some of my favorite parts of the park.

. . .

186

It was a great life, but the pay at my job was horrible, and I had student loans to pay. I also missed my family and friends. My stint in St. George, Utah, however, was enough to replenish my spirit and rejuvenate me. I returned to California ready to start building a career. I found myself living in Palmdale with my eldest brother Richard and his family. As a condition of living under their roof, Richard and his wife insisted I attend church services with them each week. I'd never been one to attend church, but I reluctantly agreed, even though I wasn't too happy about having religion forced upon me.

I put together a consulting website and reached out to my previous connections but got nowhere for my efforts. I ended up taking an outside sales position for a well-established, family-run copier dealership out of Bakersfield. The company was expanding and wanted me to develop the Palmdale and Lancaster areas. The first directive I received from my new boss was to target every church in the area.

I found it curious I was being told to target churches, but my boss explained that churches make a lot of photocopies. His logic was sound, so I went about calling on the various churches in the community. During my tenure as a copier salesman, I called upon many churches, businesses, and government entities. Despite having a vast territory, despite my efforts, and despite generating an abundance of proposals, I closed very few of the proposals I wrote. I was barely scraping by financially. I felt as if I was battling a force that was purposely trying to control me, that relished in my failures, held me back, and prevented me from getting ahead financially. Unfortunately, I had an abundance of failures.

· · ·

Heroes Wanted

One of my worst experiences while working for the copier company was on one of the days my boss rode along with me on sales calls. He had been on me about hitting specific churches in the area. As we pulled into the parking lot of a church I had called upon a week earlier and wasn't able to get in front of a decision maker, we saw two box trucks. They were offloading a number of brand-new copier machines! It was like a scene from a comedy, except I was the star idiot being humiliated and excoriated. Experiences like I just described would mar my career as a copier salesman and my career in general.

While I languished financially and was unable to generate sales to improve the quality of my life, my relationship with my boss and my fellow sales associates at the copier company was legendary. Our personalities clicked. Whenever we'd get together as a group, we'd entertain ourselves, talking and laughing for hours on end. My boss and co-workers were good people, and I would have welcomed an opportunity to build a career while working with them. However, I was always in conflict. I never had any extra money. Whenever we went out for drinks or dinner, I would have to watch every penny. Usually, my boss would cover my expenses because he was an awesome individual. I loathed the fact that I wasn't self-sufficient. I wasn't raised to let other people take care of me.

Eventually, I realized I wasn't cut out for outside sales. I was spectacular with inside sales, but outside sales just wasn't my cup of tea. I managed to secure a position as a software trainer and moved back to Sacramento. When I returned to Palmdale to visit Richard and his family, I dropped in on my replacement, and he shared with me how every business in town he called upon had my business card and knew me. While I couldn't close enough sales to survive, my replacement was doing quite well.

Stoppable

I didn't fare much better with my subsequent employment opportunities, either. Despite having an extensive business background, being incredibly talented, knowing more than most managers about customer service and sales, and being a technology genius, I was forced to start at the bottom. I was being prevented from utilizing my God-given skills, talents, and gifts. When I was going to college, I took on substantial student loan debt because I believed within a few years of graduating, I would be able to retire the debt because of my high-paying job. High-paying jobs always managed to elude me.

The software training position I was hired for was for a new software program designed to help automotive repair owners operate their businesses more efficiently. During our initial rollout, I discovered my role was really more of a business consultant than a software trainer. I was paid very well, and I thrived in my new position. Unfortunately, the founder of the consulting firm had other business interests he wanted to pursue. Although I could handle all aspects of our consulting projects with minimum supervision, I was not an expert in the automotive repair industry. The company's founder was the expert and was well-known in the industry. Without him, I could not envision the firm surviving. I was forced to move on.

My next gig was at Best Buy. My belief in taking care of the customer by providing them with an incredible shopping experience clashed with corporate's statistical models. As long as sales were within the acceptable limits of the bell curve, all was fine. If the numbers weren't acceptable, then all hell broke loose.

. . .

Heroes Wanted

Based on my life experiences, statistics took away the human factor and degraded the customer experience. I was raised to take care of the customer. Sales and profits were made when they were kept happy. I wanted to ensure that every customer who came into the store received world-class customer service. I was at odds with the statistical models, which were resigned to accepting a percentage of customers who were not happy. As far as I was concerned, even though the reports showed we were technically making money, we were actually missing out on sales and losing customers.

Perhaps the most significant challenge I experienced working at Best Buy was their unwillingness to discipline or remove problem employees. Management refused to do anything about insubordinate or habitually late employees. I was instructed to try and be their friend and coach rather than discipline. I learned that I wasn't a good coach or friend. I believed that if someone showed up to work and didn't want to do their job after additional coaching, if there was no improvement, then it was time for that person to move on. Our sales numbers were always poor, and our store went through several different managers, but problem associates were never replaced or disciplined in all the time I was there.

I was offered a position as a general manager for a lighting showroom, and I took it. To this day, I believe my experiences at the lighting showroom were all needlessly contrived. My entire tenure with this firm was marred in turmoil. There were two company owners with two different visions for the company, and I was caught in the middle. One week, I'd be in favor with one of the owners. The following week it would be the other. The owners would constantly fight, and I knew better than to choose sides because, in the end, they were family, and I knew who would lose. I was constantly stressed out trying to appease them both.

. . .

In addition, I had to deal with employee complaints, sales associates not returning customer calls or following up on orders, incorrect merchandise being ordered, upset customers, and in one instance, a sales associate who was providing customers with quotes, that included our costs and markup. When one of our customers presented me with a quote that included all our privileged financial information, I could have died right there on the spot.

Eventually, I became so stressed out that I started to get physically sick. I was still trying to get any one of my businesses launched but just wasn't having any luck. I just couldn't figure out why I wasn't making any progress on God's plan. My existing life was in sharp contrast to the one I envisioned. God had provided me with all of these incredible visions, and here I was, unhappy and very stressed out. It's as if I was missing something or not getting it. I felt like I was living in a really bad reality TV show, where the sole objective of the show was to humiliate and demoralize me. I was frustrated beyond belief. But then .... in 2007, something incredible happened.

I got a toothache. Having no dental insurance, I was forced to ignore my bad tooth for as long as possible. Eventually, the pain became so intense that my entire head began to throb, and I couldn't think or focus. My dentist at the time wrote me a prescription for Vicodin until I could come in for treatment. For the first time in a very long time, I felt happy and content. From that moment forward, I would treat my mental pain and anguish with Vicodin. In fact, I was able to get through the next several years of my life with not much more than Vicodin and a cheap bottle of wine.

. . .

Heroes Wanted

I knew my career as a general manager was not going to last. I was in a no-win situation. I enrolled in a local trade school to obtain Microsoft Certifications. The school was phenomenal, the staff was fantastic, and I was on my way to becoming a Microsoft Certified Systems Engineer (MCSE). As I predicted, one day, there was a blow-up between one of the owners of the lighting showroom and me. At this point, I didn't care anymore, and I was fired. Within a few weeks, I had an opportunity to work for Apple, Inc.

I can honestly state that Apple was one of the best companies I ever worked for. My first computer was an Apple, and I always loved their technology and philosophy, even though I hadn't used an Apple product in decades. At Apple, I felt I was at home. Apple made great products, and best of all, Apple valued and treated their customers exactly the way I believed customers should be treated. During my entire time working for Apple, I never once had a manager confront me about doing too much to take care of our customers.

At Apple, I learned about different metrics. I wasn't being held accountable for sales, but my time was tracked. There were several different metrics that advisors would be held accountable for. Fortunately for me, I loved my job and was compensated handsomely, so I was motivated to learn these metrics. In addition, I always had great managers. I'd receive the coaching necessary to correct any deficiencies in my metrics.

I learned two important things about my personality at Apple from two different managers. The first manager called me out on the way I processed information. During our one-on-one meeting, she flat-out told me, "Jim, it takes you several days to process information. I'll say something to you on Monday, and you'll be like, "Nope, that's not me," or "That's not how I do things," but then by Friday, you're like, "Oh yeah, I see what you're talking about." What an insightful and accurate observation. I never realized this behavior, but being called out on it has helped me tremendously.

The second manager pointed out that I was struggling to perform my daily responsibilities because I was processing and focused on issues that were three levels above my pay grade. My manager's observation was another great insight. I'm a problem solver, and given my extensive business knowledge and entrepreneurial spirit, it would make sense that I operated at a higher level than what I was being paid for.

Even though I had a great job with Apple, I was still obsessed with trying to launch one of my business ideas that God had blessed me with. It got to the point where I could no longer learn new things. My brain was full. It was an interesting phenomenon that I'd never experienced before. In addition, at this point in my life, I started to be cognizant that something wasn't right. I was missing something.

I had always gone on the assumption that after graduation, money would be there for me. I had no idea where it was going to come from. I just took God's word on faith. I never really asked people for money. I just shared my ideas and would wait and see where the conversation went. Now that I believed something was amiss, I reached out to family and a friend for some seed money to start DebateMe.com. It wasn't even that much, but both responded with a flat refusal.

I then reached out to a former Napa Valley College professor and presented DebateMe.com as a pilot program to help students develop debating skills. I used my apple.com email address to intimate that

Heroes Wanted

Apple was behind me. I got nowhere, but my eyes were opened. For my efforts at bluffing, I started to receive an abnormally high number of escalated calls, where the customer was unreasonable and demanding. As long as customers didn't address their anger toward me, I'd do whatever I could to assist them. I even tolerated cursing as long as it wasn't directed at Apple or myself. These calls were different, though. They were attacks on me, and I didn't have the skill set to deal with them. I'd take it personally, but I'd have to refrain from engaging in sessions of juvenile tit-for-tat. I also knew these calls were fake.

Any time a demanding customer had the type of issues I was dealing with, they'd call back either the next day or within a few days at the latest. As a conscientious support advisor, I'd check these difficult tickets after a few days to see if the customer's issue had been resolved. None of the escalated tickets causing me grief ever called back. Statistically improbable. I ended up taking stress leave, and once I realized it was my job causing the stress, I resigned rather than milk the system for all it was worth.

When I graduated from college, I was going to be unstoppable. I was a visionary, blessed with innovative visions for technology-based businesses, and I was determined to set the world on fire with my greatness. Despite my best efforts, success miraculously avoided me, yet failure, humiliation, and poverty arrived in spades. It was as if the universe was conspiring against me to ensure I would never get ahead financially while mocking me, tormenting me, and laughing at me.

I truly believed I would set the world on fire with my greatness, but the only thing I managed to set on fire was my own ass. It would take me many years of pain, suffering, and poverty, as well as cost me my relationship with God, before I figured out that it wasn't the universe or God that had failed me. My struggles were the direct result of Satan and his minions orchestrating my defeat.

Religion

My boss from the copier company, if you recall, directed me to solicit churches in the Palmdale and Lancaster areas. During one of my cold calls to a church in Lancaster, I met a pastor to whom I took an immediate liking. I couldn't comprehend why I was struggling financially and was forced to start at the bottom when I had so many different business concepts that God had bestowed upon me. I was hopeful that a pastor might be able to shed some light on my experiences and help me understand where I was with my relationship with God. In addition, I looked forward to sharing my personal experiences with God with the church.

I met with the pastor and was so impressed with him that I agreed to attend Sunday worship services at his church. It turned out to be an eye-opening experience for me. The worship team was spectacular, the music was inspirational, and everyone around me was singing about how much Jesus loved them and how much they loved Jesus. The pastor's sermon hit home, was inspirational, and by the time worship services had concluded, I was filled with the Holy Spirit. I felt renewed, invigorated, and amazed. I was amazed because all of these people were attending church in order to feel like I felt when God met me out in the desert. I had maintained a connection with the Holy Spirit for over six years, and here were all of these fine folks attending Sunday worship services in order to feel the presence of the Holy Spirit. It was an amazing experience for me to realize that all of these people were communing with the Holy Spirit every Sunday in church.

· · ·

I began attending regularly. For the first time in my life, I actually looked forward to going to church. I also continued to meet with the pastor. I shared with him the details of my personal relationship with God. I asked him questions about my relationship with God, and while his answers pacified me, they never really provided me with peace or resolution. God had promised me a compelling life upon graduation, and it wasn't materializing.

Instead of moving forward, I found myself stuck at the bottom. For the next several months, I continued to attend Sunday Services and expanded my participation in the church to include projects, events, and fellowship. I actually felt like I was part of a church family. No matter what my week was like, I could count on the Holy Spirit showing up at Sunday's worship services.

When my copier career ended, I moved back to Northern California. While I attempted to find a new church home, nothing grabbed me or inspired me like the church I had left behind in Lancaster. In fact, the more exposure I had to different churches, the more skeptical I became of organized religion. The church promoted itself as an expert on God. I incorrectly assumed I'd find the answers I was looking for from a priest or a pastor. I didn't.

I found that revealing any experiences I'd had with God were dismissed out-of-hand unless those experiences were in alignment with church doctrine. At one point, while attending a Maronite Church in the Sacramento area, I showed up for Mass one Sunday and was surprised to encounter a visiting English-speaking priest among the predominately Lebanese-speaking congregation. He apparently had been brought in to hear my confessions. Talk about weird. This was. Not being aware of any sins I'd committed, I informed the visiting priest that I had no confessions to offer.

Compounding my skepticism about finding a church family was the pressure from my family to find a church home. I was flummoxed by my family's sudden obsession with religion. Growing up, attending church was never a priority. Now all of a sudden, my brothers and sister were embracing religion.

Subterfuge

Prior to my encounter with God in 1993, my memories of my parents, brothers, and sister were ones of loss, missed opportunities, bad decisions, failure, anger, and manipulation. Through God's grace, I was able to forgive my family and my past. When I left Zion National Park in 1993, I had embraced the vision of the future God had planted in my heart. I couldn't wait to share all of my amazing, life-changing experiences with my family. I wanted to give my parents, brothers, and sister hope. I would show them that we didn't have to be looked down upon by other family members. I was going to show them that we didn't have to be losers, we didn't have to be poor, and we didn't have to fail. I was going to bring my family with me on the spectacular journey God had shown me.

For several years, my relationship with my family flourished. I established meaningful relationships with my nieces and nephews. I turned my family on to Zion National Park. My nieces and nephews would go out to dinner with me, we'd go camping, to the movies, and we were all getting along. I finally started to understand what my mom meant when she would break into tears, start praising our family members, and then declare how much she loved all of us. Family was important.

. . .

Heroes Wanted

I used to dream of how I would orchestrate a surprise meeting with my brothers, sister, nieces, and nephews and inform them of my financial success and how our lives were about to be changed forever. I looked forward to erasing our past and never having to suffer the indignation of being looked down upon by the Maroun family ever again. I dreamt of uplifting my entire family.

When my mother passed away in 2010, her previous speeches about the importance of family hit home with me. It was during the last 15 years of my life that I really enjoyed hanging out with my family. I was looking forward to spending endless summers with them. Unfortunately, with my mother's passing, my brothers' and sister's attitude toward me changed. They started to act aloof and behaved as if I had somehow wronged them, but they weren't willing to confront me. They now acted with an air of superiority. The fact that their attitudes toward me changed after my mother's passing made me incredulous. Whatever they were up to, it had to wait until after Mom's death.

Over the course of the next few years, their arrogance, deception, and trickery would lead to the eventual destruction of our relationship. Their behaviors after my mother's death caused me to cast doubt on previous interactions. For example, I can remember having dinner with Richard and my nieces and nephews at our favorite sushi restaurant. We're all drinking, eating, and having a fantastic time, except for Richard. All night long, he's glaring at me.

Throughout the night, I kept asking him about it, and each time he assured me that nothing was wrong. A short time later, both he and his wife instigated an argument with me. At no time when my mother was alive did either of them, or anyone else in our family, ever confront me or complain about my behavior, actions, or attitude. While I quickly moved to address their grievances, their actions proved my apology fell upon deaf ears. Something was amiss. As the years progressed, my suspicions grew, but I was always provided with false assurances that everything was a bed of roses.

One night, I was speaking on the phone with one of my older cousins from Ohio. When I was much younger, he had owned a successful chain of music stores. He was the age of my older brothers and sister. They had all hung out together growing up while I was just the baby of the family. I have memories of him from childhood, and I looked up to him based on the stories I heard about him while I was growing up, but I never really had a relationship with him or knew him very well. I did visit him and other relatives in 1993 during my cross-country excursion.

During the course of our phone conversation, he blurts out how much Richard loves me. It was an awkward statement, and I should have called him out and asked for details, but like many other conversations I had during this time, I just let it slide by. It wasn't until a few days later that his words sunk in and sent a shudder down my spine. What the hell did Richard do on my behalf, out of love for me, that I was unaware of and was brought to the attention of our cousin, who I rarely saw? Knowing Richard as I did, I became incredibly suspicious.

Perhaps one of my most torturous memories is when Shawn and I were at a shopping mall. Shawn gets this spontaneous idea to call our aunt. As soon as he gets her on the phone, she starts laughing at me and calling me a jackass in Lebanese for trusting my brothers. Shawn can hear her, and he's laughing hysterically as he turns red with embarrassment. I didn't press the issue, and she was too busy laughing and calling me a jackass to explain what she was talking about.

I had no assets. There was talk of inheriting some property in Lebanon from my father, but my father never benefited from this property that was his inheritance from his father. As far as I was concerned, the property in Lebanon was a pipe dream. I was focused on God's plan. To the best of my knowledge, my brothers had nothing on me. Besides, I was raised to trust my older brothers. It was all part of our Lebanese culture.

As the years progressed, I never got a straight answer from Shawn or my aunt as to why she was laughing at me and calling me a jackass for trusting my brothers. My aunt responded that she just liked to laugh sometimes. As for Shawn, whenever I confronted him about anything, his response would make even the most crooked politicians blush. As the years progressed, I began to wonder and doubt myself.

Was it prudent for me to sign a blank signatory card at Shawn's request? I was told it was so my two brothers and I would have control over my mom's checking account after she passed away. While I was told the sum in the account was only $10,000, I was never given a closing statement after her funeral. What did my brothers do that would cause my aunt to call me a jackass for trusting them? Even more interesting was that both of my brothers transitioned from being objects of scorn on my dad's side of the family to being respected.

. . .

One of the most infuriating experiences I've had to endure was on the one-year anniversary of an uncle's death on my dad's side of the family. A special service was being held at the Maronite church in Millbrae, California. Afterward, we all sat outside for lunch. At the time, my wife was on crutches, and I was still suffering from severe back and shoulder pain from a recent car accident.

Out of nowhere, one of my cousins approaches me and whispers in my ear that my car crash resulted from me behaving stupidly. I couldn't believe my ears. I was involved in a single-vehicle car crash, and I was the one driving. I know who caused this horrific crash, and I also know the circumstances surrounding it. I certainly didn't need my self-righteous cousin, who had little to no relationship with me, getting all sanctimonious on me. She was so confident. Someone had put her up to her little speech.

When it came to encounters with potential investors, I was equally frustrated and haunted by memories of conversations. God was answering my prayers and bombarding me with visions for numerous businesses. As noted earlier, my brain was constantly on overload, working a million miles a second processing information, identifying opportunities, and trying to figure out a way to bring any one of these numerous visions to life. As a consequence, when interacting with potential investors, I may have been more focused on what I was going to say or honing the message I wanted to convey instead of listening. I was blinded by my dedication to following God's plan. I ignored or minimized warning signs, and as a consequence, I found myself broke, isolated, irrelevant, and haunted by memories of inter-actions that seemed awry.

Inheritance

I can still remember the day my father passed away in 1995. My uncle counseled me, my brothers, and my sister on how to secure our father's inheritance in Lebanon. On that day, my uncle was like a Guardian Angel. Over the course of the next few years, I truly believed a reconciliation between my aunts, uncles, and my family was taking place. There were numerous overtures, and I welcomed every opportunity to strengthen our family ties.

My father's passing devastated his brothers and sisters. They would often speak of his death in disbelief. I had a genuine interest in learning more about my dad's life, his family history, and the country of my birth, Lebanon. My visits with my aunts and uncle were now pleasant, and there was incredible encouragement and support for me to finish my college education. For my part, I was at the zenith of my spiritual connection with God. I was filled with the Holy Spirit, unstoppable, and for the first time in my life, I wasn't intimidated by my dad's side of the family.

In regard to my father's inheritance, I never expected to see anything ever come of it, nor did I ever depend on it. I was skeptical of my father's inheritance for a good cause. I'd spent my entire life listening to my father talk about the property his father owned in Lebanon. My father dreamed about selling the property in Lebanon and becoming a millionaire. In the end, other than inheriting the most valuable lot, my father died poor and never benefited from his father's inheritance. I had no illusions that I would somehow fare better than my father in regard to property in a distant land. The way I saw it, if an inheritance did materialize, it would be an additional blessing.

. . .

My focus was on obtaining a college education and then creating the technology empire God had planted in my heart. An illusory inheritance from Lebanon was not a priority. In fact, I remember during church service for my father, one of the priests approached me afterward and assured me that I would never have to worry about money. I found the priest's statement curious. I knew I didn't have to worry about money because God had already shared this information with me. I knew that when I graduated from college, there would be money available for me to fund my businesses.

During the time I was pursuing my college education, I had a lot of financially successful friends from Napa Valley. I was meeting influential people in the Sacramento region, my uncle was highly successful, and I never had any expectation that any of the people from these groups were obligated to invest in me. What I did know is that God was telling me money would be available for me after graduation. I had visionary concepts that would upend entire industries. My expectation was that whomever I shared my business concepts with, someone would eventually take an interest and partner with me to bring any of these innovative visions to life.

Throughout the years, my uncle would summon my brothers and me for a conference about the property in Lebanon. At no time was I ever provided with an official appraisal of the property's value. Instead, I was inexplicably informed that it was worth anywhere from $25,000 to 300,000. In addition, I was told that I could not own property in Lebanon, so I had to sign over my share of the property to my brothers. As this was regarding property inheritance in a foreign country that I'd never seen, and for the sake of unity, I trusted my uncle, aunts, and my brothers unconditionally. I signed over my share to my brothers. I never doubted the wisdom of my actions because I was focused on the visions God had bestowed upon me. I was focused on God's promise and on making a fortune. I wasn't counting on an inheritance from Lebanon. I saw no downside to trusting my brothers or my uncle.

Eventually, my family's actions, behaviors, and attitudes started to raise alarms. At one of the meetings regarding the property, one of my aunts was visiting from Lebanon and desperately wanted to tell me something. Her English wasn't good, and my ability to speak Lebanese, outside of a few curse words, was virtually non-existent. My uncle forbade anyone from translating. My aunt was furious, and I was nonplussed. Again, I was focused on God's plan, yet, what did she want to tell me, and why did my uncle forbid it?

At another meeting to discuss my father's inheritance, my uncle was boasting about the obnoxious prices he paid for these beautiful Persian rugs he had acquired. Like many of the meetings before, nothing productive came from this meeting, but I didn't go home empty-handed this time. During our visit, my uncle mocked me by presenting me with a worthless 1K Lebanese Livres while Richard and Shawn looked on laughing. I accepted it because I thought having a piece of foreign money was cool.

At one point, I learned that my uncle purchased all of the other properties in my grandfather's inheritance from all of his other brothers and sisters. My uncle now owned all of these connected properties except for my father's parcel, which was supposed to be the best out of the entire lot. I soon learned our parcel was no longer more valuable than the other parcels, either. I then learned my uncle wasn't interested in purchasing our parcel.

. . .

During my last phone conversation with my uncle, I remember he was furious because he found out Shawn was trying to have the property in Lebanon independently appraised. My uncle began ranting that we were somehow trying to pull one over on him and alluded back to 1972, when my father, Shawn, and he had had a falling out. He vowed that he wasn't going to allow that to happen again. I was seven years old in 1972 and was oblivious to anything that transpired between my brother, father, and uncle. I was indifferent to the fate of an inheritance I may never see because it was in a foreign country. I was more concerned with the fact I wasn't able to get any of my business concepts off the ground. The money God had promised me was not materializing. Someone out there was ignoring God.

Not to be outdone by my father's side of the family, after my mother passed away in 2010, I was informed by Shawn that there was a potential inheritance from my mother's side of the family. Shawn informed me that my cousin, one of my mom's favorite nephews (and who was the inspiration for me to enter the real estate industry), was told many years ago by my aunt, my mom's sister, to look into property belonging to my grandfather, their father, in Lebanon. My cousin investigated as asked but kept the findings to himself until after both my aunt and mother passed away, denying both aunts their inheritance. Shawn explained that my cousin felt it would be better to divide the property among all the cousins.

My grandfather on my mother's side, whom I was named after, was dedicated to the church and to the Lebanese community. He helped many people in his lifetime, and his daughter—my mother—died poor, having been denied her rightful inheritance. Two inheritances, two different sides of the family, affluent family members, the Maronite Church, and all kinds of less-than-righteous behaviors, actions, and manipulation, are the legacy of my parent's death. I already pledged to God that I would never fight over money or property ever again in my life. I was focused on God's plan then, and I'm focused on God's plan now.

A Clear Conscience

One day, I was having lunch with a close friend from college whom I hadn't seen in years. I held this person in high esteem because she introduced me to the Sacramento Entrepreneurship Academy. During the course of our lunch, she informed me that she had divorced her husband because, among other things, he was involved with illicit drugs. The details of her tale reminded me of my own experiences with Shawn, and at times I felt compelled to share my personal experiences I'd had with him.

As our conversation continued, I became suspicious. The similarities in our stories were uncanny. I had once met her husband, and I couldn't imagine him being involved in the drug trade. He was just as responsible as she was, just as civic-minded, and, as I remember, a very hard worker. What she was sharing with me didn't make sense. I felt as if I were being set up, and she was trying to prod the details of my past out of me. I never revealed my history to her. If she wanted to know the details of my past, all she would have had to do was ask and not dance around the subject.

Sometime later, I'm having a phone conversation with my best friend from Napa, Brad, and coincidently our discussion is directed toward my past involvement with Shawn's illicit dealings. The difference this time is that Brad had met Shawn, he knew Shawn had gone to jail, and he had witnessed me working my ass off trying to legitimatize the cutlery business and take care of Shawn's wife, child, and our mother. He also witnessed how my family sabotaged my efforts and tried to destroy me. In addition, Brad and all of my other Napa Valley acquaintances witnessed my true character—who I really was—as I attempted to start my new life, free from Shawn's influence.

In the entire time that I knew Brad, he never once inquired about my past or about my life before Napa. When he asked about my level of involvement with my brother's illicit drug dealing, I provided the same narrative I've shared in this story. I then asked Brad, based on our relationship and time spent together, if at any time he thought I had ever misrepresented myself or if I ever gave the impression of being someone who would choose to be a drug dealer or be involved in anything illegal. His reply to all of my inquirers was a resounding, "No!" When I walked away from my brother's lie, I left behind a lifestyle that was not my choice. It was a lifestyle I wanted nothing to do with, and it was only by the grace of God I escaped unscathed.

Over the next few years, I was inundated with innuendos about telling the truth. These references would come up in conversations with acquaintances and managers. I began getting a complex as I tried to figure out to what the person may be alluding. Were they insinuating that I wasn't being truthful in some manner? I was never provided with a specific example. I abhor liars and deceitful people and try to avoid them whenever possible.

To be accused of being less than truthful without directly confronting me is a perfect way to torment someone like myself that overthinks every situation. I go into self-analysis and start to second-guess myself. Did I lie about something? Who did I lie to? Was I aware I was lying? What was the context of my lie? I can go on and on with the self-analysis. What I do know is that I'm one of the most honest people you'll ever meet on this planet, and it's because of my honesty

Heroes Wanted

I'm easy to take advantage of. I'm not perfect, nor do I claim to be, but I'm certainly not a habitual liar.

During my in-depth self-analysis of all the times I was less than truthful, I could only come up with two references that had anything to do with my past and drugs. During my freshman year at Sacramento State University, I was applying for a scholarship, and there was a question on the scholarship application about whether or not I had ever dealt drugs. Without even blinking, I responded with a "no." What a weird question to ask on a scholarship application.

The only other time I was asked about my involvement with Shawn's illicit activities was in 1995. I was at the zenith of my spiritual relationship with God. I was attending Napa Valley College, I was succeeding academically, and I was laying the foundation for a successful future. My father had passed away three days earlier, and I found myself standing before my father's brothers and sisters, being interrogated about past activities with Shawn. Specifically, I was asked about my involvement with Shawn's illicit activities.

My father's side of the family was highly religious, conservative, and dedicated to serving the Maronite church. I was standing before people with a high moral character who have looked down upon my father, mother, brothers, sisters, and me since I was a child. I thought about when I was 18 years old and how my cousin disparaged me by lying that I was selling drugs with my brother. As I stood before the high council, all I could think about was how Lebanese culture and family pressure forced me to go to work for my brother Shawn, who tricked me into a lifestyle I wanted nothing to do with. I did my best to get Shawn off drugs and focus his efforts on our legitimate business. I had reached out to God every day for help and protection. I had beaten the devil, started a new life, encountered God in the Utah desert, was attending college, and was laying down the foundation for a bright future. Yet, here I was, standing in front of the high council of morality that was looking for a yes or no answer.

I couldn't help but wonder what they were going to use my answer for. I knew right off the bat that any information gleaned from this interrogation would not inspire them to look further into the war on drugs. I knew they weren't interested in fighting the injustice taking place under the guise of the war on drugs. I knew they weren't interested in starting drug rehabilitation facilities to help addicts recover. I knew they wouldn't use my answer to honor God and make this a better world.

Their only reason for asking me such a question during this time of spiritual and personal growth in my life was to satisfy their own egos, belittle me, make me feel lesser, and ignore all of the great things God was doing in my life. The depth of shallowness of these righteous Christians, to so willingly discredit everything I was currently experiencing, and was working for so that they could impugn my character, was unacceptable to me. I do not answer to the high morality council of the Maroun family. They are not my judge, nor is the Maronite church. I answer to God alone.

It was my life, my experiences, and my story to tell, and I would tell it on my terms. I wasn't about to let them hijack my narrative in order to condemn me. The intimate details of my life are to be shared if and when I want to share them, not dictated by the high morality council of the Maroun family. My experiences living under my brother's lie were between God and me. God used my experiences to open my eyes to the enormous injustices taking place in the drug war. God had absolved me of any wrongdoings I had committed and was partnering with me to make this a better world. Within seconds of the high counsel of moral authority asking me about my involvement with Shawn's illicit activities, I replied that I had nothing to do with them and that in the six years I worked for him, I was focused on his legitimate business. As you've previously read, my answer wasn't far from the truth. If I had been actively involved in Shawn's drug distribution business, I would have been sitting in a jail cell beside him.

I went through hell freeing myself from my brother's tentacles. When I started my new life, I never looked back. He conned me into a life I never would have chosen for myself. I licked my wounds and moved on with my life. Even now, some 30 years later, I cannot express how painful it was for me to have to recall all of the shit my family put me through. I didn't get away with anything, and God made sure I walked away from that period in my life with nothing, so He could meet me in the Utah desert and build me back up into His champion.

Trashing My Relationship with God

As my post-collegiate career faltered, I eventually began to blame God. After all, hadn't He promised me that money would be there when I graduated? There was no cash. There were no strategic partners, and there weren't any God-inspired businesses I could launch without significant resources. Why wasn't I getting ahead? Why was I stuck? Why couldn't I launch any of my business concepts, and why was everyone bugging me to attend church?

I became livid. Nothing I did was improving my situation. On the one hand, I had my faith in God and God's plan, but success kept eluding me. It was as if I were being purposely held back. I started to believe that God was sabotaging my life and letting me down.

Outwardly I appeared angry and hateful toward God. Whenever someone suggested I attend church or even mentioned God, I would reply with a few choice words as I began to rebel. I felt God had betrayed me. He had blessed me with incredible visions of what could be and various business concepts. He had made promises to me that He didn't keep. I no longer wanted Him in my life; I wanted nothing more to do with Him. I was rebelling against those who kept suggesting my lot in life would improve if I attended church.

During this dark period in my life, which began around 2006, I began to disassociate myself from God. I'd spent my entire life contemplating things like the difference between good and evil and doing what was right vs. what you could get away with. I believed in making this a better world. I believed in being fair and honest. I cared about injustices being perpetrated against the populace. I cared about tragic events and the plight of victims that had nothing to do with me. I was focused on launching businesses that empowered people and made this a better world.

When God met me out in the Utah desert in 1993, we planned my future, which entailed success after success. I was going to be unstoppable. At no time during any of my communication with God was any of the bullshit I was currently experiencing ever mentioned. My frustrations grew as I observed those who don't care about God or care about doing good in this world were thriving. Those who were doing evil were prospering. I cared, while they didn't, and they prospered. I no longer wanted to have the emotions, feelings, and focus I always carried around with me every day. I no longer wanted to care, and purposely began to sever my connection with the Holy Spirit. I wanted to be like everyone else and live a life where God wasn't in my life every day. In this, I largely succeeded. God honored my wish to cease communications between us, and it would be a very long time before I had an encounter with the Holy Spirit again.

In reality, as angry and frustrated with God as I may have been, I could never bring myself to give up on God entirely. I could not comprehend why my life was so miserable and why I couldn't realize the visions God had bestowed upon me. I was resentful at suggestions that I was being tested like Job or that I needed to attend church. The church was adamant about controlling my experiences with God, dictating the terms of my relationship with God, and since I had a personal relationship with God, I didn't see a need to kowtow to church doctrine.

So was God really testing my muster? My muster was previously tested when I went to work for my drug-dealing brother. Satan had already won Shawn's soul, and he was eager to bag mine as well. With God's help, I defeated Satan. It was ludicrous to insinuate God was somehow testing my muster once again, especially since I was at the stage in my relationship with God where a technology empire was to be built. God provided me with the visions needed to build a technology empire, not further test my resolve to serve Him. I was frustrated, confused, and angry, and I directed my anger toward God for my plight. We had a solid relationship, and now He was absent from my life, and our relationship was dormant. God would not come back into my life again until March 29th, 2015, when out of nowhere, he intervened on my behalf and stopped me from taking my own life. Had it not been for God, Satan would have been triumphant, and this story would never have been told.

A Collusion of Coincidences

I believe one of the greatest tragedies that resulted from the squandering of my life was preventing me from being able to bring Debate-Me.com to fruition. It would have been the first social media platform to market that would have allowed the masses to interact with the mainstream media. DebateMe.com would have promoted open, honest debate about our society's challenges. Rational thinking, identifying fallacies, finding common ground, and working together would have been a few of the cornerstones of the DebateMe.com platform.

Politicians, government leaders, corporate leaders, public figures, high school teachers, students, and the general public would have had access to a platform to debate any and all topics and issues. Debate-Me.com would have been a clearinghouse for identifying the best solutions to any problem or challenge.

Absent from the DebateMe.com platform would have been character attacks and fake news. Given today's toxic political environment and dishonest media, I believe it wasn't by accident that DebateMe.com was shunned. It doesn't seem like honest debate or truth is very popular in today's social media-obsessed world.

As the years go by, I've been forced to witness variants of my other original business concepts come to market. CNN's Heroes, and Amazon's new series about everyday people who are making an impact, are similar to the websites I wanted to launch back in the late 1990s that would recognize and honor those individuals who, without fanfare, would go about their daily business of making this a better world. Another concept I pushed for back in the 1990s was to celebrate America and what made America great. Fox News has several new shows dedicated to these same concepts. We now have Truth Social, and Elon Musk, playing the guardians of free speech and debate, which I would have started back in 2002 with DebateMe.com.

Having the incredible gifts and talents God had bestowed upon me purposely squandered has been nothing short of living in a nightmare. To say that I've been beaten down would be an understatement. My ability to trust others or have faith in starting a business has been completely destroyed. I went from having a spirit of entrepreneurship to a spirit of defeat. I've been robbed of my dreams, drive, purpose, and confidence. I'll never have the satisfaction of looking back on my life and recounting feelings of success that comes from starting a successful business, setting and achieving milestones, overcoming challenges, turning my dreams into reality, and creating the lifestyle of which I've always dreamed. My lifetime achievement will be defined as having my ass handed to me.

Compounding the pain of having my life squandered is being denied the ability to be a good provider for my wife. Unfortunately, my wife came along for the forced poverty ride that had been imposed upon me. Like me, my wife is far from perfect. Our relationship has not been flawless, but my wife has a spectacular heart and is a great human being. I pledged to God that I would take care of her by making sure she is always safe and will always have a home. In 2019 we separated, but I couldn't bring myself to file for a divorce. Today we remain separated, but we get along better now than ever.

Another major point of hurt in my life is the loss of my friends from the Napa Valley. I met some spectacular people there. Some I remember, and some I don't, but I'll always be grateful for the hospitality, friendships, and acquaintances I cultivated while living in the Napa Valley. I found sanctuary in Napa, and I created meaningful friendships with people who loved me, and I, them. Somewhere along the lines, our relationship was poisoned. I lost contact with people who inspired me, lifted me up, and assisted me on my journey through life. I never got to thank them properly for their generosity and love.

Another group of friends that I lost was my high school classmates. I attended my 30th annual class reunion, my first one, and had a blast reconnecting with old classmates. I visited Half Moon Bay and Montara and checked out my old haunts. I even looked up one of my father's friends. The entire experience was overshadowed by the feeling that everyone was holding back, as if there was a secret everyone was in on except for me. It was sad, especially with my father's friend. I wanted to engage in conversations and memories about my father, but he seemed aloof.

I went from everything was going my way to everything working against me. I'm a huge believer in signs from God. I also believe in coincidences. Unfortunately, there have been a statistically improbable number of coincidences taking place in my life that have put me on the losing end of the stick. Satan and his minions have effectively squandered my life, neutralized me, isolated me, and made me irrelevant.

I'll never get to be a technology billionaire, I won't be that powerful billionaire that drives humanity to evolve, and I won't get to be the guy that changes the world. While God has provided me with everything that I prayed for, I've been prevented from fulfilling the commitments I made to God. In light of my persecution, God has graciously absolved me of my obligations to Him. He is well aware that I'm a faithful servant, and I strive to make this a better world every day. When I depart this world, I will take great comfort in knowing that my destiny remains unchanged. I'll be taking my place among God's most trusted and battle-tested Angels.

Part Two
The Evils of This World

Chapter 14
Abominations To God

Desensitization

We see the sensational news headlines. A child has gone missing, only to be found dead days, weeks, months, or even years later. The details fit an all-too-common narrative. She was abducted, raped, tortured, and then murdered. These once taboo, horrific crimes have become commonplace to the point that society has become desensitized. The days of these terrible crimes sparking mass outrage, public outcry, demands for accountability, and even mob justice are remnants from a bygone era. The desensitization of these horrible crimes, along with society's apathy, has allowed evil to thrive unabated.

For its part, the mainstream media does a fantastic job of sensationalizing these horrible crimes yet sanitizes the details to make the story more palatable to a broader audience. Consider the definition of the words rape and murder. Rape basically means unlawful sexual intercourse without the victim's consent. Murder is defined as the intentional and unlawful killing of another human being. We hear about a young woman who was forced into non-consensual sex and then she was murdered. Yes, the story is unsettling, but we have bills to pay, shopping to do, kids to pick up, and jobs to get to. We have other, more important things to do with our time and focus. Without much effort, our brains have been tricked into diluting and processing a horrific crime into a sanitized, impersonal experience.

We're further desensitized about these horrific crimes because we live in a civilized society. We have placed our trust in numerous government agencies that are supposed to protect us from monsters and bring the perpetrators of these horrible crimes to justice. Between our dependence on government, our hectic lifestyles, and the media feeds we choose to follow, we mindlessly go about our daily business, following the daily narrative that's been provided to us without question.

Other than saying a brief prayer for the victim, and the victim's family, as well as taking a moment to be grateful that God is looking out for our family members, we just don't have the time or motivation to give serious consideration to the plight of victims of abuse, rape, and murder. We've placed the horrible crime in God's hands, and we're now free to continue on with our everyday activities.

The Screams of Children

For me, there's nothing benign, unoffensive, or desensitized when I read about a predator that has abducted, raped, and murdered a little girl. I get incredibly emotional. I don't get to skim over the details. My train of thought doesn't just process the term "little girl." Instead, when I hear the term "little girl," I imagine an innocent child full of life, wonder, happiness, playfulness, curiosity, adventure, and mesmerized by the incredible world around her. I can see her smile and hear her laughter, and if I were to look into her eyes, I'd see the miracle of God's creation looking back at me.

As I learn more about the demise of this innocent child, I vicariously explore what that child must have experienced. Starting with the terror of being abducted and yanked away from the safety of her parents to being terrified, crying as she is tied up and blindfolded by a stranger. I can hear her whimpers, her cries, and her pleas for help from God, her mommy, her daddy, her favorite superhero, while she's being savaged by a monster intent on sexual gratification. I'm horrified at the thought of what could be going through her mind as she's lying there helpless while her entire world has been upended, and she experiences wave after wave of pain and terror.

Her screams for help go unanswered. No one has come to her rescue. Having satisfied his sexual desires, her captor, her rapist, now becomes her executioner as he slowly begins to choke the life out of this defenseless little child. I see this little girl as she struggles to breathe and lashes out with her hands, feet, and body as her soul is violently forced out of her body. The last remaining hours of this little girl's life were spent in pain, suffering, and abandonment. My heart sinks, and I'm reduced to tears, knowing that no one was there for that little girl in her time of need. For me, what I've just described is outrageous, completely unacceptable ... and preventable.

The above thoughts were very close to what I went through when I first read about Girl X back in 1993. I'm plagued by these same types of thoughts when I hear about other vicious crimes against innocent human beings. Take a moment and Google Jessica Chambers[2] . Nineteen-year-old Jessica Chambers, who had ambitions of becoming a nurse, was doused with a flammable liquid and set ablaze. Jessica was discovered emerging from the woods near her burning car, wearing only her underwear. Over 93% of Jessica's body was burned. A first responder described how she found her with her outstretched arms saying, "Help me, help me." The first responder went on to describe how her hair was fried like it had been stuck in a light socket. Her face was black, and her body was severely burned. She died hours later at a Memphis hospital.

Look up Brittanee Drexel[3]. Without her mother's permission, Brittanee Drexel, 17 years old, attends spring break and goes missing. Seven years later, a witness claims that Brittanee was held at a stash house, where she was being sexually assaulted by several people. The witness further claimed that when Brittanee tried to escape, she was pistol-whipped and dragged back inside the house. The witness then states he heard two gunshots and was later told Brittanee was fed to alligators. In 2022 Brittanee Drexel's tragic case was solved[3a]. The previous stories regarding her demise were debunked.

Do a search for Gabriel Fernandez[4], an 8-year-old boy who died from repeated beatings, torture, and starvation. According to court records, the boy was habitually shot with a BB gun and forced to eat cat feces and sleep while gagged and bound inside a small cabinet. Gabriel also had his teeth knocked out with a bat, in addition to suffering a fractured skull, broken ribs, and burns across his body.

Check out baby Jazmine Robin[5] who was born prematurely at 29 weeks, stabilized and cared for by the hospital, and released healthy to her parents, only to be readmitted to the hospital two weeks later with 96 fractures, multiple broken ribs, and a skull fracture. This defenseless little bundle of life was beaten to death. No one was there to protect her.

Look up 5-year-old Lizzy Shelley[6], who was raped, sodomized, and murdered by her 21-year-old uncle. The thought of a fully grown adult male engaging in sexual intercourse with a five-year-old child enrages me. The excruciating pain, suffering, and terror that poor little girl endured just so her depraved uncle could satisfy his sexual urges. This little girl was betrayed by someone who was supposed to love and protect her and those in power who could have prevented this horrific crime from ever taking place.

All these innocent souls were reunited with God in a horrible way. Every day, God is forced to listen to the screams of the innocent, like Jessica Chambers, Brittanee Drexel, little Gabriel Fernandez, Jazmine Robin, Lizzy Shelley, and countless others.

The Selective Counting of Sins

Pornography, abortion, drug abuse, homosexuality, gambling, alcohol consumption, lust, pre-marital sex, prostitution, and tobacco use are all vices the church deems offensive to God, and are therefore, sins. With the blessings of the church, self-appointed guardians of moral righteousness take it upon themselves to identify, isolate, and ensure that individuals engaging in any of these non-church-sanctioned behaviors are made aware that they are sinners, and unless they repent, Hell will be their soul's eternal destiny. Sinners are encouraged to repent and embrace a "clean living" lifestyle, as defined by the church. Those embracing church teachings and doctrine will be rewarded for their efforts and welcomed into the flock. However, those who continue to sin shall be shunned because those lacking in moral character are not welcome in the house of God.

. . .

What I find absolutely amazing is that God created the universe from nothing in under seven days. Creating an entire universe within seven days is an incredible display of power, sophistication, and know-how, but when it comes to communicating the difference between right from wrong to humanity, apparently, God is flummoxed and is somehow dependent upon the church to inform us of the difference between right and wrong.

Even more amazing to me is the church's selective focus on sins. While dedicated to persecuting sinners engaged in any of the sins listed above, the voice of the Body of Christ is mysteriously lacking, or outright silent, with regard to the abuse, rape, and murder of children, preventing violent crimes, discouraging the exploitation of fellow human beings, and emphasizing doing what's right over what you can get away with. Incredulously, those who are genuinely evil and actively working to destroy humanity are left unmolested by the church, while the rest of us garden-variety sinners are ostracized and persecuted with zeal.

I never felt the need to condemn or vilify others because they were engaged in behaviors I disagreed with or were labeled as sins, as defined in the Bible. I remember back in the 1980s when televangelists were all the rage. Thanks to my mother, I'd catch bits and pieces of their broadcasts. At the time, televangelists, one after another, were demonizing homosexuals. The vitriol spewing from these supposed men of God was quite upsetting. Apparently, the entire decline of Western Civilization was being driven by homosexuals.

. . .

After listening to a couple of the televangelists, I was almost convinced that I, too, should hate and condemn homosexuals, but before I jumped to any conclusions, I asked for God's advice. God responded by telling me that it was none of my business what two consenting adults did in the privacy of their own homes. It was not my place to judge, and it should not be a concern of mine. God reiterated that if anyone had a relationship with Him and their behaviors were offensive to Him; then God would communicate His will to them through the Holy Spirit.

God has shown me that the church is obsessed with using sin to control the masses. The church's obsession with selective sin has denied countless millions of people from coming to know God or believe in His existence at all. As a result, humanity suffers because the church chooses to condemn and persecute rather than inspire, encourage, and guide people to a relationship with God.

My heart sinks, thinking about the prostitute that has just spent the night having sex with over 40 men, is in pain and despair, and turns to drugs to numb her existence. Pity the poor spouse that is being physically and mentally abused but believes it's her fault and has nowhere to turn. Pity the young teenage girl who is naive, confused, and is easily manipulated into dancing on stage naked in order to pay her rent. Pity those addicted to drugs who aren't aware they need help, or worse yet, cannot free themselves from the scourge of drug addiction. All of these poor souls are in need, and all are unaware of an incredible source of strength, power, and love that they can tap into from within that will help them defeat evil and reclaim control of their lives and their souls.

Actions of The Righteous

I'll never forget the story about a pastor walking through a mall and shouting out that Santa Claus was fake, but Jesus was real, in front of a line of children and horrified parents waiting to visit Santa Claus. Visiting Santa Claus and experiencing the joys and wonders of the Christmas season are family traditions, not part of some diabolical conspiracy to end the world. Apparently, for the righteous among us, there's no better way to display their love and dedication to Jesus than traumatizing young children in front of their parents by screaming that Santa isn't real, but Jesus is. In all of their wisdom, these righteous Christians have decided to take it upon themselves to purge the world of these ungodly traditions and behaviors.

Mention the words Christian or Jesus to a member of the Gay & Lesbian community, and more than likely, you will receive a skeptical, if not hostile, response. The Gay & Lesbian community has fought an endless battle against Christian persecution. Here is a group of people that want to be able to love whomever they choose freely, be in relationships with whomever they choose, and marry whomever they choose, without being admonished, persecuted, or told they're sinners that are going to burn in hell for all of eternity. Apparently, the righteous among us have no issue with blindly persecuting, and alienating the gay and lesbian community, because their Bible tells them it's their duty.

Not to be outdone, the anti-abortion, righteous Christians among us, will passionately harass, intimidate, shame, and persecute women seeking abortions. With tears streaming down their faces, these religious zealots will block access to abortion clinics and proclaim to the world that a fetus is an actual baby that needs to be protected. Yet these same righteous Christians are absent in tears, protests, and actions when a child already born into this world has been abused, raped, and murdered.

In an earlier chapter, I described an incident where my cousin, whom I really didn't have a relationship with, admonished me for my role in a single-car crash. My wife and I were almost killed. It was only by the grace of God that we both came out of the accident alive, and with minimal injuries. Yet, in the House of God, my righteous cousin felt the need to admonish me.

When my righteous cousin admonished me that day, was she going to bat for Jesus? Was my righteous cousin full of the Spirit? Was my righteous cousin winning one for the Lord? I believe the answer to all of these questions is a resounding 'yes.' On that particular day, with the blessings of her church, I believe my cousin felt morally superior, was on a mission for the Lord, was unstoppable, and felt that it was her duty to God, and to me, to condemn me and put a lowly sinner like myself in my place.

What astonishes me is that, when it comes to pimps and sex trafficking, where is my righteous cousin's voice? Why isn't my righteous cousin confronting pimps in the street by informing them that they're going to hell for exploiting other human beings? When it comes to preventable violent crimes, where is my righteous cousin's voice? When it comes to the abuse, rape, and murder of children, where is my righteous cousin's voice? When it comes to the injustices taking place in the war on drugs, where is my righteous cousin's voice? Why isn't my righteous cousin confronting our political leaders for the lack of legislation that prevents violent crimes, stops the abuse, rape, and murder of children, and humanely deals with drug addiction?

. . .

Isn't this amazing? There appears to be a pattern emerging here. There's a host of sins that the righteous among us are quick to condemn. Anything from Santa Claus, homosexuality, the consumption of coffee, tobacco, liquor, gambling, pornography, and prostitution, can bring on the ire of the church and lead to condemnation. The righteous among us are ready to confront and pounce on the hapless, non-violent, meek, docile, defenseless, minding-our-own-business sinners at the drop of a sin. Incredibly, the abuse, rape, and murder of children are not worthy of the church's attention. Allowing preventable violent crimes to continue unabated doesn't cause concern among the righteous. Purposely manipulating and profiting off of other people's misery is a non-issue. Purposely pitting people against each other, using identity politics to divide, and engaging in corruption, and a host of other nefarious activities that are leading to the destruction of humanity do not fall under the purview of the church nor the righteous among us. The voices of the righteous are silent when it comes to confronting those who are in power, are truly evil, and are intent on destroying humanity. One has to wonder if there are any passages in the Bible that specifically direct Christians to persecute the meek and ignore those who are truly evil.

Mindless Drones

Sometime during 2020, I had an interesting conversation with a young woman, discussing the challenges facing our country, and at one point, I felt we had enough in common that I revealed to her that I was on a quest to finish writing my first book. As soon as I revealed that the book was about my personal relationship with God, she told me she was a Christian.

. . .

From that moment on, I found myself listening to a mindless, babbling Christian, regurgitating pre-programmed Christian doctrine without any ability to process independent thought. For the next several minutes, I was inundated with how wonderful Jesus was and how I needed to attend this wonderful church she discovered. At first, I tried to get a word in by explaining to her what my book was about, only to have her hijack the conversation and emphatically inform me that it was Jesus's job to save the world. I couldn't get a word in, and I eventually realized any efforts on my part to engage this woman in meaningful dialogue outside of her Christian programming would be a waste of time.

In hopes of being rid of her and her incessant babbling as quickly as possible, I stood in silence for several minutes, nodding my head in agreement. There wasn't even any variety in her message, just that both Jesus and her church were wonderful. For me, the biggest problem when interacting with mindless Christians spewing out their indoctrinated beliefs is the actual absurdity of their beliefs and values. For example, when this Christian woman hijacked the conversation and spouted off about how Jesus saved the world and how much she loved Him, and How much He loved her, absent from her repertoire was any description of what she was doing to make a difference in this world.

What exactly was she doing on a daily basis to honor Jesus, other than shooting her mouth off about how wonderful He is? The abuse, rape, and murder of children, the failure to prevent preventable violent crimes, and the purposeful exploitation of other human beings are all a mockery of God's plan and what Jesus stood for. While this woman was on autopilot boasting about how wonderful Jesus was, I couldn't help but wonder what has the Body of Christ really done to honor God's blessings. My encounter with this Christian woman opened my eyes to the futility of trying to have a meaningful discussion about God and Jesus with the righteous among us if the topic doesn't jive with their religious indoctrination.

Living A Blessed Life

My wife and I spent several months saving to buy a replacement vehicle for her. We finally found a car that was in our price range, advertised as running fine, in "good" condition, with no mechanical issues. We drove over an hour to purchase the vehicle. While my wife and her son test-drove the car, I was having a conversation with the young car owner. He was telling me about his vehicle detailing business and how well he takes care of his customers by always doing an outstanding job for them. He was telling me about his wife and children. He was quite a remarkable young man.

While I shared with him some of the details of my life and our automotive challenges, he started interjecting terms into our conversation about being blessed and living a blessed life. I know from past experiences that if a Christian has to tell you they're Christian, then they're probably up to no good. However, the car was very clean, looked to be in excellent condition, and it was the car we wanted. Besides, the seller's children and wife were running around us, and his mother was sitting on the porch. The guy came across as a standup guy, a straight shooter. I chose to ignore that little alarm going off in my gut, and when my wife and her son returned from their short little ride with no complaints, we purchased the vehicle.

Within 30 minutes of driving the vehicle home, the temperature gauge went to hot. I immediately knew that we had just purchased a Subaru with a blown head gasket. As we waited for towing service, my wife found a crumpled-up bill of sale from a couple of days earlier as well as a receipt for Bars Leak, a chemical that is used to temporarily fix blown head gaskets. Amazingly, when I called the seller—a Christian living a "blessed" life—he didn't know anything about the purchase of Bar's Leaks, stated that the car was running fine, and didn't know what was happening. He explained that there was no way he could take the vehicle back either.

Fortunately for my wife and myself, I had already budgeted money to replace the timing belt on this high-mileage vehicle to ensure my wife would get years of additional use out of the vehicle. Having to do the head gasket would be an added expense, but would be manageable because we were able to both save enough money to cover the repair. My wife was devastated, but I reassured her it would be okay. Fortunately for us, we had discovered an excellent auto repair facility.

I just can't help to reflect upon the young man living the blessed life that purposely sold us a piece of junk. There he was, shooting his mouth off about being blessed, hinting at how much he loves Jesus, hinting at his Christian faith, and all the time he was getting ready to screw over my wife and me. I was using a similar product to Bars Leak to keep my wife's previous Subaru with a blown head gasket running, but at no time did my wife or I ever consider trying to sell the vehicle without disclosing its mechanical deficiencies.

Since I have a personal relationship with God, I can't fathom purposely screwing over another human being, as this Christian living a blessed life did to my wife and me. It was wrong on so many levels, but in his Christian mind, his actions were justified. I can't even imagine at what level this kid believes Jesus is telling him it's okay to pass his problems on to others and that it's okay to screw over other people. The church has a lot to account for.

Root Cause

How do you prevent child abuse, rape, murder, violent crimes, forced prostitution, theft, racism, homelessness, and every other ill that affects society? For most of my life, I've pondered these types of questions, and then God opened my eyes. History shows us from the beginning of time, those in power have used the concept of law enforcement to control and govern society. Rules are made, and if broken, there are consequences.

Over millennia, law enforcement concepts have evolved to dominate every aspect of society. Unfortunately, this is not the result of misguided efforts but rather a purposeful and deliberate attempt to control the masses. Those in power want to remain in power, and unfortunately, they are willing to do so, no matter the cost to humanity. As a result, we have numerous government institutions that control and regulate our lives and perpetuate their existence by solving nothing and placing the blame on others. In partnership with the government are entire industries that profit and flourish from the manipulation, pain, and suffering of other human beings. Civilization is deluged with unjust laws that profit the unscrupulous few at the expense of the many.

Today, those in power are not only experts at dividing society and controlling the masses, but they're operating freely, with little to no fear of the consequences of their actions. In the United States of America, we have gone from doing what is right to doing what we can get away with. Decorum has been replaced by barbarism. As a society, we have been purposely and effectively divided on just about every issue one can imagine. Citizens are no longer being encouraged to respect those with differing opinions and seek common ground. Instead, those we disagree with are to be labeled and ostracized from society altogether. Those who wish to control the masses have successfully distracted the American people from the actual causes plaguing society. It's always someone else's fault.

The common theme that has prevented the elimination of the myriad of societal ills, is humanity's failure to evolve. We have all of the world's knowledge at our fingertips, yet we constantly fail to produce better human beings. As a society, we have failed to value human life, we have failed to advance human development, we have failed at creating better human relationships, and we have failed to create and maintain government institutions that are dedicated to evolving humanity.

Unfortunately, we are governed by those willing to do or say anything to attain power, wealth, fame, and relevance. Satan and his minions are having a field day as they run amok, with no one daring to stand up against them meaningfully. Restricting the evolution of humanity while purposely allowing the destruction of civilization and allowing evil to flourish are all abominations to God.

Those in power doing evil, or who give evil a pass, will discover on their day of judgment that their allegiance with Satan was short-sighted. Their power, prestige, and wealth are limited to the span of a lifetime. The souls of those doing Satan's bidding will pay the price for their partnership with Satan throughout all of eternity.

The Church Owns It!

There is no greater advocate for prayer than the church. Christians are conditioned to pray, place their problems in God's hands, or take comfort in knowing it was God's will. If you're one of those Christians who have prayed that God would allow us to live in a world where children aren't abused, raped, and murdered, or where violent crimes are non-existent, what were your expectations?

Did you believe that one day, God would use a laser beam and vaporize all the evil predators lurking among us? Did you think one day, God would make an appearance Himself, and destroy evil, while the Body of Christ sits on its ass and does nothing? Did you just hope you would wake up one day and all the evil in the world would be gone?

For those of you who have prayed for God's intervention for all of the evil taking place in this world, know that God has heard your prayers, and God did take action. God partnered with me because I didn't place these horrible crimes in God's hands. I didn't ask God to fix it for me. Instead, I pledged to God that I would use the skills, talents, and gifts that He bestowed upon me to honor Him and, at last, put a stop to all of these terrible injustices and crimes.

I pledged to God that I would be a man of action, and with His blessings, I would be the driving force behind humanity's evolution. God was answering your prayers by taking me up on my offers. I was in a partnership with God, but apparently, the righteous among us were counting my sins—sins I wasn't even aware of—and because of my relationship with God and my unwillingness to compromise my principles, morals, or values, my life has been squandered, and I've been made irrelevant.

Human evolution has been shackled, and humanity is paying a heavy toll, while the Body of Christ is content with sitting on its ass, counting the petty sins of the meek while allowing evil to thrive unbounded. Church doctrine would have us believe the church is God's authorized representative here on earth, but claiming that the abuse, rape, and murder of children is somehow God's will is a complete fallacy. Claiming that God somehow used victims of violent crimes to provide valuable lessons for the rest of us is a complete fallacy. Claiming that a victim of any type of crime was in the wrong place at the wrong time is a cop-out. A helpless little girl that has been savagely raped and murdered wasn't in the wrong place at the wrong time. A helpless little girl that has been savagely raped and murdered wasn't put here on this earth to serve a greater purpose in our spiritual journeys, and a helpless little girl that was savagely raped and murdered wasn't being called home to God early because He missed her!

God does not idly sit back when senseless acts of violence take place. God weeps in disbelief as our spiritual leaders misdirect the faithful into believing God was somehow asleep at the wheel. Humanity has been gifted with free will. As a civilization, we make choices, we create the laws, and it is by our decisions and actions that allow evil to either flourish or be eradicated.

The church's lust for power, control, and relevance has empowered false disciples, who, in their quest to be deemed holy, righteous, and pious, feel emboldened to promulgate hate, promote division, attack others, and judge others while securing for themselves a false sense of security, that because they are members of a church, they are superior to others, and are free to screw over anyone they want.

There is no greater self-deception, and nothing could be further from the truth. No matter how blissful it feels to sing along with the worship team and praise Jesus, it doesn't mean you have a relationship with God or belong to some type of special, holier-than-thou class of people. Just because you attend church and adhere to ancient rituals, beliefs, and values doesn't signify you are abiding by God's will, have established a relationship with God, or are going to Heaven when you depart this world.

The church's quest for power, control, and relevance is an abomination to God. The creation of institutions that thrive off of the pain, misery, and suffering of others is an abomination to God. Not preventing preventable crimes is an abomination to God. Comforting those who have spent a lifetime purposely manipulating and exploiting other human beings by telling them that God forgives them is an abomination to God.

The church fails God on a daily basis while providing cover for those engaged in evil. Those who serve the church look the other way when a child is abused, raped, and murdered. Those who serve the church are not interested in preventing preventable violent crimes, and those who serve the church are not interested in stopping others from purposely manipulating and exploiting other human beings. While I attend church rarely, I've never attended a mass or a worship ceremony where those in power that do evil, or look the other way, are informed that the destination of their souls is hell. I've never seen those perpetuating evil being chastised and condemned by other members of their congregations.

On Judgement Day, how do church leaders plan to justify to God the church's apathy toward those who are in power and doing evil but are willing to denounce and persecute the meek? How are those humble servants of the Lord that lead the church going to explain to God their actions at persecuting and harassing women seeking an abortion and condemning homosexuals at the top of their voices, yet do not confront pimps, sex traffickers, drug dealers, gang members, and those in power who do evil? How do the leaders of the church plan on justifying to God scarring little children for life, screaming there is no Santa Claus, yet the same voices of the righteous are silent in front of those who purposely manipulate and take advantage of others?

There is no greater culprit for allowing evil to flourish in this world than the priests, pastors, shepherds, or whatever you call your spiritual leaders. In order to remain relevant and in control, the church spews hatred, division, and misrepresents God. With the blessings of the church, the righteous among us freely persecute the meek, docile, and defenseless while giving actual evil-doers a pass. The days of "Forgive them, Lord, for they know not what they do" are long gone. Allowing evil to thrive unchallenged is anything but Godly or forgivable. It's an abomination to God.

Chapter 15
Sins

Judgement

When I was just a child, the church instilled in me the importance of being good and abstaining from sin. I took these messages to heart. What I didn't learn, because I wasn't indoctrinated into church teachings, is how nasty the church can be toward sinners. The church loves to talk about how much Jesus loves everyone and will spew statements like, " Hate the sin, love the sinner," but experience has shown the church uses sin to divide and attack those that fail to fully embrace the church.

I have personally met religious folks, some who were friends, that have never had a drink, never used drugs, never smoked, rarely cursed and lived good, clean lives. I was always impressed with their behavior, self-control, and adherence to the teachings of their church. I was also envious of them for not having to battle addiction, contend with sin, or be generally looked down upon. These good Christians were living a clean and holy life.

. . .

In contrast, I consume alcohol on occasion, I've been addicted to a couple of different drugs, I have used several other drugs, I curse on a regular basis, and I enjoy porn every now and then. In addition, I love making people laugh, and I'm not afraid to use taboo or inappropriate humor to do so. I've overcome a cocaine addiction, a tobacco addiction, and an opiate addiction (Vicodin).

In terms of addiction, I'd say tobacco was the worst of the three and the hardest to quit. Vicodin was a very close second. I have used alcohol and marijuana infrequently and was never addicted to either of these drugs. It was during my Vicodin addiction that I consumed wine on a regular basis. I then had to use marijuana to rid myself of my Vicodin addiction.

I think it's fantastic that there are people out there who have no reference, understanding, or tolerance for drug abuse or other so-called sins in their lives. It's great that these individuals have never had to combat addiction or other self-destructive behaviors. That being said, living a life in the absence of drugs or any other type of addiction doesn't make you a better human being or superior to others. Your upbringing and environment guided you in the right direction, and you're blessed to have avoided addiction. Some of us weren't quite so fortunate.

It's not Man's place to pass judgment on the self-destructive behaviors of others or on those engaging in what the church describes as sin. If the righteous among us had a true relationship with God, they'd know the best way to counter vice (or any other activity deemed a sin by the church) would be to put their trust in God. By doing so, they would focus their efforts on encouraging others to establish a relationship with God.

When people have a relationship with God and seek Him out in times of trouble, God will guide them. God will open their eyes and provide them with a way to leave their sin behind them so they can grow and become better human beings. Condemnation, and threats of an eternity in hell, help no one other than satisfy the egos of the righteous among us.

I know with all of my heart that most of those being persecuted by the church rebel against God along with any hint or thought about God's existence. I know this because I've experienced it myself. I see other groups that are the scorn of the righteous among us, and I see how adamant they are in disavowing God's existence. Unfortunately, millions of people in need of God's love and grace are denied because of the church's need to justify its existence by controlling access to God. Profiting from the perpetuation of others 'misery, or trying to dictate the terms of what a relationship with God looks like, is an abomination to God.

My Cursing

I can curse with the best of them. When triggered—which quite frankly, doesn't take much after years and years of torment and abject poverty—I can blurt out a string of expletives that are second to none. My go-to phrase includes Jesus and God, intermixed with a series of expletives followed up by my disbelief with what just occurred that triggered me. Often, I'll find myself repeating this phrase several times per incident, depending on my stress level, current financial condition, lack of sleep, the severity of the situation, and other mental and physical factors.

. . .

My inclusion of Jesus, God, or any other noun in my cursing chain is hollow and has nothing to do with me being angry, hating, or blaming God or Jesus for my lot in life. I learned the hard way, many years ago, that bad luck, misfortune, failure, and persecution in this world have nothing to do with God or Jesus and everything to do with the righteous among us, attempting to enforce church doctrine on others. As a result, I purposely choose to use these words in a way we're not supposed to use them to offend the righteous among us that are counting my sins.

My frequent outbreak of expletives is not without rhyme or reason. For all of the Bible-reading, God-fearing Christians out there, here's a little paradox for you. By the very definition of the commandment, "You shall not take the name of the Lord your God in vain," no one should use God's name in a disrespectful way. As I've disclosed, my use of God, Jesus or any other noun in my cursing is hollow. I'm not blaming God or Jesus when I use these words. God knows this, and if God were offended, He would have certainly said something to me by now, especially as I dedicate an entire section to this subject.

Contrast my hollow chain of expletives to how you Christians gather in your churches, raise your hands to the heavens, praise Jesus with all your heart, and then go out and purposely screw people over the very next day. Doesn't that show a complete disrespect for God and Jesus? How about when the righteous among us are selectively counting the sins of others while doing nothing to stop the preventable abuse, rape, and murder of children, all the while praising Jesus. Isn't that being disrespectful to God and Jesus? How about when the Body of Christ sits on its ass and does nothing about preventable violent crimes, drug overdoses, and the numerous injustices occurring each day and gathers on Sunday to praise God and Jesus? Isn't that being disrespectful to God and Jesus?

Interesting, isn't it? I'm the one who curses, yet by their actions, the righteous sin counters among us are the ones using the Lord's name in vain. I hope that they remember this paradox every time they purposely screw over another human being and then gather in their places of worship to sing songs about how much they love both God and Jesus.

The Sex Industry

Prostitution is illegal in the United States of America, with the exception of Nevada. From a Christian standpoint, prostitution and working as a strip club dancer are both sins and are frowned upon. In some instances, if their identities are known to the church, the prostitute or strip club dancer will be prohibited from attending church or church events until they renounce their sins, repent, and embrace a clean life. I've even heard stories about the innocent children of a prostitute or strip club dancer being banned from Christian events.

There are two reasons for entering into prostitution or becoming a strip club dancer. They were either coerced, or if voluntary, were driven by a lack of viable income-generating alternatives. Bills have to be paid. Regardless of the reason, both prostitutes and strip club dancers are stigmatized. For the prostitute, irrespective if her actions are coerced or voluntary, there's the threat of arrest, trial, conviction, jail time, probation, criminal records, attorney fees, court fees, fines, and all of the mental anguish that comes with having your freedom threatened by the criminal justice system.

. . .

242

For the righteous among us, the prostitute has made a bad decision, a poor lifestyle decision, and deserves her lot. She is a sinner, broke the law, and deserves imprisonment. Maybe in prison, she'll find Jesus and salvation. For someone like me, who has a relationship with God, I know this type of thinking is ludicrous.

First of all, other human beings are profiting and earning paychecks off the misery of a prostitute. These individuals and the industries that generate profits from the prostitute's misery do not attempt to eliminate the need for the prostitute to ply her wares but instead perpetuate the conditions that force someone into prostitution to begin with.

If prostitution were legalized, significant taxpayer resources could be reinvested into creating a society where human beings were financially sufficient and would have no need to engage in a life of prostitution. Furthermore, those who still wished to participate in prostitution, freely and without coercion, could do so safely. Regulations could be established to ensure the safety of the prostitute and her customers. There is no downside to creating a society where profiting from the empowerment of humanity is acceptable and the norm.

If the church and the righteous among us weren't so closed-minded, judgmental, and all-knowing, they could participate in outreach programs that encourage people to establish relationships with God. Anything is possible through God, and both God and Jesus are capable of changing lives that are in need and want a better future. Unfortunately, the righteous among us only know God through church teachings and the Bible, both crafted by the hand of Man.

. . .

The biggest sin regarding prostitution and strip club dancers is the Body of Christ's arrogance, apathy, and refusal to do what's right. It's much easier to label someone a sinner and walk away rather than tackle the societal structures that force a human being to sell themselves sexually to survive. God weeps for those forced into the sex trafficking business. The exploitation and persecution of prostitutes and strip club dancers are an abomination to God!

Drug Addiction

I have witnessed firsthand the evils of drug addiction. I've experienced what it feels like not to have control, and to be a slave to drug cravings, that control every aspect of your life. I've witnessed, with my own eyes, how society preys on addicts and the downtrodden. For the righteous among us, who have never suffered from addiction and need to justify their apathy toward the plight of drug addiction, it's an easy out and the height of hypocrisy to condemn addicts by claiming they deserve their fate because they made poor lifestyle decisions.

Like prostitution, drug addicts have to face the threat of persecution by the criminal justice system. There's the threat of arrest, trial, conviction, jail time, probation, criminal records, attorney fees, court fees, fines, and all of the mental anguish that comes with being run through the criminal justice system. In addition, drug addicts have to contend with purchasing drugs. Are they functioning addicts, or do they have to resort to committing additional crimes to pay for their addiction?

There are ways to prevent drug addiction. There are ways to treat drug addiction, there are ways to profit and earn a paycheck from helping drug addicts, and there are ways to eradicate drug addiction without having to dilute the Constitution of The United States. I was able to overcome my addictions by the grace of God. I reached out to Jesus during my times of addiction, and I prayed to God. On God's time, I was healed and saved from addiction. God has opened my eyes to the plight of drug addicts.

Simply writing off other human beings because they've made a mistake and then profiting from their misery and suffering is an abomination to God. Satan thrives off people's ignorance of addiction, tunnel vision, and lack of empathy and compassion. As human beings, we must do better. We must be better. We must evolve humanity. It's imperative that the righteous among us, and their churches, get out of God's way. Otherwise, there's going to be hell to pay come judgment day.

Abortion

For the longest time, I was always pro-choice. I always believed in a woman's right to choose what happens to her body, and for the longest time, I bought into the argument that the fetus was just a bunch of cells and it wasn't really a baby or alive until birth. My position supporting a woman's choice was further augmented when I'd watch all of those pro-life agitators standing on street corners, blocking access to abortion clinics, and shouting at the top of their lungs how everyone involved with abortions was going to hell.

One day, I found myself watching a documentary on the development of fetuses, and during the course of that program, my eyes were opened. A fetus was much more than a clump of cells. It was an actual human being in development. It was a baby. To this day, I have no idea how I ended up watching that documentary, but I do know that without fanfare, without the righteous among us screaming at the top of their lungs that we're all going to hell, God was able to touch my heart and change my mind. Ever since I watched that documentary, it has been my belief that abortion is terminating the life of a baby that is developing inside of a woman's body.

While I disagree with having an abortion, I still believe in a woman's right to choose what she does with her own body. I'm not privy to what's happening in that woman's life. It's not my place to judge. It's not my decision to make. Most importantly, it's none of my business. I do know this, though: if the righteous among us would get out of the way, and allow God to do His work unfettered, then if a woman contemplating an abortion were to reach out to God freely, of her own will, God would provide her with invaluable counsel. Her decision would be between herself and God. Based on my personal experiences with God, I have complete confidence that if women contemplating abortion were free from harassment and persecution and were encouraged to reach out to God, the number of abortions would significantly decline.

For the righteous among us that claim it is our responsibility to prevent murder, then get up off of your asses and start protecting the babies that have made it into this world. Ensure that the babies alive today are receiving the love, care, and nurturing environment to allow them to grow up into healthy human beings. Focus your attention on the abuse, rape, and murder of children already here. Do your part to evolve humanity and get out of God's way.

We can each have our own personal relationship with God. At any time, we can seek Him out for guidance and direction. Imagine if we created a world where all children were welcome, and a woman seeking an abortion felt comfortable and at ease with her options of bringing a child into this world. With God, anything is possible, especially if we open our minds and hearts to His will and stop hindering His work.

Pornography

I'm not going to lie. When your daughters, of legal age, walk around in public with tight Spandex leggings or yoga pants that leave nothing to the imagination, I'm in heaven. I love beautiful women, and I especially love looking at provocatively dressed women. The Internet is flooded with images and videos of your scantily clad or provocatively dressed daughters doing everyday mundane tasks, or something fun, or even a TikTok challenge. One thing that can be counted on is their choice of clothing, bedroom eyes, and provocative looks.

I'd never viewed TikTok videos until a few months ago when YouTube started embedding TikTok videos into my feed. The videos your daughters are posting, or are participating in, are not designed to highlight their intelligence, critical thinking skills, or what a great mother or wife they would make. Instead, most of the videos being posted articulate your daughter's natural beauty in suggestive clothing and positions that purposely arouse men.

The Internet is also a rich source of pornography. There's an abundance of smut available for every sexual appetite. I've viewed my fair share of pornography. I've seen pictures of beautiful women, naked, partially dressed, and scantily clad, that are breathtaking and make me glad to be a man. Pornography has enabled me to vicariously experience having sex with women I'd have no chance with. I have no problem looking at your daughter's ass, naked pictures or videos.

. . .

Heroes Wanted

When your daughter decides to go out in public half naked or wears sexually seductive clothing, or post pictures of herself or videos of herself that are sexual, I don't believe it's a sin to ogle her, watch her sexualized content, or desire to have sex with her. There's only been a couple of instances in my life when God told me it was wrong to look at pornography. That being said, I don't care how beautiful your daughter is, I don't care how provocatively dressed she is, and I don't care how much sexual desire she instills in me. I know using deceit or trickery to get her into bed is a sin.

Lying to your daughter, making false promises, manipulating your daughter, or pressuring her into sex are all sins. Your daughter is a human being, and she should always be treated with respect, despite the way she dresses or flaunts her sexuality. The real problem with pornography, and your daughter's running around either half-naked or exposing her private parts for all to see, is that, as a society, we have failed to establish healthy dating practices. Most boys are not taught to respect girls, to treat them with respect, or to honor them as human beings. Girls are just as confused as boys. Madison Avenue and social media have done a tremendous job of confusing young women and men.

Interestingly, while writing this section, I had to research the difference between Spandex pants and yoga pants. All the advertisements in the search results showed only women wearing Spandex Leggings or yoga pants, and all the images focused on women's asses. If Spandex Leggings or yoga pants are so comfortable, why are they not being promoted to men? I didn't see any photos of men in Spandex Leggings or yoga pants. In addition, if these clothing lines are for working out, why are there no marketing photos of women working out in poses that are not focused on their asses?

. . .

In regard to my watching pornography pictures or videos, as I mentioned, there have only been a couple of occasions in my life when God has told me it was wrong. Back in the late 1990s, when the Internet was taking off, porn was ubiquitous. A couple of friends sent me some humorous porn videos. The first few times I saw them, I thought they were disturbing ... but hilarious. I wondered what would motivate a woman to film herself in such bizarre acts. Once I realized these poor women were being exploited, I deleted my copies and informed my friends never to send me such material again. Exploiting another human being is never acceptable to God.

If a woman voluntarily chooses to enter the porn industry of her own free will, then that decision is between the woman and God. The righteous among us would be better off spending their time creating a society that generates enough income for its members so women don't have to resort to posting naked pictures and videos of themselves on the Internet for all to see. The righteous among us would also be wise to ensure that all boys and girls grow up understanding what a healthy relationship between the sexes looks like. Once again, the righteous among us must get out of God's way.

For The Record

Throughout this book, it may be observed that my experiences in life have caused me to adopt a decriminalization approach to certain crimes that are also considered sins. For example, I do believe illegal drugs should be made legal. Part of having liberty and being free is the ability to make decisions for one's self, even if those decisions are poor choices.

By legalizing drugs, we can free up significant financial resources and redirect those financial resources toward drug abuse prevention and treatment. Drug abuse prevention entails education and the sharing of knowledge, through which we can develop better human beings. Then we will have begun the process of evolving humanity. Education and the sharing of knowledge will ensure children will instinctively avoid poor decisions like experimenting with drugs or, at a minimum, recognizing addiction and being informed of the various ways to overcome it.

By no means am I advocating for defunding the police or allowing drug addicts to shoot up in public, be homeless, or destroy neighborhoods. People must be responsible for their actions. If drug users are unable to care for themselves, provide for themselves, or have to commit crimes to support their drug habits, well then, that's when law enforcement needs to step in, with harsh consequences.

I feel the same way about pornography, strip clubs, and prostitution. Paid sex between consenting adults should not be criminalized. However, exploiting, coercing, manipulating, pressuring, or drugging someone to force them to have sex, or into prostitution, or dance naked in a strip club, or post nude pictures or videos of themselves online, should be harshly dealt with by law enforcement.

We must embrace crime prevention strategies over law enforcement, but we must keep law enforcement options in our back pockets as a harsh response to those wishing to profit off of the suffering, misery, and exploitation of others. We can, and we must do better! Humanity has to evolve if it is to survive. It is possible to create a better world, but we must first get out of God's way.

Chapter 16
Faith

Got Jesus

Have you been saved? When did you give yourself over to the Lord? Got Jesus? Those questions are asked by the truly righteous who live among us, are well-versed in scripture, are right with the Lord, and are filled with the Holy Spirit. The truly righteous among us bless the rest of us with their presence, dedication, and commitment to the Lord as they differentiate themselves from the rest of us, who are going to hell.

In the past, I've been dogged by questions like, "When were you saved?" or "When did you give yourself over to the Lord?" I've never really known how to answer these questions. Whenever I think of someone being saved, I think of Jimmy Swaggart's epic performance on national television back in the 1980s. With tears running down his face, he declares, "I have sinned." For me, his performance was overly dramatic and very ingenious. In my entire life, I've never been able to recall an "I have sinned" moment like that.

. . .

So whenever I attempted to attend places of worship, and I was asked this one simple question that separates the sinners from the righteous, I'd be dumbfounded. I've always had a relationship with God and Jesus since childhood, and there was no singular experience in my life that I could recall that was significant enough for me to claim that I had been saved. I figured maybe I was saved when God met me out in the desert. I just wasn't sure. I was equally perplexed when it was hinted that I come forward and be saved. Again, I've had a relationship with God and Jesus all of my life. Why would I need to be saved if I already had a relationship with God, who has counseled and guided me throughout my entire life?

As I write this story and reflect upon my past and the visions for the world God has bestowed upon me, I'm disheartened at the state of the world today. It is nothing like the visions God has bestowed upon me. The world we live in today is filled with people desperately compromising their values and trading their souls, so they can be a part of the "in" crowd, achieve success, accumulate wealth, or have their 15 minutes of fame. These were the exact characteristics of the superficial world I begged God to protect me from back in 1986 when, from the floor of my mother's apartment in Napa, I prayed to God and Jesus.

As previously mentioned, for several months, I weaned myself off a cocaine addiction, and all I did was eat, sleep, cry, and pray. I prayed every day for God to guide me, protect me from evil, and never allow me to compromise my integrity again. I wanted to live a productive life, a life full of abundance and contribution, without ever having to sell out or compromise my values. I wanted to live a life of serving

God by making this a better world. Most importantly, I begged God to shield me from the evil permeating our society.

I now know, without a doubt, that my recovery in Napa in 1986 was a defining moment in my spiritual journey. For the righteous among us, I would argue that this was a time when I gave myself over to the Lord and was saved. I never saw it as being "saved." I had just been through a really intense time in my life, my eyes had been opened to the overwhelming forces of evil running rampant throughout our world, and I did the only thing I knew I could do to shield myself from such evil. I reached out to God and Jesus.

My tears and pleas for help from God and Jesus weren't public, nor were they made while on my knees at the front of a church sanctuary. I wasn't gathering with the faithful at the local church, holding hands with everyone else, and singing about how much I loved Jesus. I wasn't running around in public praising Jesus, nor was I running around shouting out that I was a sinner or calling out the sins of others. I didn't seek out the counsel of a priest or pastor, nor did I confess to one that I was a sinner in need of their help. I went straight to the source, the head honcho, the CEO. From the floor of my mother's apartment, where I slept and recovered from drug addiction, I reached out to God, and God responded. I've always had a relationship with God and when I was saved, apparently, I didn't even know it.

I've always believed in the Father, the Son, and the Holy Spirit. I believe Jesus is the Son of God and that Jesus died for our sins. Throughout this book, you'll notice that in my time of need, I've always reached out to or communed with God. There are only a few times when I've reached out to Jesus. I was taught God was the creator of the universe, God was all around us, God was watching and listening, God wanted us to do good, and not sin, and God wanted a relationship with us. I learned in Bible study that Jesus was the Son of God and that Jesus preached about love and forgiveness, healed people, performed miracles, and died on the cross for our sins.

I've reached out to Jesus in times of addiction, illness, and when I physically needed to be healed. There have been numerous times in my life when I've meditated on a symptom that is ailing me and have prayed, in Jesus's name, for this ailment to be removed from my body. Jesus was a healer. Like my incredible experiences with God, I've had phenomenal results by reaching out to Jesus in prayer when I needed to be healed.

Around Easter 2023, I encountered an acquaintance I hadn't seen in years. We were standing in a grocery store parking lot, catching up on each other's lives, and I shared how I was finishing up on my book about my life and my incredible relationship with God. We had a great, positive conversation. Many of the comments my acquaintance made validated my experiences with God and gave me hope that there are people out there who want to serve God and do what is right.

At one point, our conversation turned to Jesus, and my friend asked if I believed that Jesus had risen from the dead. I replied absolutely, and then explained at one point during my spiritual journey, being opened minded and analytical, I sometimes had doubts about whether or not Jesus had been resurrected from the dead, especially when grilled by the righteous among us. After all, some believe that Jesus was just a man with a great message for the world. I could see their point of view. I could understand their skepticism. So when the righteous among us pressed me on this question, having my doubts, I took it up with God in prayer.

God confirmed for me that, yes, Jesus was resurrected from the dead. God's answer was good enough for me. I shared this with my acquaintance and then reiterated that I absolutely believed Jesus was resurrected from the dead because not only had God told me so but because of my own interactions and experiences with God. God has done some pretty amazing things for me in my life. Jesus was sent here to save the world. The messages Jesus provided to the world and the purpose of His life were significant enough to warrant Jesus being resurrected from the dead to confirm Jesus's divinity.

I explained to my acquaintance that the only people concerned about when and where I was saved are the righteous among us, trying to validate their Christian faith. It's never been important to me. God has never brought it up to me, and Jesus has certainly never mentioned it. The only ones keeping score are the religiously indoctrinated guardians of the Christian Faith.

Interpretation of Faith

I'm ignorant when it comes to differentiating between Catholics, Christians, or any other denomination that follows Jesus Christ's teachings. Based on my memories, my family attended Catholic church while I was growing up. At the same time, I remember being told that Catholics are Christians. I'm sure there are very specific distinctions between the two, and for members of those church communities, the distinctions are very important, but not for me.

. . .

Heroes Wanted

My faith is rooted in my own experiences in developing a personal relationship with God over time. A personal relationship that was developed through prayers, communing with God out in nature, and actively seeking out God. My interactions with God have all been private, in isolation, and between God and me. Whether it was in my bedroom, in my car, on my mother's bedroom floor, sitting on the side of a cliff, or staring at the mountains or stars, I was always by myself. It was just God and me, and I could access Him 24/7.

As a result of not being influenced by church doctrine, I've associated the religious meaning, or definition of having faith, as believing in God, Jesus, and the Holy Spirit. My faith has allowed me to have an incredible relationship with God, Jesus, and the Holy Spirit. It wasn't until I recently read about a pastor renouncing Christianity, that I fully realized what the religious definition of faith meant to Christians. I was unaware that church doctrine dictated that faith meant having to belong to a church, believe the Bible without question, adhere to church teachings, obey your spiritual leaders, tithe, attend church on a regular basis, confess your sins to the church, and avoid the sins of smoking, alcohol consumption, gambling, and cursing.

In contrast, my experiences and my incredible relationship with God have had nothing to do with any of these church-defined prerequisites for a relationship with God. For example, I believe there are true historical stories in the Bible that depict actual interactions with God. I believe God has interacted with humanity since the beginning of time and continues to do so today, just as I've experienced my interactions of my own. In fact, I believe my experiences with God actually validate parts of the Bible. At the same time, I can't help but believe that interspersed among the true stories in the Bible, there are others that were either hijacked, manipulated, or created by Man, in order to assert control over humanity.

. . .

I believe that sharing our personal experiences with God helps all of us to have a better understanding of God and shows how God can help us through our life journey. While I crave interactions with other spiritual people, I'm averse to people who can't think for themselves, only know God through church teachings, and can only define their relationship with God by regurgitating the church's teachings or conveying what they've read in the Bible.

Based on my observations, I'd say the church is obsessed with recruiting members to expand the church. I believe the church uses sin to create division and control the masses, and I believe in order to remain relevant and in power, the church is adamant about controlling access to God. Based on my experiences, the church is not interested in helping people develop a pure, unbiased relationship with God, free from church dependence.

To illustrate my ignorance of Christian rituals or beliefs, here is a statement I've never comprehended or fully understood—"God-fearing man." Why would anyone fear God other than those dedicated to doing evil and destroying humanity? God is the source of all life. By establishing a relationship with God, we can tap into strength and courage, allowing us to overcome any obstacles placed before us. It doesn't mean we'll come out unscathed, but we will persevere, and we can accomplish great things. God is energy. God is power. God is a restorer of spirit, and, most importantly, God is pure love. What is there to fear about that?

My Faith

I've heard and read stories about particular churches and religions that will initially be friendly toward people that do not practice their version of faith but will eventually ostracize those same people if they fail to join said church or practice said religion. I'm horrified at the thought that I may have been subjected to economic deprivation and the squandering of my life, with the idea that by being forced into poverty, I was somehow going to find God and have my plight in life improved by attending a particular church or practicing a specific religion.

For someone like me who has a relationship with God, the thought of having to coerce someone into believing the same things as you believe in or coerce someone into adhering to your own brand of dogma is incomprehensible. I mean, think about it. If you have to pressure people to go along with your beliefs, values, and morals, be deceptive, or are unwilling to tolerate the viewpoints of others, then you're doing the work of Satan, not God. Unadulterated, God sells Himself.

I know God's not looking for the holiest, pious, or most righteous among us. I know God's not looking for the person who can bake the most cookies for the church or who can recite the most scripture. At no point in my life has God ever instructed me or given me a sign that I need to attend church or belong to organized religion. I've lived a life in stark contrast to the righteous among us. I'm not committed to a specific church, I don't buy into any particular church doctrine, I don't feel obligated to abide by ancient church rituals, and you certainly won't find me raising my hands towards Heaven praising Jesus in one breath, and then condemning hapless sinners in the next.

I know, based on my experiences, that God doesn't care who attends church.

My faith, my willingness to believe, my desire to want to do good in this world, and the fact that I have sought out God throughout most of my life without the church's teachings, have allowed me to form an incredible relationship with Him. I believe God has purposely kept me away from religious indoctrination so that He could cultivate a personal relationship with me, free from the self-serving narratives being peddled by the church.

Our world is in turmoil. Our government and spiritual leaders have lost their moral compass, forgotten their obligations to humanity, and as a result, the world is in desperate need of those willing to make a stand against evil. When God opened my eyes to the depth of corruption, cronyism, and various economies profiting from human suffering and misery, I didn't pray and pass it along to God. Instead, I told God that I believed in His ability to work through me to accomplish the impossible. Each time God opened my eyes to injustices taking place, I pledged to use the skills and talents God had blessed me with to honor him and to address these abominations. God responded.

While the church seeks to control access to God, I've found that God is readily available to anyone willing to seek Him out in earnest. I believe God wants all of us to share our spiritual experiences with Him with one another. Sharing allows us to validate our experiences, as well as encourage others to seek out a relationship with God. He is accessible to anyone willing to reach out to Him. Anyone who seeks out God can establish a relationship with Him.

. . .

I cannot pretend to know how God operates. All I can do is share the details of my life and my experiences with God and encourage everyone else to seek out their own personal relationship with God. God is a powerful source of strength, inspiration, guidance, and love. Pray to God, talk to God, and commune with God. You may be surprised, like I was, to one day find out God was listening and guiding you along all of the time. All it takes is faith and a willingness to believe. Open your eyes, ears, and heart, and if you go looking for God, you'll find Him. I know all of this to be true because I lived it.

Finally, I'm here to serve God, not the church. As far as I'm concerned, the church is irrelevant and a hindrance to establishing a relationship with God, and if my values, beliefs, and relationship with God do not qualify me to identify as a Christian, well, then so be it. It's the Body of Christ's loss, not mine.

The Myth of Forgiveness

I've mentioned that I believe the Bible includes factual experiences with God, and interspersed between these true stories are stories interjected by Man to control the populace. The church will have us believe that we are to forgive unconditionally and must forgive as many times as needed to heal relationships. According to the Bible, Jesus said to forgive seventy times seven.

In life, we may trespass against someone, or someone may trespass against us. Trespasses made through ignorance or as an honest or misguided mistake should be forgiven. It is essential that we learn from our mistakes and move on. Furthermore, there will be instances in our lives where someone we love trespasses against us numerous times. In order to preserve our relationship with this person, we'll have to forgive them numerous times. That's part of growing, learning, and being in a relationship. At some point, the person being trespassed against will have to make a personal decision as to whether to continue forgiving or move on. The circumstances are unique to all individuals.

Yet it would be ludicrous to claim that those who purposely perpetuate the pain, suffering, misery, and exploitation of others so that they may profit should be forgiven. To claim that those who do what they can get away with, instead of doing what's right at the expense of humanity, should be forgiven is equally ludicrous. Allowing Satan to prosper at the expense of society or spending a lifetime destroying the lives of others will not be forgiven by God. The church is being deceptive to claim otherwise.

Based on my relationship with God, in a world where humanity is constantly evolving, our need to seek or offer forgiveness will be minimal. Human beings will have learned how to honor and respect one another. Living in a world without the need to forgive or seek forgiveness aligns with God's visions for the world. Living in a world where you have to forgive willy-nilly cheapens the intent and meaning of forgiveness and is indicative of a world that allows Satan to thrive.

Throughout the years, I've been told to forgive my family. Whenever I've asked what I should be forgiving my family for, I'd never receive a specific answer. Instead, I'd be encouraged to forgive without knowing why. Knowing how cunning the righteous among us can be, I'm pretty sure they believe they have something on me that requires them to be pious and forgiving of me. In holding with church doctrine, I must first demonstrate forgiveness toward others before I can be forgiven, just like the Bible tells us.

. . .

Heroes Wanted

In terms of my family wanting me to forgive them, we're way past the stage of forgiveness. My family has participated in the conspiracy against me and would have been equally responsible for my death had God not personally intervened on my behalf. My life has been purposely squandered; I've been deliberately forced into poverty, and every single dream I've had has been destroyed. I'm not forgiving anyone for that. I couldn't even imagine what a conversation with family members would sound like. "Hey, remember the time you guys undermined me, deceived me, forced me into poverty, and destroyed all of my dreams? Those were good times, weren't they?" Yeah, that dog doesn't hunt.

I'm hopeful that once this book is finished, it will prove to be a catharsis of sorts—the horrible way my family has treated me will fade from memory, and I'll be able to move on in peace, basking in prosperity. In terms of me owing them an apology or asking them for forgiveness, I don't provide generic, perfunctory apologies or ask for forgiveness unless I know what my trespass is and the circumstances surrounding it. I certainly won't be apologizing for manufactured trespasses against me.

I mentioned that when God met me out in the Utah desert back in 1993, He instructed me to forgive my family, and I did. When I eagerly returned from my trip around the country, I embraced my family. I wanted to share with them all of the things God had shared with me. I wanted them to be there with me when I became financially successful. I wanted my brothers and sister, nieces and nephews, never to be looked down upon again by the Maroun family. At no time since 1993 has God instructed me to forgive my family. In fact, if God is communicating anything to me about my family, the message is to stay away from them. They are toxic, and God doesn't forgive those who intentionally squander the lives of others.

. . .

A tragedy occurred between my family and me. God had provided me with innovative visions for technology-based businesses that would have been first to market and very successful. All I needed was someone to partner with, either financially, strategically or both. Had my family rallied around me, I'd have billions under my control at this very moment, and we'd be living in a much different world. I'd be using my wealth and political clout to advocate for the evolution of humanity. The church has led my family astray and has provided my family members with a false sense of righteousness and security. There are consequences for thwarting God's plan, and God will not be forgiving.

Chapter 17
Consequences

Revelation

It boggles my mind when I think back to the early 2000s and how the entire world was looking for ways to monetize the Internet while I was running around with a treasure map given to me by God but somehow managed to come up empty. Those who conspired against me thought nothing about discarding my life, dreams, and ambitions, as they callously destroyed my life.

While I've spent countless years speculating as to why I was manipulated, laughed at, persecuted, and forced into poverty, I've never really identified a motive for my life being purposely squandered. As evidenced in this book, I've speculated on a few possibilities, but the reality of the situation is that I just don't know, and I've learned the hard way that trying to figure it out is a lesson in futility. However, while writing this book, God has made it clear to me that the squandering of my life boiled down to four words: greed, jealousy, envy, and revenge.

. . .

Greed

During the mid-1990s, the Internet was the new gold rush. Entrepreneurs were staking their claims and becoming millionaires overnight. The grandiose business models God bestowed upon me were industry disruptive, innovative, and visionary. In most instances, my business concepts would have enjoyed a first-to-market advantage. I was looking at rapid wealth creation that would have easily exceeded amounts some have toiled their entire lives acquiring.

I can only speculate that there are those among the conspirators against me that were intimidated by my plans and were in fear that my quick, extreme accumulation of significant wealth would diminish their importance and the value of their wealth, as well as undermine their lifetime efforts at building wealth. In their minds, it wouldn't be right for an upstart like me to generate wealth beyond their own personal fortunes and outshine their life's work.

Jealousy

I had spent five and a half months traveling around the country on a motorcycle and claimed to have encountered God in the Utah desert. I returned to Napa and immediately began a quest to earn a college degree. During this quest, I began having innovative visions for new, technology-based businesses that were years ahead of their time. Who was I to claim contact with God out in the Utah desert without church indoctrination, church attendance, or specific church affiliation? Who was I to claim a special relationship with God without confessing my sins to the congregation, without serving the church, or without publicly telling everyone how much I loved Jesus?

. . .

For the righteous among us, especially those that read the Bible daily, can recite scripture, attend church regularly, donate their time to the church, and love Jesus more than anyone else, they know there's no way in hell my spiritual relationship with God is real, without the blessings of the church.

Envy

I had an encounter with God, and for many years I was extremely happy, content, and focused. I was on track to launch a technology-based business and be great. I was unstoppable. I had confidence in myself that was backed up by my belief and faith in God's plan. I envisioned starting a business and then bringing in a management team to run it while I would move on to the next innovative business model God had blessed me with. I would build an empire and be a tremendous force for goodness. I was going to create wealth both for myself and others.

I was going to show the world you could be good and make a fortune. I would inspire and provide hope to those who needed it the most. How dare I! Who was I to believe that I could achieve the American Dream on such a grand scale? Who did I think I was that I believed God had partnered with me and was providing me with all of these visionary business models? I needed to be put in my place.

Revenge

The survival of humanity depends on our leaders and those in power making moral decisions that are fair and beneficial to all. When I've experienced or observed an injustice taking place, I've been known to speak out because I strongly believe those in power or positions of leadership should be held accountable for their actions, inactions, or outright incompetence. Unfortunately, rather than seek to improve or do the right thing, there are those in power who will retaliate.

I once criticized the DMV's inability to process a mail-in registration without losing an attached proof of insurance card. For the next several years, my included attached proof of insurance card was always lost. It was only when I could register online did I receive any relief.

I was highly critical of my experiences at CSU Sacramento because there were far too many incompetent professors on the payroll that had no business being in front of a classroom. I've always been outspoken against the War on Drugs, and I've been critical of the government in general—especially of those in power who refuse to do what's right because they're not being held accountable. Standing up to tyranny and those who do evil has consequences.

Finally, I have my own family. During my last conversations with my uncle and Shawn, both gave me cause to believe that my plight might be tied to both of them being delusional. In my uncle's case, when Shawn and my father had a falling out with him, I was only seven years old at the time and lived on the other side of the country. Yet he threw this event in my face when he found out Shawn was trying to have our property appraised in Lebanon. Maybe he only feigned forgiveness toward my family over the years, or he didn't want to see me, the son of his brother, become more successful than his life's achievements.

. . .

As for Shawn, when he was released from prison, I offered to have a sit down with him, but he refused, stating all was good. I believed there wasn't an issue, but he is cunning and a master at manipulation. In his last email correspondence with me, he gave me cause to believe that everything wasn't all good and that he was just biding his time. In either case, my conscience is clear.

I don't believe that God was trying to console me when pointing out that the squandering of my life was rooted in greed, jealousy, envy, and revenge. Instead, I believe God revealed this information to me so that I would include it in this story as a stern warning for those who have participated in the conspiracy against me. For those who conspired against me, no matter how you spin your narrative, no matter how you justify your actions, God knows the real reason for your persecution of me. You've thwarted God's plan, and God will hold all of you accountable for your actions come your day of judgment.

Economic Deprivation

I've spent a lifetime trying to better myself. I've taken to heart the experiences God has used to open my eyes. I've confessed my sins to God. I've begged God for forgiveness and guidance. I've atoned to God for my behaviors, and God has absolved me of my sins. Apparently, having a relationship with God, atoning to God, and having God absolve me of my sins are meaningless because I didn't go through the church. I've been judged, convicted, and sentenced to a life of poverty. My life has been squandered, my dreams destroyed, and I find myself irrelevant in a world that desperately needs good people like me—people who are willing to make a stand against evil.

· · ·

Compounding my frustration is the current toxic political and media environment. As I read the news and observe social media, it is evident that the purveyors of evil have done a spectacular job of dividing the masses by pitting us against one another. I rarely find dialogue that is focused on identifying common ground, building consensus and making compromises, and tolerating opposing views in order to achieve outcomes that are beneficial to everyone. Instead, the rhetoric I'm observing is toxic. No attempt is being made to identify root causes. Instead, we're being deluged with insults and the blame game.

Voice an alternative or contradictory viewpoint, and you're immediately labeled an idiot, racist, or some other derogatory adjective. Social media is filled with vitriol, and we're constantly being bombarded with fake news. Free speech is being stifled, lies are being substituted for truth, and the P.C. police have an insatiable appetite for attacking everyone and anyone that doesn't adhere to their political ideology. I can't help feeling that the visions for the world which God originally bestowed upon me may be lost forever.

There are those in power that are experts at manipulating the masses. In their quest to remain relevant, stay in power, and maintain their wealth, they will say and do anything as they seek to divide us, and there's no limit to how low they will go. Doing what you can get away with is a tool of their trade, and it doesn't matter what you do, what you say, how many lives are destroyed, or what the costs to society are, just as long as their interests are served and they retain power. My heart sinks as I put these observations to paper.

Why am I bothering? Why am I concerned with things I have no control over or are none of my business? Why should I care about all of the injustices taking place in this world? Why should I care about the abuse, rape, and murder of children? Why should I care about preventable violent crimes or if someone is being taken advantage of? If people don't care about the state of the world, then why should I try to make this a better one?

Then there's the squandering of my life. I've done nothing wrong in my life to warrant having 20 years of my life squandered. I wasn't an evil villain planning the destruction of the world. I was a force for goodness and was doing my best to make this a better world. I was pursuing the visions God had bestowed upon me. I put a smile on people's faces, I make people laugh, and I bring joy into this world. I try to inspire and empower people, and I encourage people to improve their situations. What was the point of God partnering with me, only for me to run around for more than a decade, oblivious to the fact that I was being manipulated and played for a fool?

Magnificent

God knew that if I were to embrace the teachings of the church, then I wouldn't be concerned with ending the abuse, rape, and murder of children. I wouldn't be interested in preventing violent crimes or in changing the way society deals with drug addiction, and I wouldn't care about evolving humanity. Per church teachings, these subjects are all best left to the purview of God.

Having witnessed Man's treachery since the beginning of time, God knew that there was no way I would be allowed to be successful on my own terms and in accordance with His plan. God knew that my brothers, sister, family, and other conspirators would laugh at me, undermine me, manipulate me, and conspire against me. God knew the church wouldn't allow me to claim allegiance and prosper in His name unless I yielded and submitted to church doctrine and teachings. Most importantly, God knew I wouldn't yield or compromise my relationship with Him. God knew He could depend on me to remain faithful to the commitments I made to Him.

Back in 1997, when God explained to me why He didn't intervene when a nine-year-old girl was raped, poisoned, and left for dead, I believed His short, concise response was the end of His explanation. I was wrong. God allowed me to experience the futility of trying to do good and change the world. Satan and his minions stopped me before I even began. God has been dealing with humanity's bullshit since Adam and Eve. Human beings are inherently self-serving, superficial, and evil. God is not going to fix any of this for us. Only we, as a species, can fix this mess we've created for ourselves. God's simple response to my prayers back in 1997 has taken me over a couple of decades to fully comprehend. Magnificent!

In their zeal to count my sins, sins I'm not even aware of, those who persecuted me and squandered my life have committed a calamitous error. In the squandering of my life and by making me irrelevant, the conspirators against me have prevented me from fulfilling my commitments to God. Thereby, those who have conspired against me have inadvertently thwarted God's plan. God, in His infinite wisdom, knew this would happen and already formulated an alternative plan. As we all know, God's will shall be done!

A Cryptic Message Revisited

Earlier, I shared a very powerful message I received from God when I was at Zion National Park in Utah:

"What can't you handle? You're going to be here less than 100 years. Creation has been here since the beginning of time."

When I received this message, I was engulfed in the beauty of majestic, red canyon walls that had been in the making since the beginning of time. Zion Canyon had been here before me and would be here after me. My time here would be short compared to God's creation. What perplexed me was that if you were here for all of eternity, you could accomplish quite a lot, but if you're here for less than 100 years, you don't have much time in the grand scheme of things. I concluded that God was telling me to get the lead out.

It wasn't until I was well into completing this story that I fully began to grasp the meaning of this cryptic message God had provided me with. He was reminding me that I would be here less than 100 years, and once I departed this world, I was never coming back. The world will continue without me. This message from God turns out to be a complete blessing. I have no children. I have no skin in the game. When I'm gone, the world will continue on, and what becomes of this world is of no concern of mine. I won't be in hell forced to watch my children endure unrestrained misery at the hands of Satan.

The Demise of Humanity

The wanton abandonment of morality in exchange for doing what you can get away with is a recipe for disaster and will culminate in humanity's eventual demise. There are those in power who do not strive for the betterment of humankind. There are those among us who claim to possess a superior moral character, claim to know better, and claim to be righteous, yet do nothing to elevate humanity to a higher plane.

. . .

God has blessed me with vision, especially when it comes to technology. When I originally started writing this story, with a heavy heart, I was going to warn about the advancements taking place in biomedicine, stem cell research, mapping of DNA, robotics, drone technology, artificial intelligence, weapons systems, and computer surveillance. Our political systems lack the necessary integrity, ethics, moral fortitude, and oversight necessary to ensure none of these technological advances are used for nefarious purposes. Before I could get this book published, one of my fears materialized.

The COVID-19 outbreak and its handling validate my dire warnings and concerns. COVID-19 is a deadly pathogen that originated in Wuhan, China. The prevailing sentiment is that it escaped from a laboratory, and the Communist government did a horrible job at trying to contain it and instead relied on misinformation or none at all. At the outset, the World Health Organization was found to be less than candid about what was transpiring. As a result, the virus was allowed to spread throughout the entire world.

Here in the United States of America, some of our elected officials responded to the virus by introducing a resolution that would condemn using phrases like Chinese Virus or Wuhan Virus. These terms were considered racist, xenophobic, discriminatory, and anti-Asian. Let that sink in for a moment. The entire world has been upended with this horrific virus that may have been contained if proper protocols were followed, but they weren't. People were dying, and sadly, all that our elected officials could do was introduce a resolution calling for the use of the phrases "Chinese Virus" or "Wuhan Virus" to be labeled as hate crimes and require each violation to be expeditiously investigated.

. . .

Heroes Wanted

Perhaps the biggest scandal to come from the COVID-19 pandemic was the lack of honesty between political parties, scientists, doctors, and government leaders, concerning the proper way to contain the spread of the Coronavirus. For the first time in my life, our government wasn't unified during an unprecedented emergency. Authoritative institutions changed their positions numerous times. Disinformation and rumors abounded, and there wasn't a single source of information that could be relied upon for the truth.

Before COVID-19, how many have ever heard of the research laboratory in Wuhan, China? How many other laboratories are out there in the wild that are researching pathogens that have the potential to wipe out humanity? How many of these laboratories lack the proper containment systems in case of an emergency? Unfortunately, not all governments, scientists, or political leaders will be on the same page when it comes to ensuring that proper safety protocols are in place and are being diligently followed.

Prior to COVID-19, my biggest concern was autonomous drones and robots. The country that develops the best algorithms to keep these units from being hacked, disabled, or taken out, will be the country that controls the world. A human being will eventually hesitate and question their orders. A well-programmed, autonomous drone or robot will continue with its mission as it's programmed. There won't be an option to protest, question, or even resist. Comply with the autonomous drone or robot or be terminated.

The technology exists to program thousands of drones to swarm a target or targets. These drones can be no bigger than the palm of your hand and can be configured with stabbing weapons, explosives, bullets, or even deadly pathogens. Compared to conventional weapons systems, an army of 100K drones is relatively cheap and can be easily deployed. It wouldn't be that difficult to breach another country's airspace and release swarming drones from the air. At the same time, drones could be shipped to a country legally, and a team on the ground could attach weapons payloads and activate the drones.

Artificial Intelligence (AI) is currently all the rage. Apparently, AI technology has become practical, and there are already reports of biased AI decision-making. Imagine robots and drones autonomously performing their duties with a partisan tilt. There is much talk of AI technology upending vast swaths of our economy, especially the job market. If AI is deployed to replace significant parts of the workforce, then what happens to all of that surplus labor? How will people feed themselves and their families? None of these challenges or issues are being publicly addressed—if they're being addressed at all. I'm unaware of any governing boards setting standards for what the next generation of drones and robots will be allowed or not allowed to do. As I finish writing this book, there's talk of regulating AI, but to what end, and to whose benefit?

The scenarios I'm describing for AI, robotics, and drone technology are no longer science fiction. It would be a huge fallacy to dismiss any of these scenarios because history has shown us repeatedly that Man's ability to be evil, intent on destruction, knows no bounds. Left unchecked, the eventual enslavement and destruction of humanity is a near-certainty.

It doesn't matter how affluent or influential you are. It doesn't matter how much money you have or how much you love Jesus. There will be no escaping the unchecked evil that is gradually being unleashed upon humanity. The warning signs are all around us, but we choose not to see them. We're hoping they'll go away or someone else will protect us. We are being delusional. In a world governed by doing what you can get away with instead of doing what's right, these are perilous times. Self-denial, apathy, and indifference will be the end of us all.

An Experiment

Humanity must evolve. Our leaders and our institutions must do better. We have to get away from profiting off of others' misery. We must get away from perpetuating industries that benefit from the pain and suffering of others. We must also get away from doing what we can get away with and get back to doing what is right. We must start to solve the challenges destroying humanity so we can move on to bigger and better things. The way society is governed must be re-engineered from the ground up. We need new ways to manage the masses. We must start to treat human beings like the precious gift of life that they are and not like some commodity that can be disposed of at will.

Have any of you ever stared at the stars at night and pondered the universe? Have you ever given thought to the vastness of space? Have you thought about the irony of Man's desire to colonize space and visit other worlds, that Man is not made for space travel, and other planets are not hospitable to our survival? I have, and I've concluded that the reason Man's not made to survive in space, and the reason the universe is so gigantic, is because our planet is in a containment system.

Think about it. As a species, human beings are horrible to one another. We settle our differences through violence. We're forced to spend exorbitant amounts of money on weapons systems designed to kill people as a deterrence to those who would do us harm. We steal from each other, we abuse, rape, and murder, and we profit from the misery of others.

The evolution of humanity has been hijacked by the Satan. Instead of focusing on empowering human beings and doing good in the world, society is focused on perpetuating discourse, misery, and suffering so that others may profit. Why would God want or allow our species to expand to other planets?

How about extraterrestrial life? Any alien life form with the technology to travel through space and visit Earth would possess an intelligence vastly superior to our own. Other than to invade for Earth's resources or harvest human beings, why would an alien life form want to interact with our primitive species that prefers death and destruction to dialogue, empowerment, and evolution?

I believe that if the shackles holding back humanity were removed, and humanity was allowed to thrive and conquer the challenges placed before it, then one day, in partnership with God, humanity will figure out a way to travel across the galaxy to other hospitable planets as well as terraform other planets on the way. Until then, humanity is an experiment that must be contained.

There are much better ways to govern and inspire humanity. What's lacking are the leaders with the moral fortitude to push for a paradigm shift that will transform the way society is motivated, rewarded, and governed. Humanity deserves better, and while what I'm discussing may seem unlikely, with God, anything is possible.

Part Three
Visions of What Could Be

Chapter 18
Evolving Humanity

Valuing Life

I've pondered the ills plaguing society and dared to dream of a world in which humanity evolves, human beings are empowered, crime is non-existent, and we're all working towards the betterment of humanity. Every solution I've pondered begins with the birth of a human being. Babies must be brought into a world where they are loved, nurtured, and encouraged to flourish. As babies grow into toddlers and young children, they must be provided with safe living environments where they can develop positive self-images of themselves, develop healthy self-esteem, and embrace the morals, values, and belief systems that will empower them to grow into healthy, productive, responsible adults, who value life—and our planet.

At a young age, children should be taught about respect for themselves and for others, respect for our planet, and respect for all forms of life. As children mature, they can be taught how to settle differences peacefully and encouraged to build relationships with others based on commonalities. Children can be taught to value differences of opinion, find common ground, and work with others toward common goals. Most importantly, children must be taught that violence against another human being is never acceptable, that there are severe consequences for harming another human being; and that it's more beneficial to work out differences rather than react with violence.

Artificial intelligence, which has been the holy grail of the computing world for several decades now, is currently dominating the headlines. The time of self-learning machines capable of solving the world's problems are upon us. If you think about it, babies are actually like self-learning machines. Inputs from their surroundings dictate their behavior. Growing up, babies learn how to behave and interact with other human beings from their environments. A quick look around at the world we live in today, and it's apparent that humanity has done a horrible job.

My desire to evolve humanity by focusing on raising better human beings was revealed in my two social business ideas, Human Development and Online Nutrition & Exercise Website, which I've listed below for your review.

Human Development 1997 – Current

The concept for Human Development was to create a website where new, expecting, and existing parents could find the resources and support necessary to provide their children with love, confidence, and respect for other human beings. In addition, the offerings would include courses on nourishment, exercise, healthy self-esteem development, and ways to instill a desire to learn and be better.

Online Nutrition & Exercise Website 1999

This website portal was designed to help individuals create healthy lifestyles through a process combining healthy eating, exercise, and improved self-esteem, self-image, and self-talk. The business model included matching customers with local fitness experts and nutritionists in their areas, as well as focusing on corporate clients. My concept would have been the precursor to Web MD and similar websites.

Empowering Humanity

In addition to valuing life, the scourge of identity politics, pitting one race against another, creating discord among people, profiting off of the ignorance of others, and promoting false narratives are all abominations to God and must be purged from society. Humanity must once again embrace rational thought, engage in thoughtful debate, and respect differences of opinion. Human beings must strive to understand and tolerate different viewpoints, seek to forge new relationships based on trust and respect, and learn to set aside differences of opinion in order to work together and achieve common goals that are beneficial to all of humanity.

Satan and his minions have successfully divided humanity on just about every issue challenging society. The only way Satan will be defeated and evil eradicated from our world is by human beings finding common ground and uniting in their efforts to destroy Satan and rid the world of evil. Defeating Satan begins with our leaders and institutions. Our leaders and institutions must stop doing what they can get away with and instead get back to doing what's right.

Heroes Wanted

. . .

We have numerous government and private institutions that have built entire economies and markets off the pain, suffering, and misery of human beings. We have law enforcement, prison systems, courts, drug treatment facilities, rape hotlines, homeless shelters, victim assistance programs, parole, counseling services, counselors, and many other sub-industries that profit from human misery.

As one who staunchly believes in the power of God and that anything is possible through His grace, I personally believe that if we focused on raising better human beings and we shifted our economy from law enforcement to crime prevention, we could employ the same amount of people.

Crime prevention entails knowledge, the teaching of right and wrong, instilling morals and values, and adapting beliefs that will empower and encourage human beings to grow, prosper, and treat all with respect. Instead of economies built on human suffering, we could focus on building economies that empower humanity and drive human existence to the next level. Human beings must be empowered and driven to reach their full potential. The acquisition and dissemination of knowledge is the key to such evolution.

In my quest to switch our economy from law enforcement to crime prevention, I was blessed with the concept of The Advocate. I've included a recap of the synopsis, as well as an expanded text as to what I envisioned.

The Advocate 1997 – 2002 (Precursor to DebateMe.com)

The Advocate would profile victims of rape, violent crimes, bullying, drug addiction, and prostitution. The Advocate would tell the story of the victim's life before and after the crime, with details of how the crime impacted the victim and their family. Members/subscribers would be encouraged to attend court dates and support victims in their local communities. In addition, The Advocate would publish dedicated exposés that would identify deficiencies in the criminal justice system that perpetually enable crime and encourage members/subscribers to lobby Congress for change. Other aspirations of The Advocate would be to explore issues such as gun control, the war on drugs, the death penalty, prostitution, and other controversial issues.

Key Features:

- A public, worldwide accessible database that will allow elevated members to post and read about the abuse, rape, and murder of children, violent crimes, and drug overdoses.
- The descriptions and details of the violent crimes will not be sanitized for the sensitive reader. Instead, the horrid raw details of what the victim had to endure would be collected and catalogued.
- Victim records would include information about who the person was, what they were like, their lifelong goals, ambitions, and dreams, as well as extensive details of their lives. The life of a human being was taken, and the world will be made aware of exactly who and what was lost.
- Information about how the crime impacted the lives of the victim's family, friends, co-workers, and community would also be included.

- Information about the perpetrator would be minimal and only focus on the perpetrator's criminal record: the number of times the perpetrator was arrested, the types of crimes the perpetrator was arrested for, and how much jail time the perpetrator actually served. The names of the Judge and Prosecutors would be attached to each record.
- Geographical information would be collected and include the number of violent crimes committed regionally.
- A list of all the churches within 10 miles of the crime scene would be compiled, as well as the names of the leadership teams for each of these churches.
- The names of the current Senators, Congressman, Governor, Chief of Police, Police Union leaders, and members of the District Attorney's office would also be attached to the record.
- When crimes involve children, the names of the Child Protective Services leaders and case officers responsible for protecting the child would be attached to the record.

Reports would be posted based on the following:

- Why did this horrible crime take place?
- How can we prevent these types of crimes?
- What were the common driving factors that led to this crime?
- What are we doing, as individuals, to prevent these types of crimes?
- What are we doing as a society to prevent these types of crimes?

- How can we better serve God by eliminating these types of crimes?
- What will it take for society to change to the point that we no longer tolerate these types of crimes?
- How can the Body of Christ address these abominations to God?

The Constitution of The United States of America

The Declaration of Independence and the Constitution of The United States of America were crafted by brave, intelligent men inspired and guided by the hand of God. The founders of the United States of America risked their lives to break free from a tyrannical government to secure their liberty and freedom. These brave men did the best that they could to create a new form of government that would ensure the freedom of Man.

The Constitution was designed to protect freedom, liberty, and the citizens of this country from tyranny. The founding fathers of our nation had lived under tyranny. They knew what living under unchecked power was like. They knew the injustices of tyranny. They knew what living under a government that wasn't held accountable was like. They purposely designed a system of government that was limited in power to ensure the freedom and liberty of those the government was meant to protect.

Today, our Constitution, especially the Bill of Rights, is constantly attacked by the very people the founding fathers feared. Some in government claim the Bill of Rights or specific amendments to the Bill of Rights hampers their ability to protect us. A perfect example is the war on drugs.

. . .

Heroes Wanted

For years, the government complained about how the fourth amendment has prevented the war on drugs from being won. As a result, the American people have been subjected to no-peek search warrants, asset forfeiture, and a host of other laws that dilute our fourth amendment rights. Has the dilution of our fourth amendment rights worked? Absolutely not. The war on drugs is a complete disaster. There is no end in sight, nor is there an end to the government's insatiable appetite to whittle down our constitutional rights.

Rather than solve the challenges and problems plaguing our country, the government has allowed social ills to perpetuate at the taxpayer's expense. All the while, the government blames everyone else and claims the United States Constitution is outdated and hampering the government's ability to solve problems. In reality, if, as a nation, we adhered to the Constitution of the United States, and put people in place that wanted to make this a better world, then most of society's ills would be resolved.

I remember when I was attending Napa Valley College. President Clinton was touting the benefits of a global economy. The United States would become a service economy, and we would uplift other countries by outsourcing our manufacturing jobs. We were going to export Capitalism to the world. The economies of the world would be interdependent. It was quite an exciting time, and I thought the concept of a global economy was a phenomenal idea.

It wasn't until a few years later that I thought more deeply about globalization. When we were exporting Capitalism to other nations, I assumed that the ideals of the Bill of Rights and the freedoms we enjoy under our Constitution would also be exported or, at the very minimum, respected. My worst nightmares were realized when

Twitter warned users in the United States that their tweets might violate Pakistani law. Twitter was an American company operating under the laws of the United States that the Constitution of The United States governs. I was now aware of the dangers of globalization.

Instead of exporting freedom, we ended up importing tyranny. Today, our freedoms and protections granted to us under the United States Constitution are being undermined on a grand scale. Government agencies are colluding with corporations to bypass Constitutional protections. Right before our very eyes, the Constitution is being attacked and undermined, and no one is being held accountable.

The Declaration of Independence, The Constitution of The United States, and the Bill of Rights were all created with God's blessings. No other nation in this world has prospered like the United States of America, and there are no other people in the world that have a better standard of living than those in the United States of America.

If the guiding principles that founded this great nation are discarded, tyranny will rule the land, humanity will be doomed, and God will not intervene. The purposeful undermining of the guiding principles that founded the United States of America is an abomination to God. My dedication and love for America were represented in the Human Spirit online magazine concept, listed below for your convenience:

Human Spirit 1997 – 2000

Human Spirit would have been an online magazine celebrating everything great about the United States of America, from our

Constitution to the Bill of Rights to the Declaration of Independence. Human Spirit was designed to celebrate America's success and give all citizens a sense of pride for being a part of the greatest nation in the world.

Each issue would profile great American leaders, great Americans, and great American companies. In addition, the secondary thrust of the magazine would be to recognize America's everyday heroes – those who make a difference each and every day. Candidates would be submitted from participating colleges, high schools, and non-profits from all across America.

Dare To Dream Big

With all of my heart, I believed in the visions for evolving humanity that were given to me. While my ambitions appear to be a pipe dream, I still believe in the bigness of God, and with His blessings, the impossible is possible. Changing the world on the magnitude required for humanity to survive is no easy feat for a person without significant financial resources. God understood this, and I believe for these reasons, God showered me with an endless stream of business concepts. I would need a technology empire.

With my wealth, political clout, and God's blessings, I would build entire industries that generated profits by empowering human beings. My enormous success and wealth would inspire society to change, as I challenged the status quo and was the driving force behind the paradigm shift needed for government institutions, industry, and other stakeholders to unite and change how society is governed. I dared to dream about evolving humanity and making this a better world for all, and God partnered with me to make it so. Below are two of the primary business concepts that would have been the cornerstone of my technology empire:

Sanctuary City 1997 – Current

Victims of domestic violence and prostitution, drug addicts, and the homeless would be provided with shelter and an opportunity to have an independent, normal life. Sanctuary City is the conversion or renovation of a warehouse or abandoned building. The ground floor would consist of a mini police station, a medical clinic, a counseling center, an employment development center, a college extension, a coffee shop, a café, a community daycare center, and a public recreation center. The second floor would be a dedicated call center training facility that would be supported by various corporations. The third floor would provide housing units for those needing assistance. The fourth and higher floors would be a combination of office space and apartments with premium rents – to help cover operational costs.

DebateMe.com - 2002

I envisioned a website enabling everyday citizens to interact with mainstream media news. Any story that was published on the web, in print, on the radio, or on television would promote a DebateMe.com code. Users would log into DebateMe.com, enter the code, and then could debate the topic of the hour. Debateme.com would have been the first social media website to market. Unlike other social media platforms, DebateMe.com would have promoted rational discussion, taught people how to debate, and taught people to find common ground and build consensus. DebateMe.com was all about people coming together and finding solutions to the challenges facing our world.

. . .

Heroes Wanted

I envisioned politicians, community leaders, and business leaders sponsoring weekly debates where anyone could join in and debate topics they were passionate about. DebateMe.com was easily a billion-dollar idea. DebateMe.com would have been the first social media platform to market, and it would have focused on upholding our Constitution and backing up arguments with facts.

Chapter 19
The Future

Validation

As I mentioned at the beginning of this book, after God intervened on my behalf and prevented me from taking my own life on March 29th, 2015, I was compelled to tell the story of my life and share the incredible details of my relationship with God. After eight years, I've recently started my fourth revision. For the first six years, I wrote daily. During the past two years, I accepted a very lucrative job and didn't have enough energy after 10-hour days to write.

During my writing hiatus, my obligation to God never escaped my mind. During the last half of 2022, I started praying to God about my lack of progress on the book and my strong desire to finish it and embark upon a new writing career. I even went so far as to start purchasing lottery tickets. I needed to free up my time so that I could complete my obligation to God. When I was laid off from work in

Heroes Wanted

January 2023 because of company-wide layoffs, I was nonplussed. God had answered my prayers once again. Not necessarily how I would have liked it, but nonetheless, I'd have the extra time to finish my book.

Initially, I believed the sole purpose of writing this story was because of the incredible experiences I had with God, and that He wanted me to share with the world the visions for humanity that He bestowed upon me, as well as the game plan for evolving humanity. I dutifully went about my obligation to God. For the longest time, I gathered my thoughts, reviewed journal entries, checked notes, and documented various events in my life. It was during my two-year writing hiatus when something significant happened that I wasn't expecting, and for me is a clear validation of God's wisdom and grace. I received two revelations.

First and foremost, the telling of my life story allowed me to realize who I am, what I believe in, where I came from, and where I wanted to go. I do care about others. I am concerned about issues that are none of my business because people shouldn't needlessly suffer or live in misery. I'm inspired and I wholeheartedly believe in The United States Constitution, and I believe that we all have a responsibility to fight tyranny and injustice.

Best of all, I realized that people do like me. Every day I manage to put a smile on someone's face as I share an unexpected laugh with them. I have a lot to offer this world, and even though I've been made irrelevant, I still strive to make this a better world for all. By compelling me to tell the story of my life, God forced me to open my eyes so that I could appreciate who I am and realize that my life does have value and that I'm a good person who wants to make this a better world.

In my second revelation, God revealed to me the reason that I had His ear and why He chose to partner with me. It all began when I was a child, and with all the innocence of a child began pursuing a relationship with Him. No one was forcing me to pray and reach out to God. In fact, I don't think anyone was aware I was doing so. I spent my youth communing with God out in nature. No one else was around.

When Shawn was selling illegal drugs, and I was addicted to cocaine, I prayed to God daily to rid this evil from our lives. I focused on trying to save Shawn and make our business legitimate. I knew I would only be successful with God's help. I had no idea I was engaged in a battle with Satan. I was surrounded by evil and temptation, and I chose God. God was paying attention.

The text for the "I'm The Miracle" poster resulted from brainstorming about who I was and what I stood for. I had resisted evil, triumphed over Satan, and was starting a new life. My brainstorming revealed the essence of my heart. I wanted to serve God by making this a better world. The essence of my heart was between God and me.

I now believe my failed real estate career and eventual journey around the country on my motorcycle in 1993 were purposely orchestrated by God. I began the journey pretty much broke. I had rid myself of everything from my past life that had anything to do with Shawn. I was allowed to keep a motorcycle, a few personal belongings, and about $3,000 in cash. I walked away with nothing and embarked upon my journey rooted in faith alone. From the day I decided to resign from my position in real estate, God dispatched the Holy Spirit to guide me. In Zion National Park, God healed me, rejuvenated me, and laid out my future.

During the late 1990s and early 2000s, when people would ask how I came up with my innovative, visionary business concepts, I'd reply that they were from God. I had no other explanation. I wasn't that smart, and no one in my family had a technological background. The question no one thought to ask was why God would bless me with all of these visions. Had someone asked, I wouldn't have had an answer.

It wasn't until I began writing this book that I realized why God chose to partner with me. When God explained why He didn't intervene when a child was savagely raped, poisoned, and left for dead, I stepped up. I pledged to God that I would honor Him by preventing these types of horrendous crimes with the gifts and talents He bestowed upon me. I made the same pledges when God opened my eyes to the war on drugs and the forced prostitution of young girls. God was listening, paying attention, and took me up on my offer.

At the lowest point in my life, when I had lost all hope and Satan and his minions were about to checkmate me, out of nowhere, God intervened. On the day I was going to take my own life, God sent me a powerful message that emphatically said, "NO! You are not to take your life today." Only God could send such a simple, yet powerful message.

. . .

During what was to be my last hour, as I was wrapping up my affairs, I became aware that I no longer felt the two throbbing toothaches that had bothered me for so long. I sat in disbelief as I poked and prodded the two bad teeth and the surrounding areas. There was slight discomfort, but nothing like the intense pain I'd been experiencing. I went from a pain level of 8.5 down to below 1.0.

I've had several toothaches in my life. All of them ended up needing medical treatment. I've never had a toothache, let alone two of them, reach such an intense level of pain only to suddenly reverse course. After several minutes, I realized that God took the time out of His hectic schedule to pay me a visit. While I had lost all hope and had given up, God had not.

God communicates with us all the time through various messages and sometimes outright miracles. All we need to see these signs and appreciate the miracles is an open mind and heart. God has forced me to examine my life so that I would know that my life has value and just exactly how special my relationship with Him is, as well as the importance of my commitments to Him. I've spent a lifetime pursuing a relationship with God, and most of the time, I wasn't even aware He was paying attention. When I pledged to use the skills and talents God blessed me with to make this a better world, God took me up on my offer. How cool is that?

The Best Christmas Present

One of the best Christmas presents I have received in my life was during my previous employer's annual Christmas Awards Banquet. I was a Senior Help Desk Support Technician and part of a team that supported over 1K remote employees and company executives across the United States. I worked my ass off. I authored best practices, created new procedures, and did an incredible job supporting my bosses, my team, and all of the associates with whom I came into contact. It was the best job I had post-college.

During our Christmas Awards Banquet, when I found out there was a rookie of the year award for my department, my hope for recognition for my contributions to the department and company peaked. I was looking forward to official recognition for my contributions. I didn't win. Recognition for Rookie of the Year went to a young lady on the programmer's side of our department. I knew this woman. I had worked with her numerous times, and I knew she also worked very hard and deserved to be recognized for her efforts.

At that particular moment during the awards show, I felt we should have had two awards, one for the programmer's side and one for the infrastructure side. After about 30 seconds, I became nonplussed about not winning. I had a great job doing what I loved to do. I worked with phenomenal people, I was having the best time of my life, I was being paid handsomely, and I was extremely happy.

Our executive team and managers and associates from various divisions in the company were in attendance at our company's awards banquet. There were over 200 people in attendance, and most traveled from throughout the United States to attend. At one point, the projection system stopped working, and my boss told me to go to the front of the room and fix it. As soon as I started walking toward the front of the room, the entire room erupted in thunderous applause and cheers as my coworkers hooted and hollered for me. It was an incredible display of appreciation as well as validation of my ability to connect with other human beings. I felt honored. I was loved throughout our organization. It was the best recognition I could have ever received. In His way, God showed me what I bring to the table, and that my life has value.

The Rise of The Body of Christ

In a world where humanity is free to evolve and flourish, acquiring and disseminating knowledge will be the driving force behind our actions and economy. Increasing humanity's overall intelligence level will lead to an improved human race. Intelligent beings will embrace crime prevention policies over law enforcement. Superficial solutions will be abandoned for meaningful change.

Meaningful change will lead to a world where there no longer is any violent crime. Those crimes that can be prevented, will be. Drug addiction will be virtually non-existent, and profits that power the economy will be based on empowering human beings to push their potential to the limits. The era of doing what you can get away with will be eradicated from society as doing what is right becomes the norm.

With the acquisition of knowledge as a driving force of our new economy, cancel culture, identify politics, censorship, personal attacks, cogent dissonance, fallacies, straw man fallacies, straw man arguments, and any other type of false arguments designed to oppress the truth, will no longer be tolerated, and the purveyors of such tactics will be ostracized. Honest debate, rational thought, respect for opposing viewpoints, compromise, and a willingness to build consensus, focus on commonalities, and build solutions that benefit all will prevail.

. . .

Heroes Wanted

The greatest tool that can be used to usher in the evolution of humanity is the United States Constitution. Embracing the spirit of the Declaration of Independence, the United States Constitution, and the Bill of Rights, will require the government to return to a smaller, limited government that adheres to the Constitution and honors our system of checks and balances, thereby limiting tyranny and resulting in greater freedom and liberty for all.

Creating better human beings who value life isn't rocket science. Society has always had the knowledge and skills to develop better human beings but has lacked the will. I knew that if I were a billionaire with a technology empire behind me, I could drive the paradigm shift necessary to affect the changes needed by inspiring others to embrace the possibilities and benefits of evolving humanity. Unfortunately, for both me and humanity, Satan and his minions stopped me before I could even begin.

God has invested a lifetime in me. I was going to be the driving force behind the paradigm shift needed to evolve humanity. The visions for humanity and the game plan for evolving humanity that was bestowed upon me by God were so significant that when I had given up hope, God stepped in to intervene. By compelling me to write out the story of my life and by detailing the incredible relationship I've had with Him, God is ensuring that the information He has provided me is disseminated throughout the world.

I mentioned at one point that having squandered my life and being made irrelevant, God had absolved me of the commitments I made to Him. However, the evolution of humanity is vital if we are to survive. As such, the commitments I made to God now fall under the auspices of the church and the Body of Christ. Whereas I was just one man, equipped with God's visions, the Body of Christ is hundreds of millions strong, controls huge financial resources, and possesses exceptional political connections.

For the righteous among us, the ones who love Jesus so much and would do anything for Him, including squandering my life—it is now your time to shine and rise to the occasion. We all know Christianity is about doing what is right and being just. There's nothing more important, right or just, than driving humanity to evolve and eradicating evil from the face of the planet. Humanity must evolve, and as human beings, we must do better. Humanity can accomplish great things, and by working with God, we can achieve the impossible.

For the spiritual leaders that guide the flock, it's time for you and your brethren to up your game, roll up your sleeves, and get busy with a sense of urgency. The future of humanity is at stake, as are your souls. Don't shirk your new focus and responsibilities, and none of you will have to spend an eternity in Hell.

Judgement Day

I've pretty much made it clear that I don't hold with church doctrine or teachings. I don't need another man dictating to me the parameters of my relationship with God. I'm grateful to the Maronite Church in Ohio for introducing me to God and informing me that God is always around us, always listening, always watching, and wants us to do good, not sin. Those simple statements allowed me to establish an incredible relationship with God that has lasted a lifetime.

. . .

Heroes Wanted

I know God isn't interested in who is the holiest, most pious, most righteous, or who raises the most money for the church. I know on judgment day, God will not break out a spreadsheet and review how many times you attended church, the number of times you praised Jesus, or how many sinners you've identified and persecuted. On your day of judgment, God's not going to spring a pop quiz on you and test your knowledge of the Bible or your ability to recite scripture.

With a full heart, I know these statements to be facts because if God were interested in any of these things, He would have met one of the conspirators against me out in the desert instead of me. One of the conspirators against me would have been his champion, and one of the conspirators against me would have been blessed with visions for building a technology empire and changing the world, not me.

Based on my experiences and relationship with God, and based on the visions of the world God has bestowed upon me, I'd say on judgment day, God is going to be more interested in the following:

- Did you seek out a personal relationship with God, or did you limit your knowledge and experiences with God to church doctrine and teachings?
- What did you do to make this a better world for all?
- What did you do to evolve humanity?
- What did you do to prevent the abuse, rape, and murder of children?
- What did you do to prevent violent crimes?
- What did you do to prevent and treat drug addiction?
- Did you live your life by doing what you could get away with, or did you live your life by doing what's right?

- Did you profit from the suffering and misery of other human beings, or did you work to prevent it?
- What did you do to unite humanity?
- Were you an advocate of killing in God's name, or did you advocate for finding ways to live in peace in God's name?

For the truly righteous among us and the spiritual leaders that lead the flock, there is an extra burden being placed upon your capable shoulders. On judgment day, know that:

- As long as the church continues to give those engaged in evil a pass while counting the sins of the meek, then you, your brethren, and your congregations will all be held accountable by God.
- As long as God has to listen to the screams and cries of children being abused, raped, and murdered, then you, your brethren, and your congregations will all be held accountable by God.
- As long as preventable crimes are not prevented, then you, your brethren, and your congregations will all be held accountable by God.
- As long as the scourge of drug addiction is not prevented and treated, and as long as addicts continue to overdose, then you, your brethren, and your congregations will all be held accountable by God.
- As long as human beings are purposely being pitted against one another, manipulated, and exploited, then you, your brethren, and your congregations will all be held accountable by God.

- As long as Satan and his minions are free to destroy humanity unopposed, then you, your brethren, and your congregations will all be held accountable by God.

By having me tell the story of my life and the details of my incredible relationship with Him, God is sending a message to humanity that we have free will, and the world is what we make of it. The pain and suffering in this world is not of God's doing. God is not to be blamed. However, those who perpetuate and profit from the misery of others, as well as the righteous among us who do nothing, will be held accountable for their actions (or inaction) by God.

Evolving The Church

The news is full of stories about the decline of the church. Attendance is down, and people are dissatisfied with religion. I believe the dissatisfaction and decline in organized religion is justified. In order to control the masses, the church interjects itself between God and those seeking a relationship with God. Spiritual leaders portray themselves as experts on God. They are not. Neither am I.

Based on my relationship and experiences with God, I'd say if the church is to survive, then it must reform itself. A reformed church will be focused on serving God by advocating for the evolvement of humanity and making this a better world for all. The church will encourage all to build a personal relationship with God through prayer, communication, and communing with God out in nature. The church will advocate for doing what's right, not what you can get away with, empowering human beings, and eradicating evil from this world. The church shall be a place for spiritually like-minded individuals to gather and share the details of their spiritual journeys with one another.

It will be up to the Christians that read this story to determine if they're serving God or their Church, and if they have any doubt, they should reach out to God in prayer directly. Christians are going to have to start thinking for themselves and begin forging a personal relationship with God rather than depending on the church to spoon-feed them their spiritual redemption.

If you do not believe in God and are in need of a break, rejuvenation, or help, or if you're looking to change your life or your circumstances, then I would encourage you to reach out to God in earnest. Find a quiet place and ask God for help. Share with God your frustrations, your fears, and why you need His help. Be sincere and pray regularly. If you keep an open mind and an open heart, you may just be surprised. I know this may all sound incredible, but it just takes a bit of faith on your part. God is ready to partner with you, strengthen you, rejuvenate you, and work through you. All you have to do is ask.

If you feel the need to seek out God through a church, then, by all means, do so, but I would urge caution. Look for a church that helps congregation members build personal relationships with God. Look for a church that is focused on defeating evil and not the petty sins of the meek. Look for a church that isn't trying to interject itself in between you and God. Ideally, a church worthy of attendance would embrace the following characteristics:

- Sermons would be focused on helping people establish a personal relationship with God, along with sermons designed to address the evolution of humanity.

- The church and its congregations would lead by example, championing what's right and condemning doing what one can get away with.
- The church and its congregation would amaze non-believers with their commitment and dedication to both God and Jesus by taking every opportunity to do good in the world.
- Church leadership would advocate for the various causes necessary to evolve humanity and make this a better world for all.
- By their selfless behaviors and actions, not their mouths, the church leadership team and the congregation would inspire non-believers to want to know more about God and the teachings of Jesus Christ.
- The church would no longer blame God for not intervening when senseless acts of violence or preventable crimes take place. Instead, the church will focus on root causes, take responsibility for tolerating evil, failing to prevent preventable crimes, and for allowing criminal activities and behaviors to go unpunished.
- The church wouldn't be complicit with those who do evil or provide evildoers with sanctuary.
- Anyone approaching the church with concerns about their life, sin, God, Jesus, or the Holy Spirit shall be encouraged by the church to establish a personal relationship with God and seek out God's counsel.
- The church will not judge, condemn or alienate anyone and will welcome all seeking a relationship with God.

Until the church reforms itself and takes a hard stance against Satan, evil will continue to flourish, and millions upon millions of Christians will continue to be deceived.

God's Sense of Humor

God possesses a great sense of humor, and He certainly does work in mysterious ways. I've used illegal drugs, I enjoy tequila shots and a margarita every now and then, I curse, I enjoy looking at women's asses in tight clothing, I tell inappropriate jokes, I flirt, and lately, I've been playing "Call of Duty, DMZ," the objective of which is to explore, loot and eliminate enemy teams. Alas, I'm a human being striving to be the best version of myself. I'm far from perfect, but you won't find me pretending to be someone I'm not. Based on their supposed superior morality, piousness, and dedication to God, the righteous among us, dependent on the religious dogma that tells them how to think, believe they are justified in mocking me, discrediting me, and labeling me an unrepentant sinner.

Yet here I am, sharing my incredible relationship with God and disseminating the visions God has blessed me with to the world. God chose to partner with me over the righteous among us who bless us with their presence. I find humor in the irony, but I know precisely why God partnered with me. I didn't read about a little girl being savagely raped and murdered and then passed this horrendous crime off to God through prayer. I dared to ask God why, and when God answered, I pledged to use the skills and talents He bestowed upon me to honor him by working toward a world where little girls aren't savagely raped and murdered. God took me up on my offer.

The completion and dissemination of my life story and my incredible relationship with God fulfill my current obligation to God. I eagerly await God's next move in the battle between good and evil. I'm hopeful the release of this book, with all of the various messages from God, is the catalyst needed for driving all good people to unite in their efforts at defeating evil. I believe that those of you who have formed a personal relationship with God, who believe in doing good in the world, and who believe goodness will prevail over evil, will gather, unite, and begin eradicating evil from our midst.

I'm mindful of the visions of the world from God that I'm sharing in this book, and I fully expect Satan and his minions to launch yet another attack on me. They are cunning, and I'm fallible, but I've regained my relationship with God. I will never let the church distract me from it again. I'm comforted by the fact that, during the entire time I was writing out this story, whenever I begged God for relief, He promised me that He would intervene on my behalf once I completed and disseminated this book.

Considering that Shawn had to go to jail for seven years the last time I prayed for God's intervention, I'm confident that God will deal with Satan and his minions when they come looking for me again. Spending eternity in Hell for a relatively short stint as a villain here on Earth is not a wise investment for one's life or eternal soul.

For the righteous among us and the conspirators against me that will deny my relationship with God and work to discredit this book, keep this important fact in mind: I was already defeated and was ready to concede defeat to Satan and you guys. Thanks to the church, my relationship with God was pretty much non-existent—dormant at best. During my last hour, before I would end my life, God showed up and intervened. I'm only alive today due to God's intervention. The only reason that this story is being told is that God compelled me to tell it.

Do not be deceived into thinking I'm one of your garden variety sinners, and that there are no consequences for squandering my life.

In the squandering of my life, your actions have inadvertently stood in the way of God's plan for evolving humanity. There will be hell to pay.

For those of you sitting on your ass, counting the sins of the meek while avoiding confrontations with those who are genuinely evil, or for those who are genuinely evil and profit from the misery and suffering of other human beings, don't be angry with me and resentful of God's messages. Be angry with your spiritual leaders because they're the ones who have been lying to you. By fulfilling my obligation to God, I've done all of you a huge favor. God is doing you a huge favor, too, by giving you an opportunity to avoid spending all of eternity in Hell.

For those actively doing the work of Satan, a final warning: You may feel powerful, you may be handsomely rewarded financially, and you very well may be untouchable in this world. However, you need to realize that Satan was an Angel, who God kicked out of Heaven. While evil is currently thriving and destroying humanity, goodness will always prevail.

Satan and his minions prosper because humanity allows them to. Satan and his minions may be cunning, but they are no match for God. He allows free will to rein, but come judgment day, those who worked for Satan shall join him in the depths of Hell for all of eternity.

God's New Champions

A few years ago, I enjoyed a conversation with the daughter of a Christian pastor. This woman was well aware of and leery of mindless Christian zealots and equally as frustrated with them as me. We engaged in a great conversation about faith, developing a personal relationship with God, our own experiences with God, and about how we can all have different experiences with God that differ from church doctrine.

While we may not have seen eye to eye on every subject, we were both able to share the details of our beliefs and our experiences with God and discover the beliefs and values we had in common. Since we both had personal relationships with God, we were receptive to listening to each other's experiences. Our brief conversation allowed us to validate each other's relationship with God. I believe our encounter made us both better human beings. It was a perfect example of God's magnificence and how He works through us.

Upon further reflection on our encounter, God's wisdom became clear to me. The world is full of incredible people who can think for themselves, who believe that goodness overcomes evil, and who want to do what is right, not merely what they can get away with. My experiences with God, my relationship with God, my struggles, and my commitments to God will all resonate with people wanting to do good in this world. Those who have a personal relationship with God, or are seeking a personal relationship with God, will be inspired by my story. They will form their own takeaways from my story, seek to strengthen their faith in God, and double down on fostering a personal relationship with God. God is waiting for the next champion, or champions, to step up and go on the offensive against Satan.

For those of you who do not know God, I'd like to share the following with you to illustrate the power of partnering with God. While I've experienced my ups and downs while writing this book, as I get closer and closer to completing this enormous task, something wonderful has occurred. My relationship with God has returned to a level I haven't experienced since God met me out in the Utah desert. In my time of despair, doubt, and need, the Holy Spirit appears, and I find myself filled with a sense of purpose, strength, and comfort in knowing that I'm serving God. I suddenly find myself again motivated to continue documenting and writing this book. I take comfort in knowing that God has a plan no matter how bad things get. Humanity is going to evolve, and humanity is going to unite in its efforts to make this a better world for everyone.

My life, my relationship with God, and my incredible experiences with God are a testimonial that we don't have to accept the world in which we live. I dared to ask God how I could help change the world, I pledged to use the skills, talents, and gifts God bestowed upon me to achieve those ends, and He took me up on my offer. While I've described a utopian world that seems a pipe dream, with God's blessings, anything is possible.

Through telling my story, God is providing the world with a roadmap for evolving humanity. How great would it be for humanity to unite in its efforts to make this a better world for all? What can be more inspiring than becoming a hero by saving a child from being abused, raped, and murdered? What can be more fulfilling than being part of a solution where preventable violent crimes are prevented? What can be more rewarding than knowing that you are actively participating in the growth of humanity and that by your actions, we will all become better human beings?

For those of you who are like me and have cultivated a personal relationship with God without being corrupted by Man's influence, I encourage you to remain steadfast in your relationship with God. You and I are kindred souls, and just as much as we depend on God, God depends on people like us to set aside our differences, focus on our commonalities, and unite to defeat evil and make this a better world for all. For those of you who do not know God, know He exists and is a source of unimaginable power if you decide to open your heart and seek him out. God is always in search of champions. If we can dream it, then we can make it happen. The time for all good men and women to unite in defeating evil is upon us.

Epilogue

I've been described as very stubborn. I couldn't agree more. I believe God purposely made me stubborn so I would focus on my relationship with Him and not be distracted by Man's agenda. I have no doubts that my life would have improved had I humbled myself and kissed my rich uncle's ass. I'm confident that had I picked a church, attended regularly, attended Bible study, embraced church doctrine, and lived a life free of what the Bible calls sin, I would have been a successful businessman and pillar of the community. Likewise, I'm sure if I had indulged my family's superiority complex and acknowledged how everyone in my family, especially on my dad's side, was morally superior to me and better than me because they all attend church, I'd still have a relationship with my family. Thankfully, I chose to honor my relationship with God over their pettiness, religion, and ego.

It all comes back to those six months I spent in Napa in 1986, when I prayed, cried, and begged God to save me from the evils of this world. I loathed that I was living in a superficial world devoid of God, and I promised God I would never compromise my values or beliefs again. I begged God to allow me to serve Him and to be a force for goodness. As I reflect upon my life, I cannot express the euphoric feelings of joy, happiness, and gratitude that overcome me from knowing that God had answered my prayers.

The truth of the matter is that if any of the churches or religions I've experienced were representative of God, then I'd already be a dedicated, practicing member. I do not need man dictating to me the parameters of my relationship with God. Absent in my life is my desire to commune with other like-minded, spiritual beings that want to share their experiences with God, encourage others to build a relationship with God, and unite in our efforts to defeat Satan and his minions.

While those who have manipulated and played me would like to believe they are smarter than me, they are not. Like Satan, they are cunning. Being cunning doesn't equate to superior intelligence. For those very few who conspired against me and are more intelligent than me, they will one day come to know that they are not smarter than God. God has outmaneuvered them in every play. Satan has misled them into believing that since there is no recourse against them for their actions against me, surely they're righteous. Nothing could be further from the truth. God is not dormant. God is watching, and there are consequences for thwarting God's plan.

Other than satisfying their egos and attempting to reinforce their dogma, nothing beneficial has come from the squandering of my life. I've chosen to live my life in accordance with my relationship with God. The conspirators against me have chosen to live their lives in accordance with what the church dictates to them. In my world, the abuse, rape, and murder of children are entirely unacceptable and preventable, as is every other type of senseless violent crime. In my world, humanity evolves to make this a better world for all. For the conspirators against me, the only thing important to them is power and control.

While God partnered with me to eliminate all the horrible injustices perpetrated against humanity, the righteous among us saw fit to squander my life because they could not control me or force me to adhere to their dogma. As I shared with my family during my last email correspondence with them, I have a personal relationship with God, and I'm wagering the remainder of the pitiful life imposed upon me against their eternal souls that my relationship and experiences with God will trump their ancient religion, beliefs, rituals, and church doctrine.

I'm 58 years old. I'm more than halfway through my life. With the completion and dissemination of this book, I've fulfilled my obligation to God and look forward to leaving my dreadful past behind, and begin a new chapter in my life. I've spent a lifetime pursuing a relationship with God. I've served God, and God has used me for His purpose. Once I depart this world, my suffering and painful memories of a life purposely squandered will come to an end. I'll be spending eternity in Heaven, and I'll never return to this planet to assist ever again. For those who conspired against me, you have thwarted God's plan, and He will hold you accountable on the day you depart this world.

How Great Would It Be if 100 Million Human Beings:

- Stood in unison and demanded that our leaders stopped doing what they could get away with and started doing what's right?

- Committed to doing what it takes to ensure children are no longer subjected to abuse, rape and murder?

- Demanded that humanity evolve?

- Set aside their differences and worked together to make this a better world for all?

- Stopped passing the problems of this world off to God and instead took action to fix what humanity has created?

It Begins With You!

From person to person, to community to community, we can begin a grass roots movement that inspires, encourages, and unites humanity in our quest to defeat evil and make this a better world for all.

If any part of this book resonated with you, then please reach out to your family, friends and colleagues and encourage them to pickup a copy. In addition, please consider writing reviews on Amazon and other social media platforms.

Visit www.jamilmaroun.com for more information

God is looking for Heroes.
Will you heed His call?

Vaya Con Dios,

Jamil "Jim" Maroun

Acknowledgments

To my wife Heidi, thank you for the plethora of memories of us wearing galoshes and eating macadamia nuts on a boat while watching Beluga whales swim by, with you sporting your bulbous bouffant and brand new mukluks. God believes in you, loves you very much, and is waiting for you to reach out to Him. You're an incredible woman with a wonderful heart. I love you with all of my heart.

To the Vestibules, thank you for assembling select words my wife deems essential for any piece of literature to be considered great, into the lyrics of a song called Bulbous Bouffant [7].

For Andrea, Vicky and Rich, I'm forever grateful for your dedication to your profession, to humanity, and the extreme kindness and guidance the three of you have provided me with. People like yourselves are the ones that make a difference in this world each and every day.

To the Napa Valley College faculty (1994-1997), during my journey of personal growth, I felt very fortunate to have encountered so many incredible professors, instructors, assistants, counselors, and administrators that strived to make this a better world by helping other human beings reach their potential. Napa Valley College is the epitome of doing what's right to make this a better world for all.

For my friends, co-workers and acquaintances, from Napa Valley (1986-1997), the person you met was the real Jim Maroun. I never passed myself off as someone I was not. It saddens me that our relationship was poisoned. I miss all of you, have great memories and I'm extremely grateful for the experiences and love.

Visionary Business Concepts Expanded

I've spent my life dreaming about ways technology could change our lives. For the curious, below is a list of the various business concepts I've entertained throughout the years.

DebateMe.com

DebateMe.com would have been the first social media platform to market and would have allowed the general public to interact and debate any topic found on mainstream media. The DebateMe.com platform would have promoted honest debates based on facts and logical thoughts.

Storybook

A new, unique, engaging, and fun way to collaboratively create and distribute fiction.

Online Music Store 2007 – Current

My visionary, new online music store would engage consumers, increase their purchasing options, and provide them with a greater, deeper, more satisfying musical experience, all the while increasing and expanding industry profits.

Business Class Desktop 1998 – 2010

An operating system specifically designed to be business-centric by enhancing the workflows of business professionals.

Consumer Class Desktop 1985 – Current

Another advanced, consumer-centric operating system with an enhanced user interface that creates a premium end-user experience.

Call Center Cube 2007 – Current

An innovative upgrade to the traditional employee cubicle that maximizes workspace, increases employee efficiency, and, most importantly, keeps employees' morale high by keeping employees engaged.

Virtual Employees 1990 – Current

My virtual employees' concept was a precursor to today's work-from-home environment. Imagine needing assistance in a store, and at the end of the aisle is a video monitor. With a push of a button, an employee appears onscreen, ready to answer questions.

Retail Command Center 2004-2005

Inspired while working for Best Buy. I envisioned utilizing technology to track customers as they walked through the front door until they checked out. Customer movements would be tracked on a computer screen where a manager could then direct sales associates, whose movements were also being tracked on screen, to departments filled with customers.

Shooting Range

I believe this to be one of my most creative and best innovations. I've developed a concept that elevates target practice into something more exciting, competitive, engaging, and satisfying for consumers while providing range owners and firearms manufacturers with increased profits.

Brick & Mortar Music Stores 2010 – Current

A chain of revolutionary brick-and-mortar boutique music stores never before envisioned. A music enthusiast's dream, with revenue streams and more significant profit margins to satisfy the entire music industry.

Electronics, Robotics & Drone Retail Store 2012 – Current

A visionary retail concept that educates and engages youth by providing them with challenging and fun exposure to electronics, robotics, and drones.

Police Robotics & Drones 2014

From the safety of their police vehicle, an officer launches several drones that encircle a car. One of the drones approaches the driver's side window, and the driver holds up a driver's license.

Mega Entertainment Complex 1999

An indoor arena of various flight, car, and vehicle simulators integrated into video game ecosystems. A gamer's paradise and a place for families to gather and have fun.

Harley Davidson Marketing Concept 1983-1984

Identified a marketing model for Harley Davidson motorcycles based on a cool factor that wouldn't be realized by Harley Davidson until the mid-1990s.

Robot Concept 1985 - 1986

Inspired by my passion for computer technology and Apple's

recently released Macintosh computers, I envisioned a Mac computer mounted on caterpillar tracks like a tank. Several sensors feed into a CPU for basic mobility. I envisioned software that would recognize and classify objects to differentiate various obstacles the robot would encounter.

Self-Generating Computer Code 1985 – 1992

I envisioned minimum computer code that, when compiled, could only be interpreted for a specific purpose and would automatically generate needed code to accomplish a task. The goal was to reduce file size and increase coding efficiency. This was more of a mental exercise than a business concept.

Motorcycle Touring 1994

Based on my 5 1/2 month journey across the United States on my motorcycle, I envisioned an adventure-type vacation that allows people to ride motorcycles, camp, and explore America's scenic beauty.

Electronic Business Cards 1997

Basically, a single PowerPoint slide that looked like a business card and could be emailed to clients.

Virtual Model Cars 1994 - 1995

Just like a model car kit put together with glue, only on your computer. Cars would be assembled with various parts and configurations. Finished cars could be virtually raced with outcomes determined by the various components used to build the vehicle.

Grocery Store Customer Service & Sales Training 1995 – 2000

While performing my duties as a meat clerk, I observed that customers were highly receptive to meal and food suggestions I recommended, especially when customers didn't know what to make for dinner. I devised engagement scripts for store employees to use to engage and enhance customer experiences by providing meal suggestions based on the customer's current needs. It was as simple as having employees share their favorite meal ideas.

Grocery Store Television Network 1998 – 2000

The same concept as listed above, only video displays would be strategically placed throughout the grocery store and play short videos of meal suggestions. Kiosks would be nearby so customers could print out recipes and coupons. Food distributors and producers would pay sponsoring fees to have their products featured.

Retail Video Store Network 1999

The grocery store television network concept only expanded to include the retail industry. Automotive, clothing, consumer electronics, sporting goods – any retailer. Videos of the latest fashions, trends, products or DIY videos would play continuously. Each video display would be the perfect salesperson.

Real Estate Website Portal 1997 – 1998

At the time, most Realtors hadn't heard of a website, and a single webpage with contact information often represented those that did. My vision included the following:

- A current listing page.
- Past sales page.
- Selling tips page.
- Buying tips page.
- A title company page.
- A home inspector's page.
- A lenders page.
- A page with links to relevant community resources.

Visionary Business Concepts Expanded

Web-Based Real Estate Office 1997-1998

Computer terminal based – clients would come into a showroom and peruse listings via computer. Monitors mounted on walls would cycle through listings and other real estate related videos.

Platinum Websites 2000

A business concept I developed with three other students at the Sacramento Entrepreneurship Academy. At the time, a basic website cost between $1,500 and $3,000 to have developed. Platinum Websites was going to sell pre-packaged website templates to the public at a cost of $600.00 each.

Online Video Services 1999 – 2000

While working for a startup with video technology, I brainstormed several video-based website themes that would allow people to post videos of themselves. Basically, youtube.com before there was a youtube.com.

Valentines Day Video 1999 – 2000

I envisioned a web-based business model that would enable companies like Hallmark and florists to utilize emerging video and internet technology to allow people to send Valentine's greeting videos to loved ones.

Liquid Energy Drinks 2001

In order to increase sales for a dietary supplement health company I worked for, I proposed the company package their liquid vitamins and minerals into "shot" type bottles to be sold at convenience stores.

Mobile Document Scanning 2002

Inspired by Canon's latest high-speed scanners and document management software, I recognized a huge business opportunity to provide onsite scanning and archiving services for real estate, law

326

offices, and the medical profession. However, at the time, privacy laws quickly killed this concept.

Court Cases 1997 – 2004

A wickedly fun concept initially designed for law students but with definite potential for consumer markets.

AutoTechSuperstarts.com 2003

A job posting board and resource center for automotive technicians. The strategy was to provide online customer service and business training to automotive technicians to increase their value to potential employers.

Tablet Retail Checkout 2004

Based on tablet pc handwriting technology, I developed a retail checkout process while working at Best Buy. The concept was each sales associate would have a tablet with them, and when a customer made a purchase, complimentary products, and services would automatically be presented during the checkout process.

Jeep Off-Road Resource Website 2005

Designed to be used with off-road retail specialty parts websites, this module would allow off-road enthusiasts to connect online geographically by zip code to share their passion for off-roading with others, create personal profiles, post pictures of their rigs, post pictures and videos of their favorite spots, as well as organize runs together. A community for the off-road community – linked to commercial retail sponsors.

Idigya.com 2006

A dating website concept geared towards young adults with a unique screening process that emphasizes personal safety.

Apartment Complex Maintenance System 2004 – 2007

Visionary Business Concepts Expanded

Allow tenants to create maintenance requests online and track their progress. Allows Apartment managers and owners to track maintenance requests in real time. Other services included a maintenance worker time tracker and a place for residents to gather online – classifieds, blogs and other community-related social events.

iPod Touch/iPad Meeting App 2009

An incredible concept to enhance the way people attend and interact with presentations/meetings.

iPad Rental Tours 2009

Inspired by the beautiful Napa Valley. Users would rent iPads that came pre-loaded with map routes targeting specific sites. When the iPad was near places of interest, videos or messages from the site would appear to further enhance the visitor's experience.

Boutique Meat Shop 2010

A traditional butcher shop featuring fine meats, sausages, and wine coupled with a BBQ dining area. A gourmet meat lover's paradise.

House of God Coffee Shop 2013

Inspired by my niece's incredible photography talents and her love for Jesus. I envisioned a bohemian-style coffee shop where my niece's incredible artwork could be displayed along with encouraging scripture and personal writings. House of God Coffee would be a place to visit for a quick rejuvenation and be reminded about what's really important in life.

Apple Consulting Business 2012

Capitalizing on my extensive business background and knowledge of the needs of business owners, I devised a concept for a consulting group with a retail location that specializes in
Apple technology.

QuitMakingExcuses.com 1997 – 2013

Based on my years of business experience, customer service, and sales strategies, I envisioned an online employee training program geared towards those new to the employment market.

Lighting Showroom 2012 – 2013

A futuristic lighting showroom designed to transform living spaces and create new worlds.

Pinball Emporium 2012 – Current

A way for the family to spend a day together having fun and playing games.

A "Best Buy" Retail Store Concept 2010 – Current

A re-image of the retail industry that creates superior consumer experiences and allows brick-and-mortar stores to compete and beat internet stores.

Electronics, Robotics & Drone Education Platform 2012 Current

The study of electronics, robotics, math, science, computer programing, engineering, and all related fields are of strategic national importance to our country. I envisioned a curriculum that is engaging and ignites students' imaginations.

America Innovates, Entrepreneur Boot Camp & Vetting Camp 2013 – 2014

Three reality TV shows. The concept was to launch a new business each week, with each reality show tracking three distinct parts of creating and launching a business.

Class Reunion 2013 – 2014

Visionary Business Concepts Expanded

An innovative and fun way for former classmates to celebrate and enjoy class reunions.

Spaceport 2013 – 2014

An earth-based hotel that simulates what it would be like to live in outer space. A complete entertainment experience rivaling Disneyland or Universal Studios.

Bibliography

1. Crime victim Girl X
CNN Interactive (1997), 'Ex-convict charged in sexual assault of Girl X,.', CNN, 4 April, Available at: http://www.cnn.com/US/9704/04/girl/ (Accessed: 3 June 2021).

2. Crime victim Jessica Chambers
Sarah Fowler (2017), 'Her hair was fried like it had been stuck in a light socket': Rescuer traumatized after seeing Jessica Chambers',, USA Today -The (Jackson, Miss.) Clarion-Ledger, 11 October, Available at: https://www.usatoday.com/story/news/nation-now/2017/10/11/jessica-chambers-mississippi-murder-trial/753723001/(Accessed: 6 March 2020).

3. Crime victim Brittanee Drexel
Tribune Media Wire (2016), 'FBI: new details in case of teen who was abducted, gang-raped, shot and fed to alligators',, Fox13 Salt Lake City, 30 November, Available at: https://fox13now.com/2016/11/30/new-details-in-case-of-teen-who-was-abducted-gang-raped-shot-and-fed-to-alligators-fbi/(Accessed: 6 March 2020).

3a. Crime victim Brittanee Drexel Update
Amir Vera and Jamie Lynch (2022), 'Remains of 17-year old 17-year-old girl who went missing in 2009 found in South Carolina, sheriff says' ,, CNN, 16 May, Available at: https://www.cnn.com/2022/05/16/us/brittanee-drexel-case-remains-found/index.html (Accessed 11 June 2023).

4. Crime victim Gabriel Fernandez
Garrett Therolf (2016), 'How officials failed to save Gabriel Fernandez from years of abuse, torture', Los Angeles Times, 8 April, Available at: https://www.latimes.com/local/lanow/la-me-ln-gabriel-fernandez-torture-case-20160407-story.html (Accessed: 6 March 2020).

5. Crime victim baby Jazmine Robin
Miya Shay and Jessica Willey (2019), 'Parents arrested after death of premature baby with 96 fractures', ABC Eyewitness News 13, 25 June, Available at: https://abc13.com/parents-arrested-after-death-of-premature-baby-with-96-fractures-/5361944/ (Accessed: 6 March 2020).

Bibliography

6. Crime victim 5-year-old Lizzy Shelley

Elaine Aradillas (2019), 'GGirl, 5, Was Killed by Uncle, Who Gets Life in Prison: 'Never See the Light of Day', People/Yahoo Finance, 25 September, Available at: https://finance.yahoo.com/news/girl-5-killed-uncle-gets-202337941.html (Accessed: 6 March 2020).

7. Terence Bowman; Bernard Deniger; Paul Par'e. (1994). Bulbous Bouffant[Song]. On *Sketches Songs & Shoes*. CD Baby CO; CD Baby Sync Publishing, and 2 Music Rights Societies.